RUSSIA AND THE RUSSIANS

RUSSIA

and

THE RUSSIANS

Edward Crankshaw

NEW YORK · THE VIKING PRESS · 1949

CONTENTS

v

I

THE WORLD AND THE U.S.S.R.

THE WORLD AND THE U.S.S.R.

IN a small book about Russia, written when the war was at its
height, I undertook a brief survey of the history of Anglo-
Russian relations from the sixteenth century, when they were
first inaugurated, to the Intervention, when they temporarily
ceased, in order to indicate, very lightly, certain lessons which
could be learnt with profit for the future. The future, by
which I then meant the end of the war in Europe and Asia, is
now the present, and the lessons have not been learnt. They
will not be repeated here; and I refer to that earlier book only
because it has a direct bearing on this one, which is neither more
nor less than an attempt to produce a picture of the Russian
people, their culture, and their political ideas, against the background of the unchanging conditions of their landscape and
their climate. Something of this kind seems to me badly needed
to serve as a firm anchorage for our thoughts and speculations
about the impact of Russia upon the rest of the world.

In that earlier book, after considering the monotonous and
gloomy regularity with which the birth and recurrent rebirth
of good-will between our two countries has been succeeded by
the resurrection of suspicion, hardening quickly into hostility,
open or concealed, and after some attempt to suggest reasons for
this dire and inflexible rhythm, I tried to show that if we were
not very careful we should find the same thing happening at the
end of the war (which then seemed a long way off), and I went
on to suggest that one of the first steps we could take to
strengthen ourselves against the inevitable shock of disillusion-
ment to come was to disillusion ourselves a little in advance and
try to think of the Russians as ordinary human beings instead
of as a nation of masked demigods. I was writing in 1943, shortly
after the victory at Stalingrad, when the agitation for the so-

called Second Front was at its height both in Moscow and in London, and when we, the average Englishman or American, were extending to Russia a warmth and passion of admiration unprecedented in the history of alliances. Nothing Russia did was wrong; nothing we did was right.

To return from Moscow to London at that time was an odd and unmanageable experience. You left the company of a battered and weary nation struggling on with a weary war, making the usual muddles and mistakes associated with wars and nations, groping on from day to day, like any other nation, but enduring privations unimaginable by us, now weakening, now regaining strength, wondering what it was all about, but saved from demoralization in moments of blackest despondency by the very real fact of German soldiers sprawling all over their own cherished soil; you left this people, tired of the crowded tubes and trams, sick to death of the blackout, weak through undernourishment, often to the point of starvation, and hanging on blindly while their beloved Red Army recovered from its appalling initial defeats and, by sheer weight of numbers and machinery and by occasional strokes of brilliant generalship, at last halted, and then beat back, the inglorious invader, their readiness to die and be hurt outweighing, in the long run, their multifarious inefficiency; you left this familiar scene and returned to London, then convalescing between blitzes, but also shabby, weary, and blindly hanging on, and were immediately treated as a visitor from another planet inhabited by a rarefied and immaculate race fighting with utter unanimity and unflagging inspiration and precision, showing boldness where boldness was needed, prudence where prudence was needed, and supported by a civilian population which laboured, starry-eyed, and never muttered or harboured a dark thought. Whereas we . . .

And the odd thing was, the Russians were admired too much and at the same time not enough. Their efficiency and their enthusiasm were absurdly exaggerated in our eyes; but in London at that time it was as much as one's reputation was worth to say so. Their endurance, on the other hand, their capacity to muddle through, their sacrificial doggedness in circumstances of

almost inconceivable privation and desolation, were never fully
realized, and are not realized to this day. But then one could
say little about it; one could say, for instance, nothing at all, for
fear of giving comfort to the enemy, about the hundreds of
thousands who had starved to death in Leningrad. It is now
possible to speak more freely. Then, all one could do, and in
the most general terms, was to plead that unlimited and unin-
structed hero-worship was both dangerous and unhealthy, and
that if we insisted on believing for reasons of our own that the
Russians had achieved the sort of perfection hitherto denied to
ordinary mortals, we were laying up for ourselves a rough
awakening, the sudden shock of which, coming unexpectedly,
would throw us off balance and might very well end in the
resumption of that ancient and insensate cycle of friendship
followed by enmity, with results this time calamitous. That
forecast, as I see it, reflected pretty accurately the present state
of affairs.

Returning home while the war was still in progress, I expected questions about Russia of every kind. On countless matters of fact my answers were ready; but I was far from ready
with opinions: so many impressions, so many strong emotions,
called for tranquil contemplation at a distance from their
source. By now, impressions have had time to crystallize, contradictory emotions have resolved themselves. The questions assisted this process. These were not at all what I had expected,
and they were astonishingly limited and repetitive. The questions which were *not* asked told much more of the bottomless
ignorance of most of us in face of Russia than those which were
actually put. Later, on a short visit to the United States, I
found an even more extreme state of affairs, aggravated by the
American's almost total lack of objective curiosity. In England
there were three main questions. In America there was only one.

The English questions were: Why do the Russians fight as
they do? How do they manage to fight as they do? Is Russia still
a socialist country (they said Communist, but meant socialist)?

The American question was: Shall we have to fight the Russians?

There were, of course, other questions; but these were the main heads. I was never, for instance, asked *how* the Red Army fought, but always how it managed to fight *as it did,* the questioner taking it for granted that he knew how it fought, which I found surprising.

That was at the height of Russian fame, during the year after Stalingrad. Nowadays there are more questions, some with a strongly derogatory flavour, and all symptomatic of our unwarranted surprise at finding, on closer inspection, that the Russian is not an angel. Nowadays the sort of question I am asked is: Is Russia out to dominate the world? Is Russia a democracy *or* (always *or*) is Stalin a dictator? Is the M.V.D. really a Gestapo? Is it true that Russians at home are not allowed to mix with foreigners? Is it true that the forced-labour camp is a flourishing institution? Why is the Red Army so undisciplined? Why are their habits so disgusting?—these last questions from members of His Majesty's Forces who have served in Germany and Austria.

I have not revisited the United States, but Americans over here still limit themselves to a single question, the same one as before, but cast in a more definite form: *When,* they now ask, shall we have to fight the Russians?

All these questions, the British ones, are asked by those very people in whose eyes only two years ago the Russians could do no wrong. We have come to the reaction. The pendulum is now putting all its weight into the return swing. We have admired the Russians. There are those who would now have us hate them. And just as our admiration was based in misconception, so will be our hatred, if we allow it to develop and mature; *our* hatred, the hatred of the people of Britain and America for the people of Russia. It is the very thing which has happened so often in the past. It is in the first beginnings of happening again today. It is the apotheosis of silliness. It is so silly that if the budding fact were not there beneath our eyes it would be inconceivable. But there it very much is, in the full process of becoming. And the Russians are not helping any. . . .

One can only echo sadly the words of one of Daudet's characters: *"Cela vous donne une fière idée de l'homme!"*

Our hero-worship of Russia was silly. We had not, the great majority of us, the faintest idea of what it was we were worshipping. But at least it was generous. And if we retain the generosity and season it with sense we can still arrest the dismal process which nature, tedious, limited, and blind, takes it for granted we shall dully obey. For are we really prepared this time, now that at last we have attained the dignity and responsibility of full self-government and like to think that we are no longer a mob played upon by professional spellbinders—are we really prepared to submit ourselves to this primitive and tedious play of action and reaction? Are we really content to sit back passively and allow ourselves to be used as the raw material for the bleak and senseless repetition of an idiotic superstition? Time alone will show; and this time, unless we use our wits, with a bang which will scatter the lot of us into our component dust and leave this planet free for the inventive genius of the lesser known tribes of the Amazon and the Congo. And worse by far, worse to infinity, than the physical disaster, will be the disgrace, the shame, of being its author. For just as we admired the Russians on no better ground than that they held and beat back two hundred German divisions, so, if the fatal process develops, we shall find ourselves hating them for the following edifying reasons: (i) cross-purposes about the meaning of democracy; (ii) failure to understand that Russia, America, and Britain are the three effective powers, with the rest nowhere; (iii) dislike of Mr. Molotov's manner; (iv) distaste for the drinking and sanitary habits of the Red Army troops in Berlin and Vienna; and so on. . . . If it is seriously considered that these reasons and others like them justify a war to end civilization, well and good. If not, let us try to see what lies behind these things—and, while we are about it, what lay behind the Russian victory which we once admired so much.

Death and destruction, blood, tears, and famine have been the price of past failure of the people who live in Great Britain to comprehend the people who live in Russia, both lots of

people being the most unwarlike in the world. They have fought
the Russians actively only twice; but war is only one aspect of
destructiveness, and may, in itself, at times be necessary. The
war we have just survived was necessary, or could only have been
avoided by complete domination of the German people by the
rigorous use of force. It was necessary because one set of people
living in one part of the world set out deliberately, and by naked
force, to impose their inadequate conception of life upon the
rest of the world. We had, in the end, to resist by naked force.
But there will not be for many, many years, perhaps there
never will be, another deliberate attempt at world domination
by force of arms. Any war which broke out between Russia and
the West would be a war of accident, a war precipitated by fear,
or umbrage, or exasperation. And if it happens, it will be because we allow it to happen, because we shall have proved that
our lives are lazy and brutish and deserve to be short, because
we shall have proved that we are mental and emotional slovens,
finally and irredeemably deserving of the swift and extravagant
retribution to which we can now look forward with so much
confidence, and better vanished from the scene, for all our partly
realized splendours; since we shall, in a word, have proved
ourselves incurably afflicted with what the Russian critic,
Herzen, called the inertia of the spirit, that same quality which
the great German novelist, Jacob Wassermann, called *die
Trägheit des Herzens,* which causes everything to die.

On the threshold of the Atomic Age, which will be the
apotheosis of Technical Man, and may very well be also his
extinction, some two thousand years, furthermore, after the
birth of Christ, the future of the world lies absolutely, and for
the first time in the history of the world unambiguously, in the
hands of a clearly limited number of powers—three of them,
and only three—Russia, America, and Britain. Between us we
can make or break the whole civilized world, and in the shadow
of this staggering and unprecedented concentration of power
no other nation counts for anything at all, except in the form
of a moral influence for good or evil. For, if the three great
nations behave themselves in an adult and sensible manner,

their might can immediately neutralize the most venomous and persistent attempts elsewhere to disturb the peace. Any world war of the future, then, must be the sole responsibility of America, Russia, and Britain. For once, for the first time in history perhaps, it is impossible to pass the buck. This responsibility, the responsibility for the future of the world, is inescapably fixed upon our joint shoulders, and we cannot shake it off. Nor will any attempt to dilute this terrible and magnificent responsibility by dragging in the so-called United Nations help us in this matter at all. It can do nothing but cloud the stark issue, which must be starkly faced. Decisions will be made in Washington, Moscow, or London which will determine whether a white civilization is to continue, gradually drawing into it on an equal footing the coloured races of the world, or whether the human race will have to make a fresh start, which may take a million years, in isolated pockets of jungle, steppe, and desert.

One would think that these three great nations, shrinking arbiters of the destiny of the world, would approach their august task in a spirit of high dedication. One would think that the smaller nations would be overcome with relief that theirs was not the ultimate responsibility for the future of mankind and would be hanging upon each word or gesture of the unique and fantastic trinity, going about on tiptoe and scarcely daring to breathe for fear of disturbing the fateful deliberations of the absurdly inadequate representatives of the fearful and aspiring race of men. Instead, one sees—what one sees. And the only evidence of awareness of the reality of the situation on the part of any of the three powers, namely, Russia's insistence on the special position of those three powers, goes for nothing because of Anglo-American woolly-mindedness aggravated by the fatal incapacity (fatal, that is, so often in the past) of the Russians to explain themselves in straightforward language, which drives them into the employment of a sort of totemistic code of significant or symbolic actions—like a tramp's chalk-signs—to which no one possesses the key.

We were discussing present realities. We may not like these realities. We may not like the notion of controlling the fate of the world. But our likes and dislikes are neither here nor there. The fate of the world is in our hands, and sooner or later, in time, or just too late, we shall be forced to recognize this fact. Any pretence that we can share our responsibility effectively with Sweden or Argentina, or even with France, is at best self-deception, at worst hypocrisy. These nations, and all others, will have voices; and in the case of some particularly, and in the case of others when they produce a worthy idea, we shall welcome what they have to say—but we shall welcome it in the spirit with which Mr. Churchill used to welcome the comments of private members of the House of Commons when he was fighting the war against Germany and Japan.

We then, as nations, are responsible. For responsibility does not cease with the nondescript and gallant Mr. Attlee, the amiable and jumpy Mr. Truman, the gently purring tiger Marshal Stalin. The people also count for something, and it is useless to rail at the levity shown in high places if we do not do our part, each of us individually. And one of the first and most imperative things we must do is some hard thinking about Russia—in order to decide whether we want to fight and conquer her or reach a vital understanding. Unless we can reach a *modus vivendi* with the Russians our civilization will not survive the next critical half-century. That much is self-evident. There are only two ways of achieving a *modus vivendi* with another country, just as there are only two ways of achieving a *modus vivendi* with another human being: by conquest or understanding—or, in the old-fashioned monosyllable, love. Conquest is simple enough. It is the German way, and it might very well have succeeded. I have no doubt at all that if America and Britain today set out to conquer Russia they would meet with swift and gratifying success—and without the atomic bomb. But conquest is not, traditionally, our way. And that leaves only the other way, the way of understanding, or love, which is more difficult, but which has the advantages of bringing about more permanent results and also of being the method enjoined upon us by the religion, or system of ethics, or what have you, in the light of which we are now, after twenty centuries, just beginning to strive to live.

For this is the inescapable antithesis. Conquest or love.

Is it necessary, at this time of day, to justify that poor word love, that dusty monosyllable which holds the germs of all goodness and all greatness? Perhaps it is. Let us, then, put it this way. Why do the Americans and the British not unite to conquer Russia, whom we seem to fear? Let there be no mistake about it—that is where our immediate material interest lies. A victorious war against the Soviet Union—and, if undertaken now, it would be victorious, for reasons which will become plain later on—would make us joint masters of the world. Together, if it took us that way, we could sack the globe and live in splendour on our spoils. Or, if we saw farther and cared what happened to our grandchildren, we could so organize the world on mass-production lines that the general standard of living would be immeasurably raised. And, contemplating this enticing prospect through the eyes of a material idealist, what a prospect for this battered planet! Unified world government without fear; a stern but benign authority beneath whom all would prosper as never before—until at last the grave would come to stand for relief from satiety. And how insignificant the initial bloodshed. . . . And could we not, and particularly America, argue as speciously as in the past we have argued about the Indians and the Zulus and as America has argued about *her* Indians and the Filipinos, that the world outside our dominion is not fit to govern itself and that we must rule that the world may prosper. . . . Well, and why not? By our standards, and particularly American standards, every other country in the world, including Russia, is populated by poor, benighted savages eking out brutish days in unplumbed squalor. . . . And when it came to the turn of the British, as it would—when, having conquered Russia with our help, America decided that *our* continued sovereignty made the world untidy—who should we be to say that we liked things better as they are, echoing the Hindu widow or the witch-doctor of the Niger valley? Oh, yes, America could do it, first aided by us.

Then why not? We say, we progressives, that what the world needs for prosperity and peace is a central world authority. Here then is the way to get it. The Romans had something like it, and it counted for a good deal. Napoleon tried it on a limited scale, and failed. Hitler tried it on an unlimited scale, and only just failed. America, first aided by us, then absorbing us, could succeed with unopposable ease and a subsequent benevolence unprecedented in the history of conquerors.

Why, indeed, not? You may say idleness, inertia, muddled thinking, fear of the incidental suffering, the short-sightedness of vested interests, the lack of bold and logical imagination. But I do not think the probable failure of the English-speaking nations to appear as world conquerors will be due to any of these causes, although all of them confuse and blur the issue. No, the real reason for our restraint will be, quite simply, that we think conquest by force of arms is wrong. Because we are developing a moral sense to which we pay a good deal of lip-service, and, when it comes to a final showdown, a quite surprisingly heavy tribute in practical behaviour. We believe, in short, that aggression is wrong.

This is a belief which derives from the New Testament, which attributes to Jesus Christ a system of living based on love. Others before Christ had intimations of this conception; but it was he who gave it what would nowadays be called a global voice. I do not know how many of my readers are Christians, or how few. But one thing must be clear to us all, and that is that for two thousand years Western civilization has been groping towards a philosophy of love based on the teaching of the New Testament, which only in the last century or so has begun in any way to be properly understood. And this conception, to put it at its lowest, is opposed to wars of conquest. It is also true to say, I think, that in the West we are showing signs in our daily life of believing that Christ was right and the pagans wrong. The very fact that in a book of this kind I can freely suggest that the English-speaking nations may refrain from setting out to conquer Russia because they think it wrong is a proof of that; a century ago, when all men professed themselves Christians and the Church was strong, a Ricardo or a Bentham would have had a fit at any such suggestion.

But, as a faith, belief in the wrongness of aggression is still woolly in its head and weak on its legs. The question still is whether we can carry it to a decent and firm conclusion. Because the only argument against conquest is love. If we are to abandon love—then for heaven's sake let us conquer, and substitute the London police system and the plumbing of Fifth Avenue for the M.V.D. and the cess-pit.

Where, then, does that bring us? Simply to the position from which we see that we have either to love the Russians or to conquer them. And because I do not think we shall deliberately set out to conquer them—which from every point of view but the highest would be the reasonable solution—I suggest it is high time we paid some attention to the problems of loving—or, to come back to our less terrifying word, understanding—or, to go back to the first step of all, toleration.

Understanding is more than admiration. We thought we admired the Germans (some still do); but we did not, and do not, understand them. It is better to understand than to admire. Our private and subjective emotions, embodied fluctuation, are apt to lead to trouble when let loose on even so small and commonplace an understanding as marriage. How much greater the disaster when the relations between two nations are involved. Let us have less of passion and more of the spirit of the marriage of convenience in our foreign attachments; for understanding (after toleration, which is a general attitude of mind) is the first step to love—which, once more, is greater than admiration, or infatuation.

And I would qualify even further. Understanding is an unattainable ideal. The most we can do is to try to understand, and to keep on trying.

To those who say that understanding must be mutual, I would answer that there is no must about it. It would be very nice if it could be mutual, because then there would be no more problems of this kind. But although it takes two to make a quarrel, only one is necessary to avoid a quarrel. We shall talk later on about appeasement. For the moment it is enough to remark that this horrible word, a dubious label for cowardice in face of a bully, now shows every sign of driving from our language and our thought one of its finest and most sturdy flowers: the word conciliation.

It is a word which implies interaction between two or more firm points of view, a deliberate adjustment of differences. It demands self-knowledge as well as knowledge of the other side. And it demands sufficient clarity of head to know when to give way and when to stand firm. Finally it demands the courage to stand absolutely firm on the points which matter and to give way with good grace on the points which do not.

II

THE MIGHTY PLAIN

1. THE SPIRIT OF THE PLAIN
2. THE PLAIN AND HISTORY
3. THE PEOPLE OF THE PLAIN

1. THE SPIRIT OF THE PLAIN

RUSSIA is a country of light and sky; Moscow, its capital, is a city of light and sky, its buildings part of a tremendous and luminous skyscape. When the sky is overcast, Moscow is nothing. On such days, which are frequent, all Russia is shapeless, and you see at once how much it depends on the modelling of the horizon and the radiance of the sky to provide the hard outline and the movement, in a word, the character, which is absent from so much of the landscape. On a winter's day in the great plain, when the cloud is spreading out for snow, there is no horizon at all: the whitish snow which has already fallen to cover an infinity of slowly undulating plain merges indistinguishably with the whitish sky from which snow will soon fall. And when it begins to fall, more often than not in the form of a powdery, dry fragmentation, all that happens is that the whitish shroud wraps itself more closely round, with claustrophobic effect, until, finally, the nearest dark object, and then you yourself, are totally enveloped in a uniform whitish element, which is manifest only as a whirling vortex, a blinding of the eyes, and a bitter stabbing of the cheeks. Then nothing is palpable; nothing has shape. But when the snow ceases to fall and the cloud-ceiling lifts, breaks up into distinguishable cloud-shapes, and finally dissolves before the face of the sun, the change is as dramatic and exciting as a transformation scene. What, beneath the clouds, was characterless and shapeless is now an immense and glittering landscape spreading to remote horizons beneath a sky of purest azure which seems to take its radiance from the reflected dazzle of the sunlight shining upon the all but limitless fields of snow, which may stretch three thousand miles from east to west, from the Pacific Ocean to the Elbe.

What was shapeless now has exquisite definition, and although
the great plain is still the great plain, and therefore fundamentally monotonous, it is now broken up into the most delicate patterning by the conjunction of woods, clumps of trees,
slight tiltings of the surface of the earth, villages and solitary
homesteads, still white but clearly shaped beneath the snow.
There is no middle distance, no softening haze. Far away, beyond the point where previously land and sky had merged, the
sun catches the gilded cupolas of a monastery church, and white
walls gleam warmly against the colder whiteness of the snow
and in brilliant contrast with other walls in flat colour-wash
of blue or pink or green. And the more you gaze the more aware
you become of the plain's innumerable departures from monotony, and you see that each shift of emphasis is marked by the
prismatic brilliance of the snow, which may be violet in the
shadows or rosy-flushed on the slopes that face the sun. And
there, quite close at hand, in what a moment before had seemed
a grey monotony of flatness, is a hidden ravine, one of the deep
scourings which break up the surface of the steppe into number-
less sudden folds. And on the side of the ravine which faces the
sun is deployed a small village, each wooden cottage with its
own fenced garden, its poplar tree, its elaborately fretted
window-frames, its nesting-box for starlings raised up on a
pole: the snow-cushioned roofs stand clearly against the snow
background, the defining shadows gleaming as violet light.

All this is typical of the Russian landscape, which is either
crystal clear and defined with the utmost sharpness, producing
its effect with slight and delicate touches on the background of
monotonous immensity, or else grey, characterless, and shapeless. It is a country which takes its very shape from the light and
the sky. And what applies to the rural landscape applies equally
to the cities, which are subject to the same laws. The great
Russian sky vaults them as impartially as the forest and steppe,
putting them in their place as sudden concentrations of urban
agitation islanded in this boundless expanse of natural earth.
Just as London takes its character from the marooning oceans,
which send their sea-wrack scudding low above the city spires,

so Moscow lies marooned in this endless plain, a glittering speck beneath that immaculate and Byzantine sky, which stretches from Kiev to Vladivostok and takes no account of cities.

So that the first impression you get of Moscow, in spite of ferro-concrete outcrops, is of a rambling mass of low-pitched roof-tops, armoured against the snow with their characteristic red iron-sheeting, huddled together to form positive warrens, or villages, of crooked, tunnelling lanes and complicated court-yards—all this crouched, as it were, beneath the weight of the sky, and then drawing back to form broad avenues and open spaces which welcome the irresistibly flooding light and enable the eye to group the works of man against the sky. So that even the multi-storied concrete buildings of the last decades, squarely reared up above the general roof-line, do nothing so much as emphasize their own insignificance against the mighty sky, like a triumphal archway, leading nowhere, in a desert. Perhaps it is for this reason that the traditional Russian architecture, with its high-shouldered churches surmounted by rounded cupolas, or the celebrated onion and pineapple domes derived from Byzantium and Asia Minor, has sought to establish the power and invention of man not by raising buildings which float up from the earth, their slender arches rising to lofty spires, but, instead, has made its point with broadly patterned interruptions of the flat horizon, creating fantasy of the most formal kind which is firmly based upon the surface of the plain.

I have started with a generalization about the Russian land-scape, not for its own sake, but because nothing could be more absurd than to try to visualize a people in a vacuum, or with no background to relate them to. We ourselves, when all is said, are very much the products of our landscape and our climate. And who could make sense of the problems of the Eskimos without some idea of the properties of snow and ice, or explain the Italian Renaissance without an appreciation of the hill-sequestered cities of Tuscany, or the rich loot of the Po valley with its guardian fortresses? Certainly when we think of Russia we must evoke the image of the mighty plain and its exacting climate, which have dominated and conditioned the lives of the Russian people for countless generations, and will continue to dominate them until man succeeds in shutting out the sky. The plain is a positive influence. It has certain characteristics which are faithfully reflected in the make-up of its inhabitants. I do not say that aspect for aspect the people have been moulded in the image of the plain, but I do say that certain characteristics of the Russian temperament, latent perhaps in the temperaments of all peoples, have been brought out and magnified by their physical environment, which has therefore helped to make them what they are.

And in this generalization of the winter landscape of the plain we already begin to see certain features emerging which are also features of the Russian people, and have been from time immemorial. I mean particularly the qualities arising from its immensity, its lack of light and shade, its habit of appearing as all brilliance or all greyness. All these find their reflection in the Russian character, and the keynote of them all is immoderation. Later on, as we come to look at the Russian people in their daily life, we shall see again and again these qualities emerging and singly or in elaborate combination giving rise to other qualities, all with the keynote of immoderation, and all working together, sometimes in harmony, sometimes in destructive opposition, to shape the history, the institutions, and the perennial aspirations of this tremendous people, which add up to form the great and fascinating human complex which we label the Russian Enigma.

Long ago in Moscow I began to arrive at some kind of an appreciation of what Russia was and had been and might become. That appreciation had been attained for the greater part unconsciously in the midst of other, more immediate preoccupations, not by reading books—although these were needed in their place—and certainly not by contemplating model farms and crèches, or learning statistics by heart. That appreciation had slowly crystallized in a long series of sudden minor flashes, in a word, by *feeling*. I believe that all the explaining in the world will get us nowhere unless we can experience the *feel* of Russia. And the feel is dominated by the mighty plain.

The plain is immense. Its immensity is such that it never for
one moment allows you to forget the insignificance of man in
face of nature and the universe. It arouses, not only in the newcomer to Russia, but also in the Russians themselves, a sense of
cosmic consciousness and the emotions associated with the large
and insoluble problems of human existence. We, in these islands, are faced in the last resort with the same infinity and the
same universal rigour, but while for us the first and last things
are concealed by a thousand accidental, man-made circumstances, for the Russian they are not. They are perpetually present. As we have seen, you cannot shut out the plain even from
the proudest cities, which are islands lost in its immensity and
subject to its laws. So that even in Moscow, the old and new
metropolis, where there are distractions enough, one would have
said, to shut nature out and limit awareness to the rules and
laws of man, the broad avenues and open spaces keep your daily
life constantly vulnerable to the impact of a universe above
the lives of men, represented by the limitless sky above, which
speaks of limitless space, and never allows you to forget the
universe and your ignorance in face of it, keeping alive perpetually the sort of emotions felt in contemplation of the stars.

Even at night in the very heart of the city the presence of
the plain is no less real. In the dead stillness of a frosty winter's
night you hear from far, from near, the deep, mournful, yet
mellifluous and muted bellowing of the great steam locomotives circling the city or setting out on their tremendous, weighty
journeys to link one huddled speck of humanity with others
scattered widely on the flat plain beneath the stars. . . .

This emotionalism, from which you cannot escape, and
which itself partakes of the quality of immoderation, you will
find in Russia's literature, her music, her endless speculative
conversations over endless glasses of tea, and, indeed, in a thousand details of her daily life. Other lands may be considered
always as societies of men and women, individual societies, with
the follies and nobilities of such, and deriving their existence
from the interplay between one another: men and women combined into societies apart from nature and in despite of her.
We regard these societies as we regard our own, thrown up in

sharp and uneasy focus against the vague and menacing back-ground of human, of animal, of organic, of cosmic conscious-ness. But with Russian society the background becomes the middle distance, like the vegetation of the tropics, unceasingly threatens the foreground, and sometimes envelops and de-vours it.

All this may be considered nebulous and highfalutin. Perhaps it is. But unless you are prepared to think in terms of moods, or simply to let yourself *feel*, Russia will remain a country without meaning. Later on we shall have something to say about quali-ties precisely the opposite of these, or apparently precisely the opposite, the sort of hard matter-of-fact realism, for instance, for which the Russians are so famous. For nowhere in the world is there a national temperament so profoundly at odds with itself as the Russian. And to appreciate this dualism you have to feel it rather than explain it; and the plain is a source of such feeling, as it is a source of the dualism itself.

The plain is not only immense, dwarfing human-kind and reducing their differences, one from another, to insignificance. It is also limitless and formless, inviting infinite expansion. And just as we may see in the hard matter-of-factness of its people a strong reaction away from the metaphysical implications of immensity, so there are interesting examples of their attempts to escape from the destructive and enervating influence of the formless and the infinitely expansive. We can see this in a variety of spheres, always working in conjunction with other forces, since in life there is no purity of means or motive. We can see it in the political sphere in the institutions of Tsardom and serf-dom. We can see it in the social sphere in Peter's impassioned attempt to create an artificial and clear-cut society in a brand new capital which by sheer weight of stone and elaboration of limitation should shut out the disintegrating influence of the great plain—St. Petersburg, which, as well as a window to the West, was a gesture of defiance, like a city built in the shadow of a volcano. We see it in the aesthetic sphere in the stilted and repetitive formalism of ecclesiastical art, in which the subject matter is rigorously restricted and the treatment of every detail minutely prescribed; and, later, in the classical ballet, which is ruled by the same sort of laws. We see it in the religious sphere, in the Orthodox Church, in the total absence of evangelizing and the impassioned preoccupation with ritual and form. We see it in the sphere of human intercourse, which, apparently expansive and informal to the point of absolute naturalness, is yet regulated by an elaborate and wholly arbitrary code of manners so rigidly adhered to that its unconscious infraction by a foreigner may produce a misunderstanding which may lead to a war.

And all this—autocracy, artificiality, restrictiveness, and formalism—is in direct and often violent opposition to the true spirit of the people, independent to the point of anarchy and expansive to the point of incoherence, who, perceiving the need for limitations in human society, but having no inborn sense of limitations, surround themselves with restrictions of the most arbitrary kind. That is one aspect of the Russian dualism. Later on we shall be considering the qualities of the Russian peasant, and we shall find that nothing could be easier to prove than that he is a born co-operator—and that nothing could be easier to prove than that he is a selfish individualist. An impressive exposition of the Russian character and state could be built up on either hypothesis; but, unfortunately, neither would be true. The truth, as we know, the truth about a single human being or about a mass of human beings, is beyond human apprehension. To approach it as closely as may be we have to rely on reason, but reason which does not spring from the emotions is an academic exercise, useless in all but academic problems. The Russian people are not an academic problem. They are human beings of flesh and blood and feeling and perception, all nourished by the great Eurasian plain, which runs to extremes.

The plain is also severe. So far we have looked at Russia under snow, which is reasonable enough. Most of us who do not know the country habitually think of it in terms of snow—with memories of Vereshchagin's painting of the rout of Napoleon's army or, more recently, of the reports of the German débâcle in the dreadful winter of 1941. But the snow is only one extreme: the others are heat and mud. And these three extremes of climate condition the lives of the Russians and have helped to shape their character as much as any other single factor. They also heighten the effects of immensity and formlessness. So that to the influence of the plain itself we must add the influence of its climate.

Because of the snow and the mud the peasants are without their land for six months of every year. For four months the snow lies heavy. For a month in spring and another month in autumn there is mud, limitless, bottomless, body-and-soul-annihilating mud, mud caused by the autumn rains and the first melting snowfalls, and mud caused by the great spring thaw. This mud makes the great plain, which has little stone for road-making, impassable. For perhaps six months in the year, then (in the north for less, in the south, of course, for more), the peasant works his land. For another four months he can move about freely; but the land and everything belonging to it is buried deep in snow. For the remaining two months he is immobilized and confined to his wooden hut: in spring until the sun dries the mud and he can go about on wheels; in winter until the snow covers the mud and he can get out his sledge. This harsh, ineluctable rhythm which imposes upon him the fiercest activity in summer alternating with aimless winter idleness has also marked his character.

For the winter of the plain is not merely an affair of snow and mud; it is also an affair of cold, cold that is no longer a matter of relative temperature or a climatic condition, but an element in its own right, as absolute and self-sufficing as water or earth or fire. But although this cold is the enemy, which kills when it finds you off your guard, it can be barricaded out, and it is. So that the effect of the winter cold is on the character rather than on the body. There are plenty of illusions about the Russian's resistance to cold. We heard a good deal about the effect of frost-bite on the German army before Moscow in the winter of 1941; what we did not hear was that some of the Russian formations suffered similar casualties almost as severely. Their superior mobility was due partly to special winter clothing and partly to their limitless capacity for endurance, not to their resistance to cold as such. For the plain fact is that you cannot lie out in a ditch at 30° C. below for days and nights on end without getting frozen, whether you are a German or a Russian. This is not a question of toughness, but of elementary physics. The toughness comes in when you lie out in spite of being frozen.

This the Russians, in time of war, will do; and then their endurance is heroic. But in normal times they will go to extreme lengths to avoid the cold, so that their winter life is, by our standards, soft; and there can be no doubt at all that this natural evasion of the cold, as an enemy not to be trifled with, has helped to produce that familiar Russian lethargy which results in part from spending the winters indoors, cut off from all normal work, and in an overheated atmosphere. The Russian capacity to endure is, in fact, far less a product of winter cold than it is of summer heat, which is also extreme. The job of getting in the harvest, under a malignant sun and on a diet of black bread and *kvass,* calls for more endurance in a few weeks than the Russian peasant is normally called upon to display all through the winter, when he either lounges idly indoors or wanders off, wrapped up against the cold, to do winter work in the towns.

But the real toughness of the Russians—who take toughness for granted, do not dwell on it, and get away from it to the softer delights as soon as they possibly can, like Elizabethan Englishmen, or like modern Englishmen hardened in modern war—is developed by generations of resistance to hunger. For hunger is another feature of the plain, or part of its aspect of severity. In the north, in the forest zones, there is not much food. The soil is poor in the forest clearings, and the old inhabitants ate fish and honey and the flesh of animals they trapped for furs. These are now called the consumer provinces, and they formed the greater part of the old Russia, or Muscovy. Nowadays the people of this area buy grain, which comes from the producer provinces of the south, first from the wooded steppe, then (and comparatively recently) from the true grassy steppe with its famous black earth. And it is here, in the steppe, that the continental climate of the plain makes itself felt most disastrously. There are two horrors: early frosts and summer drought. All through the long winter the young winter corn lies beneath the blanketing snow, to stand up strongly and swiftly when the earth dries off in spring. But each year the late autumn is a trial of suspense. For if the hard frost comes before the snow, the autumn sowings are wiped out. And then you can do nothing, nothing at all except sit and wait through the long winter until the late spring. The frost came first in 1941. It helped to stop Hitler's army, but it also ruined immense tracts of desperately needed autumn sowings.

There is at least a chance of recovery after an autumn frost. But from drought in summer there is no recovery. Although the black earth is the most fertile soil in the world and almost unlimited in extent, it is also, perhaps for lack of woodland, all too rainless. And a serious drought beneath that scorching, continental sun will wither everything growing, like fire. When that happens there is nothing to be done. Your crops burnt up in late summer, there is no second sowing. Your animals sicken and die. You yourself must struggle along as best you can, helping your neighbour and being freely helped by him, until the next harvest. And if, as sometimes happens, the next harvest is also bad—well, then you get stark, staring famine, with all its terrible consequences in the way of aimless blind migrations in search of food and work, and the epidemic diseases that arise and sweep through a disorganized society.

That, too, comes from the plain, and even local famines are exacerbated by the nature of the plain, which, providing no stone for hard roads, makes an impossibility of rapid distribution.

It may well be that the reader at this stage is asking what the domestic and agricultural problems of the primitive Russian peasant have to do with modern Russia, the U.S.S.R., with its Five-Year Plans, its up-to-date machinery, its huge constructional activity, and all the other paraphernalia of the great socialist experiment in which the new men and the newer women think in terms of tractors rather than one-horse sledges and devote their dreams to the increased production of pig-iron rather than to autumn sowings—and, if farming still must be, to combine-harvesters and experiments with arctic wheat rather than to the patient teasing of clods to coax from them their daily bread.

But it has everything to do with it. In the first place, there are still plenty of primitive Russian peasants with their one-horse sledges sitting out the Russian winter by their stoves, or plodding off to work in the towns or on the nearest construction job while the earth lies under snow. In the second place, most of the people whom we think of as "new" were peasants only yesterday, and, as such, are immemorially old. You cannot begin to understand the way the Russians work their machinery or fight their mechanized armies without a more than abstract awareness of this fact. Twenty-five years ago four-fifths of the population of Russia were peasants of one kind or another, the sons and daughters, usually illiterate, of generation after generation of peasant forebears, and still using, except in certain prosperous areas of steppe-land, the old wooden, wheelless plough which superseded the ploughing stick in the fourteenth century. Now only half the population consists of peasants. But that still leaves nearly a hundred million of them. Most of these live today on collective farms, or *kolkhozes;* but the number of collectives that find themselves anywhere near a railway or a metalled road are few indeed. Further, except in a spectacular handful of exceptionally prosperous farms, there is nothing magic about the word collective. It simply means that the land which was once cultivated in bits and pieces by a number of different owners is now communal property and farmed more economically, scientifically, and with respect to division of labour. But the men and women who make up the collective do not inhabit an ivory tower in the middle of the steppe: they go on living in the same old huts, or *izbas,* leading much the same old life, except that it now has a common focus for work and play and politics. And still they are (and always will be) more concerned with the progress of the winter wheat than with the latest statistics from Magnitogorsk.

As for the other half of the population, the other ninety million who are no longer peasants—the great majority of these started life as peasants or came from peasant families and, until the other day, were exclusively peasant in outlook. These are the people who now run the machine-shops in the Urals, the Ukraine, and in deep Siberia. The most brilliant of them have become doctors, scientists, teachers, army officers, bureaucrats, diplomatists, and all the rest, to take their place with the sons and daughters of the relics of the old Tsarist bourgeoisie, of the Revolutionary intelligentsia, and of the urban proletariat who made the Revolution—themselves only one remove from peasants.

The Russian peasant is an extremely variable, as well as complicated, sort of human being. Later on we shall regard him in more detail. But first we must grasp the fact of his ubiquity. We shall come to the Revolution in due course; but it is not the least bit of good talking about the Revolution and how much it has changed, or added to, the Russian people unless we have some idea of what there was to change, or add to. The great mistake so many of us have been making is to think of the Revolution either as a blueprint of a social upset, a practical exercise in Marxian theory functioning in a vacuum, or else in terms of the social life of Great Britain or America with their immense weight of what used to be called the middle classes and educated workers. Such a conception is fatal to any understanding of Russia. Without some idea of the conditions of life of four-fifths of the Russian population as they lived twenty-five years ago, we can appreciate neither the limitations nor the real and astounding achievements of the U.S.S.R. as it faces us today. Hence my insistence on the character of the ordinary Russian, who was—and, in effect, still is—the peasant, who dwelt in the great plain and was its creature.

We have already seen how the immensity of the plain, which you are never allowed to forget, acts as a constant reminder of the littleness of man in face of the universe, and now, in considering the climate of the plain, we add to immensity, severity. The ever-present universe is seen to be inimical. So that the natural elements in which the Russian lives his life themselves embody for all to see not merely the vastness of space but the ruthlessness of an impersonally hostile universe which, with its unchanging laws of life and death, can never be disguised. And this too is reflected in the Russian character. For just as the limitless nature of the plain itself is an invitation to take the line of least resistance to infinity, to move away and ever away from restrictive authority whether physical or spiritual, so the severity of the ever-present universe, with which we are all faced, but which the Russian, by the very land he treads, is never allowed to forget, can only be answered in one way by the individual man or woman, and that is to band himself together with others, to sink his own individuality in a common cause, in order to survive at all the cold and the drought, which, when they strike, strike on a deadly scale. It is the plain, too, which gives him a speculative attitude towards life and death, as well as a ready acceptance of the facts of life and death—for you cannot live your life in the immediate shadow of infinity and be uninfluenced by the tragic sense of life or untouched by fatalistic resignation. At the same time it also gives him clear and matter-of-fact assessment of the conditions of survival and unlimited flexibility of mind and spirit and behaviour, resulting from the sense that once survival, the supreme and only reality, is assured, nothing that man can think or do is likely to be of importance in face of the monstrous universe. And bound up with this is the famous Russian breadth of spirit, an easy acceptance of everything under the sun and a boundless tolerance of and sympathy with the shortcomings of his neighbours. And here we find slipping into the complex mosaic of character the total absence of hypocrisy in the make-up of the Russian. He knows too well that when affliction comes it falls on good and bad alike; he is never tempted to call misfortune the reward of sin. And here, too, in face of infinity, is the ready acceptance by an independent spirit of the impositions of absolute authority, authority beneath which, as beneath the overwhelming bitterness of the elements, the differences between ordinary men are seen as nothing, so that all men are equal beneath God and the Tsar. And again, another piece of the mosaic, partly as a corollary to the arbitrariness of the plain, partly as an outcome of the immemorial physical rhythm of alternate fierce summer activity and winter idleness, we find unlimited boldness of thought and action surging up in tremendous waves, coupled with a tendency to throw up the hands when the struggle seems too long and too hard, to shrug and murmur: *Nichevo!* For what, when all is said, and against that overwhelming background of insensate and indifferent nature, does anything matter? It will all be the same in a hundred years, we are apt to say in moments of lucid resignation. The Russian has only to look up at the sky, or out at the unending plain, to have it heavily borne in on him that it is all the same today.

By now we should have some idea of the highly generalized physical background of the Russian people, the two hundred million men, women, and children, who somehow withstood the assault of the finest and most determined army in the history of the world (for that was what the German army was in 1941 and 1942), and who, before that, had carried out the most complete revolution in the history of the world (a revolution which was really three separate revolutions, culminating in the establishment of a new kind of civilization), and who, before that, for countless generations had lived a life as hard and restricted as the life of any people in the world (with one or two exceptions, such as the Eskimos and the Patagonian Indians). Now, finding their feet, standing up against this immemorial background and glorying in this new sensation, they present themselves to the bewildered West as the Russian Enigma, which we find personified in Generalissimo Stalin, a Caucasian hill-dweller, and Mr. Molotov, who comes from the middle of the great plain.

It is a very generalized background. There are other aspects of Russia besides the forest and the steppe, and the monotony of the plain is sometimes broken up by little hills and majestic river valleys. But all aspects have one common factor. All, above all, are *exacting*. And we should try to visualize the sort of life we ourselves should have to live if we inhabited those regions —the stunted tundra of the far north; the conifer forest belt below that, which leads to the mixed forests farther south; then the wooded steppe, and the open grassy steppe, which flattens

gradually into the salt desert bordering the Caspian. For all
these people, save the hill-dwellers on the southern and eastern
fringes and the nomads of the desert steppe, no matter how they
may differ in detail, have had to submit to the domination of
the plain, individually, and as a people. And the plain has left
its stamp on them. It has also made for an amazing homogeneousness in its population, because, through the centuries,
it has been slowly peopled by the exploring peasants of old
Russia, who might plod with their families a thousand miles
and settle down in some favoured fold of the immense plain
indistinguishable from the corner they had left when they set
out on their journey. And today the traveller may go a thousand miles across the surface of the plain and everywhere find
the same people in the same situations doing the same tasks in
the same way and with little variation in local customs or
local accent to tell him that he has moved from one side of
Russia to the other. This makes among the Russian people
for a profound community of thought and feeling, which is
manifest in many ways, as we shall see.

I do not wish to suggest that in sketching some of the qualities of the plain which find themselves mirrored in the Russian
character I have attempted a logical synthesis. On the contrary.
These qualities do not arise neatly out of one another in a simple chain of cause and effect. But they exist, and they combine,
as I have said, in the most complex interplay, sometimes harmo-
nizing with one another, sometimes setting up a stiff tension of
opposites, sometimes mutually destructive, sometimes sharpen-
ing each other.

I have listed only some of the qualities which reflect the
physical aspects of the environing landscape and climate. There
are plenty of others; but the ones we have touched upon should
be enough to give us a palpable background to our reflections
on the nature of the Russian people. That background is the
great Eurasian plain, with its limitless space and its pitiless
climate which make Russia the battleground of the human soul,
a vivid substantiation of the darkest and most dazzling ob-
scurities of the universe. It is not only her literature which is

both terrible and sublime, but also her whole life. And unless we are prepared to think about Russia in terms of emotional hyperbole, we had better not think at all.

Nevertheless, the Russian is very much a creature of the earth; and to bring this chapter down to earth, we shall take notice of one more quality inspired by the great plain. And that is patience. When we talk of Russian idleness, of the Russian's apparently total lack of time-consciousness, we should remember that for him waiting is not, as for us, an irritating interruption in a swift sequence of activities: it is itself activity, as real and as valid as any other. It is a definite occupation, with its own laws and its own very prominent place in the general scheme of life. We should remember that the ancestors of our contemporary Russians have for centuries under direst compulsion developed the art of doing nothing, not merely for days and weeks, but for months, for the whole winter through. Unable to read, even if they had anything to read; unable to work, with no common centre—except the village vodka shop, where once in a way they could relieve the tedium of waiting by getting drunk—with no wireless, no politics, nothing at all but a hut with one room and the shelf above the stove, or the stove itself, or the floor, to lie on—with nothing to do except fuel the stove and fodder the animals—they waited the winter through, in preparation for the intense and often fearful struggle of the summer. The Russians know how to wait. On the one hand, perhaps they wait passively too easily. On the other, they use waiting as a positively dynamic instrument of policy. They know how to wait because for centuries they have had to wait for the melting of the snow, as a full-time occupation, or, if they did not, go mad.

2. THE PLAIN AND HISTORY

BY now it should be clear that the people who inhabit the great Eurasian plain, the Russian people, must, in the course of centuries, have developed very distinct characteristics which distinguish them sharply from the peoples of the more sequestered regions of the West. We ourselves, if we were set down as a nation in the middle of the plain, would have to adapt ourselves or perish; and slowly we should find our national character changing. So strong and irresistible is the influence of climate and soil that any collection of people submitted to the Russian climate and the Russian soil would in time come to share certain characteristics now peculiar to the Russians themselves.

But by no means every characteristic. Climate and soil are not the whole story. We have only to look at any of those curious spiritually autonomous communities of alien races which huddle together in scattered enclaves throughout the Russian lands to see that it is possible for foreigners to share for centuries the habitat of the Russian peasant and, in many particulars, his way of life, without becoming Russian, though not without developing the qualities necessary for survival in that setting. I think, for example, of the Volga Germans who, until 1941, when they were deported lock, stock, and barrel to an unknown destination in Siberia, had for at least two centuries colonized and farmed the Volga steppe-lands in the neighbourhood of Saratov with a mixture of Teutonic efficiency and Russian endurance. I happened by chance to get a glimpse of this mass deportation while it was in progress. It was very much like any other mass deportation in Eastern Europe under emergency conditions: long-settled families suddenly ravished from their homes and driven in draggled, dazed procession to the railway,

33

there to be herded into sealed freight-cars with no room to lie down, with no apparent sanitary arrangements, and with, to say the least, inadequate food. The weaker would probably die where they stood on that interminable journey into Asia, with the wait at every siding an instalment of eternity. To all appearances these unfortunates were indistinguishable from Russian peasants. They might have been a train-load of dispossessed *kulaks* being taken away to the mines. It was extremely cold: the winter of 1941 began too soon. But there was no lamentation. The Volga Germans had learned that much from the plain. They stood wedged in their vans, the fortunate ones gazing out impassively through the bars in the top half of each door, and waited like Russian peasants, because there was nothing else for them to do.

But they were not Russian peasants. For generations they had kept themselves to themselves. Their way of thinking was un-Russian. Their tidiness was un-Russian. Their methods of farming and their domestic life were more efficient, provident, and economical than those of their Russian neighbours. They were, in a word, more prosperous. So that not everything about the Russian can be explained in terms of climate and soil. There are, obviously, other factors; there are, for instance, history and race. Of these two, it seems to me that the first is immeasurably the most important in differentiating the Russian from the rest of the world. I suppose most people would disagree, declaring for race, whatever that may be, echoing Disraeli's "Race is all." It is so much easier and more definitive. The Russians are Slavs. The French are Latins. We are Anglo-Saxons (or is it Teutons?). Of course all the differences between us are explained by our different races. . . .

But are they? I do not profess to know what race is. When we find anthropologists and ethnologists still arguing hotly about first principles it is surely better for laymen to disregard racial problems until the experts are agreed. . . . The Russians are Slavs no doubt; but in the blood of the Great Russians, the people who have made Russian history and to whom we refer in all generalizations about the Russians, there is a great deal of Finnish stock, which is not Slavonic at all, which is not even

Aryan. And even if we contemplate the pure Slavs of Little
Russia, the Ukraine, what does that tell us? The people of Kiev
are Slavs—and so are the people of Warsaw, Prague, Sofia,
Belgrade, and Zagreb. So also are a large number of the inhabitants of Chicago. . . . The French are Latins. But so are
the people of Spain, of Italy, of Mexico, of Quebec. . . . The
people of Basutoland are Negroes; but so are the people of
Harlem and Haiti. . . . As for the people of Germany, and
the people of England . . .

The Russians undoubtedly are Slavs, and we are not. But
this is a book about Russians, not about the Slavonic genius;
we are more concerned now with considering the differences
between the Russians and ourselves than with determining the
common denominator of the Russians, the Poles, the Czechs,
the Bulgars, the Serbs, and the Croats. And I think it would
be better to think of the Russians as Russians (which is quite
sufficiently exacting) and to speak of the Russian rather than
the Slavonic temperament—at least for the time being. Doubtless race, for what it is worth, is responsible for much of the
difference between the Russians of the Volga and the Volga
Germans; but we are on far safer ground if we stick to what
can be seen. For two hundred years the Volga Germans have
shared the physical home of their Russian neighbours; but what
they have not shared is their history, which has also been conditioned by the plain.

It has been a history of suffering, oppression, and defeat—
now at the hands of barbarian invaders, now at the hands of
Western conquerors, now at the hands of native autocrats. Russia has had her great victories. We know of some of them. But
even her victories have sprung from the bitterness of a defeated
people clinging in blind agony to gutted homes and ravaged,
blood-soaked fields. "The history of Russia," declared Stalin
in 1931, with absolute truth, though with deliberate oversimplification for his immediate end, which was to save the
first Five-Year Plan from breaking down at the very moment
when Japan was invading Manchuria—"the history of Russia
is the history of defeats due to backwardness. She was beaten
by the Mongol khans. She was beaten by the Turkish beys. She

was beaten by the Swedish feudal barons. She was beaten by the Polish-Lithuanian landowners. She was beaten by the Anglo-French capitalists. She was beaten by the Japanese barons. *All* beat her because of her backwardness—military backwardness, cultural backwardness, agricultural backwardness. She was beaten because to beat her was profitable and could be done with impunity."

We shall have more to say about backwardness later on. For the moment the point is this: that, as far as the Russian character is concerned, to the influence of the cruel elements which, in the mighty plain, find scope for their natural expression, must be added the cruelty of predatory man, who also, in this vast arena with no ready-made barriers, finds scope for *his* natural expression. Thus already, and without particular instances, we see, for example, that Russia is not the same as Canada—and without invoking race.

The most important of all the beatings listed by the head of the Russian State and also the most important event in the history of Russia was the impact of the Tartars early in the thirteenth century. They came in 1223 and they remained in control of the Russian lands, under successive khans, and with an irregular rhythm of alternating aggressiveness and passivity, until 1480. For a century after that they maintained a standing threat from the Black Sea region, and in 1571, in the reign of Ivan the Terrible, they raided up as far as Moscow, which was burned. But even the final repulse of the Crimean Tartars was far from being the end of the Tartar story, and the effects of their domination of Russia are still apparent in every fibre of Russian life today and in the Russian attitude towards the rest of the world.

Few things have been more disputed by historians than the extent to which the Tartars influenced the development of Russian history and Russian institutions; but if historians paid less exclusive attention to records and more to common sense I think there would be less wrangling among them about this and many other antique problems. Not that one can blame the historians. They are limited by ascertainable facts. Unless they are to write history out of their own heads (which some, of course, have done) they have to go after the facts, for which, inevitably, as with all things upon which a man's whole activity depends, they come to have a totemistic regard. Even this would not be so bad if we all knew what we meant by facts. But we differ so much about this that, in the end, the only thing we should all agree in calling a fact is an authenticated contemporary record, which may or may not be accurate. So, automatically, all contemporary records become facts, and nothing but a record is a fact. This kind of scholastic jugglery not only blots out common sense, but also narrows the field of speculation and enquiry in a most arbitrary manner. So that too often what should be the all-engrossing study of mankind is degraded to a sort of academic puzzle-corner.

But it is possible to hold quite another conception of the nature of a fact. It is possible, for instance, to believe that the ascertainable facts of history embrace more than the surviving records. It is even possible to believe that many of the undisputed records can be more misleading than the wildest and most irresponsible fantasy, unless they are considered in the light of facts which are not commonly regarded as facts at all. The Eurasian plain, for example, is a fact as valid as Magna Carta or the Declaration of Independence, and a good deal more informative. Further facts are the immensity of the plain and the formlessness of the plain. Facts of this kind are of immeasurably greater importance in the development of the Russian people than, for instance, the precise moment or manner in which the dominion of the grand princes of Muscovy hardened into the Tsardom. And this is because, taken in conjunction with another sort of fact, such as the fact of the Tartar domination of the Russian lands for two and a half centuries, they made the institution of Tsardom, and an absolute autocracy, inevitable and necessary. And as for the Tartars themselves, the bare fact that they did dominate and exact tribute from the Russian princes for a period equal in length to the span between Elizabethan and Victorian England, a period, moreover, which covered the formative years of modern Europe, contains in itself so many implications which, though they may not be recorded, must be as plain as a pikestaff to anyone not wholly lost to the world, that one wonders how so many admirable historians find it difficult at all to make up their minds about the extent of the Tartar influence.

It is, of course, because they do not see the wood for the trees. It is also because the sort of influence they look for is the concrete kind amenable to documentary demonstration. And because there is nothing much to show that the Russians borrowed customs, institutions, devices or words from their inflammable and barbaric oppressors, and because the Tartars let religion alone and, once they had burned down the great cities and destroyed a freshly burgeoning culture, left the people very much to themselves, provided they paid their annual tribute, some historians conclude that Russia, after all, was not materially influenced by her subjection to Asiatic overlords which lasted for a quarter of a millennium.

Why the Russians should be expected to have adopted Tartar specialities it is impossible to guess. They hated them. During the five years of their hideous subjection to Germany the French did not borrow many German words or customs. Why should they? But the influence of the German occupation during those five years, a breath in history, is past computing and will make itself felt (but not recorded and sealed in documents for the benefit of future historians) for centuries to come. And so it was with the Tartars, as anyone with a shred of imagination cannot fail to see, their influence being so much greater than the German influence on the French not only because it lasted so much longer, but also because it operated upon an embryonic and less organized society. In a word, the effect of the Tartars on the Russians of the plain was to change the whole course of their development. So much so that without their impact there might never have been a Russia as we know it, for reasons which will later appear. And that is what I mean by a historical fact. A nation cannot be subjected to a barbaric conqueror for two and a half centuries without finding its character changed —its *national* character—and therefore its whole line of development reorientated. It simply cannot. And that is what I mean when I say that to understand our friends the citizens of the

Soviet Union we have to go back to the plain, which formed the characters of their ancestors, and to the Tartars, who, operating on this character, decided the character of their state. So it is always the plain. For the Tartars themselves came from the plain and because of the plain, with its open Eastern gateway in the Kirghiz Steppe and its total lack of barriers to swift-moving horsemen.

In saying that the Russian autocracy was the direct and inevitable and necessary consequence of the Tartar invasions and the nature of the plain I do not in the least mean that it had to turn out in every particular as in fact it did. Obviously, it might, together with other features of Russian life which spring from those causes, have developed in any of a multitude of particular ways; but in fact, as one would expect, the precise way in which it did develop and the precise form it did take were also due to certain particular aspects of the Tartar dominion and, again, of the topography of the plain.

The precise way it developed is of great interest to us now because, itself conditioned by the character of the people of the plain in conjunction with certain external stresses (*e.g.* the Tartars), it in its turn proceeded to influence the national character which in the first place had influenced *it*. And so on for ever and ever, until this moment of time in which we find ourselves. Facts of this kind are so obvious that they should not need stressing, but there are so few signs today that they form a part of the common mental armoury that perhaps I may be forgiven for stressing them here. And this means that we shall have to run through a little history, which is nothing but the adventures of the people of Russia in their early adolescence, the same people who confront us today in their early maturity —or, if you like, in the act of changing their habits.

The Eastern Slavs, from whom the Russians are descended, inhabited the forests of the Dnieper basin and had a great centre at Novgorod. They were trappers, beekeepers, fishermen, lumbermen, elementary agriculturalists, and traders. They lived in scattered communities in forest clearings by the banks of rivers, which served as their highways, and they appear to have had strong tendencies towards egalitarianism. The city of Lord Novgorod the Great had a highly organized republican society. But, as far as one can make out, the people lacked the faculty, or the desire, to organize the separate communities into a compact, centralized, and hierarchical society. Suddenly, in the year A.D. 862, we find these communities submitting to the rule of foreign princes from the north, and developing into characteristic medieval principalities. These strangers, from whose line the Russian Tsardom ultimately sprang, were Vikings from Sweden, Rurik and his two brothers. But they were river Vikings, long accustomed to using the Dnieper as a convenient route to the Black Sea, and thence to Constantinople and beyond. It is pretty obvious that they took the lands of the Dnieper basin as a means of securing their trade and plunder route and increasing their own wealth. But the legend which says that the Slavs themselves invited them to come and rule their lands, which were rich but anarchic, is, as we see, remarkably true to type. At any rate, they came and they settled, and soon the centre of the Russian lands had moved from Novgorod to Kiev. Here the grand prince had his stronghold, superior to all the appanage princes who held territory in the neighbouring lands. And here, in the tenth and eleventh centuries, long before Moscow meant anything at all, we see the Eastern Slavs developing along familiar lines, in fairly close parallel with the more advanced countries of the new West. They also had rich and fruitful contacts with the West. The princes married with the West. And although they took their Christianity from Byzantium as a by-product of a military campaign against that city, which was always in their thoughts, the culture of the new state, as exemplified above all in its buildings, in its code of laws, and in the distinguished figure of Yaroslav the Wise, who was responsible for most of these, could hold its own with most Western cultures of that time and resembled them very closely. In spite of the Rome–Byzantium cleavage, which then meant nothing but geographical accident, and only later came to mean a very great deal in the development of Russia, Kiev could regard herself as European.

But her immediate undoing was the appanage system with

its disintegrating influence on real estate. There were too many younger sons, and they all had their share of the Russian lands. One of these, Andrew Bogolyubsky, Prince of Vladimir-Suzdal, sacked and conquered Kiev in 1169, and that was the end of any hope of Russian unity, destroyed ironically enough by a man who had some sense of the need for it and refused to divide his own lands according to custom. But Vladimir-Suzdal never truly replaced Kiev and there followed years of fraternal and wholly unconstructive strife.

It was this internal disruption of a unity laboriously sought by the great princes of Kiev which made the Russian lands all too easy for the Mongols to overrun. They came first, under Genghis Khan himself, in a loot and plunder reconnaissance in 1223, and then, fourteen years later, in great strength and with a far deeper thrust, which took them for a time into the heart of central Europe. They receded from central Europe, but they held the great Russian plain so that the lost identity of a young and promising people had to be recovered beneath their domination, and its unity forged in spite of them and yet with their unconscious aid.

It is possible that sooner or later there would have arisen a Russian prince strong and wise enough to subdue all the others and absorb their territories into his own by conquest or marriage had the Mongols never come. It is more likely that they would have fallen to a conqueror from the West. This kind of movement was going on all over Europe, the emergence of the type of born potentate with a lust for power as such, wholly different from the princes who loved power as a means of securing the objects they required for the gratification of their own extremely vital senses. The new kind of ruler belonged to an alien type. He was as different from his boisterous predecessors as our new oil magnates are different from the typical nineteenth-century merchant. In both cases it is a difference in kind rather than in degree. There is no mystery about the motivating forces of the ordinary successful business man: we all of us have our share in them. He wants money to buy things with. But the motivating forces of a Rockefeller we do not share and they must remain to us for ever incomprehensible. They have no

roots in normal human experience. They have no connection
with the gratification of normal human desires and needs. And
the men in whom they operate stand outside the pale of common humanity. Such were the Habsburgs, their incorruptible
ambition a unifying force of Western Christendom. What satis-
faction they received in return for the blighting of their lives
in the service of their own devoted tyranny they and heaven
only knew. And such were the early rulers of Muscovy, Princes
before they were Tsars, beginning with the real founder of
the Great Russian State and the Empire of All Russia, Ivan
Kalita, who in the first half of the fourteenth century secured
a privilege from the Mongol Khan Uzbek, in his golden pavilion
at Serai, near Saratov, on the Lower Volga. The privilege he
received, partly in return for the assiduity of his pilgrimages
to the Golden Horde, and partly as a result of a fortunate conjunction of circumstances, was to act as the trusted agent of the
Khan for the collection of tribute payable by the other Russian
principalities. The particular circumstances referred to were,
firstly, the situation of the city of Moscow, which was the capital of Ivan Kalita's minor principality, in a central position
and near the headwaters of a great river system, and, secondly,
the weakness of Ivan compared with the rulers of other principalities, such as Vladimir-Suzdal and Tver. Such a man, the
Tartars thought, would be more amenable and less likely than
others to make trouble. They were right about immediate
trouble, but they made the same mistake which modern historians make in misjudging the qualities required in a ruling
house of the fourteenth and fifteenth centuries. The day of
irresponsible filibustering, as we have said, was over. The new
societies required, for a number of reasons, to be developed
in larger units than heretofore, and the sort of man to answer
this need was not the swaggering, strong-arm warrior prince but
his measly-looking younger brother with a terrible and brooding lust for power for its own sake, to be obtained by diplomacy
and guile. These conditions were fulfilled by the scions of the
minor house of Moscow, who bamboozled the Tartar khans into
thinking they were weak and pliant, made Muscovy, beneath
Tartar protection, the seat of the grand prince and of the

Orthodox Metropolitan, and in due course pulled all the principalities into their orbit and rose up and drove the Tartars out. That took them nearly two centuries to achieve.

Thus, unlike the rulers of the West, the founders of the house of Russia laid their fortunes not as a result of marriage and conquest, but by favour of an Oriental autocrat. And this fact influenced the whole development and character of the Russian Tsardom to the day of its end, and colours the government of the Kremlin to this day: the interplay of ruled and rulers is so intricate and close that you cannot change the general direction of the one simply by cutting off the head of the other. . . . What kind of a state should we have if the royal house of England, instead of rising from a struggle of character, ambition, loyalties, and treachery to be first among its peers, with the active support of other houses of good standing, and with the consequent standing and automatic checks to the growth of autocracy, had been placed upon the throne by a Moslem invader whose power was absolute? Where would Debrett be today? Even taken quite alone and regardless of other circumstances, the particular genesis of the Russian autocracy would be enough to explain a good deal of what followed, such as the phenomenon of a weak and irresponsible nobility and the development of serfdom. Taken together with certain features of the Russian character reflected in the nature of the mighty plain, from which the Tartars also sprang, the pressure is irresistible. And we must remember, too, still another Tartar influence. They isolated Russia from the rest of Europe, so that the decisive growth of the Russian state and the Russian institutions took place behind a Chinese wall, and in this isolation every natural quality which could distinguish the Russians from the rest of the world was magnified and hardened; so that when at last the genius of Peter the Great broke down the barrier between Muscovy and the West, succeeding where Ivan the Great in the fifteenth century and Ivan the Terrible in the sixteenth had passionately tried and failed, she was a fully-grown society, set in her ways which she had developed in solitude to meet the peculiar challenge of the East, and glorying in her apartness. For was Moscow not also the Third Rome?

The first Rome had apostatized. The second Rome had fallen to the Turk; and behind the impenetrable barrier of the bordering states, looking westwards, she, Moscow, had succeeded to the heritage of Constantine, jealously nourishing the pure, the authentic spirit amidst her forest gloom and in the shadow of the barbarian.

Thus was the holy Tsardom born, and thus it continued.

"Wielders of a power purchased by an unspeakable baseness of subjection to the khans of the Tartar hordes, the Princes of Russia, who in their heart of hearts had come in time to regard themselves as superior to every monarch in Europe, have never risen to be the chiefs of a nation. Their authority has never been sanctioned by popular tradition, by ideas of intelligent loyalty, of devotion, of political necessity, of simple expediency, or even by the power of the sword." Those words were written in the year 1905, nearly six hundred years after the elevation of Ivan Kalita, when the Tsarist autocracy which he founded showed the first signs of cracking under the bombardment of Japanese cannon. They were written by a Polish patriot who was also a man of an acute political intelligence not always associated with Poles, Joseph Conrad, the great novelist. I quote him at length because he expresses so admirably what is really the common conception of the Russian Tsardom, but in his case pointed by hereditary suffering.

"This despotism," he wrote again in the same magnificent essay, "has been utterly un-European. Neither has it been Asiatic in its nature. . . . The Russian autocracy as we see it now is a thing apart. It is impossible to assign it to any rational origin in the vices, the misfortunes, the necessities, or the aspirations of mankind. This despotism has neither a European nor an Oriental parentage; more, it seems to have no root either in the institutions or the follies of this earth. What strikes one with a sort of awe is just this something inhuman in its character. It is like a visitation, like a curse from Heaven falling in the darkness of ages upon the immense plains of forest and steppe lying dumbly on the confines of two continents: a true desert harbouring no Spirit either of the East or of the West."

The emotional, the rhetorical truth of that last passage is beyond dispute. And if we confine our vision to the later Tsars, above all the ineffable sterility of the first Nicholas, who ruled all Russia like a blight, and his inferior successors, we cannot dispute the intellectual truth of it. To all appearances the Tsardom, as manifested in the wild caricature of a tyrant, the lunatic integrity of Nicholas, was precisely a visitation and was felt as such not only by impassioned Poles but also by millions of his own stunned masses and the small handful of the Russian intelligentsia who had brains to think with and mouths for articulation. But the first Nicholas was not the whole of Tsardom. To find the reasons for the visitation we have to go farther back. We have to go back to the plain, and to Ivan Kalita, who founded in collaborationism a dynasty which survived the overthrow of the occupying and protecting power.

I have quoted Conrad, I repeat, not because, as a historian, he is a reliable authority, but because he gives, with his customary superb sweep, what may be called the *outside* view of the Russian autocracy. Better than any other writer he has, in a few words, summed up the idea of the autocracy as it must appear to those who regard the history of a nation or an institution as an arbitrary series of accidents. At the same time he gives the spiritual atmosphere of Russia as it must appear to a liberal Western intelligence who lacks emotional sympathy with the Russians. "A brand of hopeless moral inferiority," he continues, "is set upon Russian achievements, and the coming events of her internal changes, however appalling they may be in their magnitude, will be nothing more impressive than the convulsions of a colossal body. Her soul, kept benumbed by her temporal and spiritual master with the passion of tyranny and superstition, will find itself on awakening possessing no language, a monstrous full-grown child having first to learn the ways of living thought and articulate speech. It is safe to say tyranny, assuming a thousand protean shapes, will remain clinging to her struggles for a long time before her blind multitudes succeed at last in trampling her out of existence under their millions of bare feet." And finally: "The conceptions of legality, of larger patriotism, of national duties and aspirations, have grown under the shadow of the old monarchies of Europe, which were the creations of historical necessity. There were seeds of wisdom in their very mistakes and abuses. They had a past and a future; they were human. But under the shadow of Russian autocracy nothing could grow. Russian autocracy succeeded in nothing; it had no historical past, and it cannot hope for a historical future. It can only end. By no industry of investigation, by no fantastic stretch of benevolence, can it be presented as a phase of development through which a Society, a State, must pass on the way to full consciousness of its destiny. It lies outside the stream of progress. . . ."

In those passages there is so much truth in detail, while, as a whole, they seem to me so hopelessly wide of the truth, that I can think of no better starting-point for a consideration of modern Russia. Perhaps if Conrad had lived to watch the rise of Stalin he would have thought of Russia less in terms of a dynasty and more in terms of a nation. For he was writing about an abstraction; but it is the sort of abstraction inevitably projected by Western intelligences thinking about Russian life in terms of their own experience. Tsarist autocracy meant one thing to the Poles, another thing to the common people of Russia as imagined by the Poles, and still another thing to the common people of Russia *as they were*. What they were, we in Britain and America can never know; but by contemplating them as they are today in the light of their physical and historical environment, we can at least to some extent discover what they were not.

Stalin and a thousand others have attributed the misfortunes of Russia to her backwardness. Conrad and a thousand others have attributed her backwardness to the autocratic blight. It would, I think, be more accurate to say that the Tsars were themselves due to Russian backwardness. In which case, where is the cause of the backwardness? What, in any case, do we mean by backwardness in this context? Russia is a hundred years, two hundred years, or whatever the latest estimate is, behind the democracies, plutocracies, or whatever the latest label is, of the West. We all know that. A thousand travellers have told us so. Stalin himself has told it to the Russians. So it must be true. But what do we mean by backwardness? Russia produces less pig-iron per head than we do, a fact which seems to go to her heart; but she produces more music. Her sanitary arrangements are reminiscent of the eighteenth century; but she has steam-baths in every village and knows how to warm her houses. Her peasants were illiterate until the other day; but they knew how to dance. She had the secret police; but for centuries she had no capital punishment. . . .

It does not seem to me that this is taking us very far. Let us start again and think of the people who have called Russia backward. What would Stalin mean, faced with the Japanese war-lords in the East and the threat of Hitler in the West? He would mean, of course, backwardness in utilizing the resources of the country, in productive capacity, in standards of living. That is pretty plain. When every Russian produces so many hundredweight of pig-iron per head per day they will cease to be backward. They will be forward. Or at least abreast. But abreast of what? Why, of America of course. We can tell the Americans are not backward by the amount of pig-iron they produce, which is stupendous. So that what Stalin means by backward is materially undeveloped. But did Conrad, the patriotic Pole, and all the other nineteenth- and twentieth-century liberals think of pig-iron when they spoke of Russia's backwardness? I don't think they did. They, I imagine, were thinking in terms of the more venerable and respectable of what we have been taught to call the Four Freedoms: freedom of thought, freedom of speech, freedom from Tsars. Russia was backward because she lived under an autocracy and was not allowed to think for herself: that, of course, led to the untidiness and squalor of the peasant *izba*, just as in twentieth-century Germany it led to the untidiness and squalor of the Nazi domestic interior. . . . Or did it?

That, at any rate, is what they must have meant. Backwardness in production, and backwardness in social development. And, of course, both Stalin and Conrad, by their particular standards, were perfectly right. Russia was, and is, bad at making pig-iron; and America is much better at it. Russia was, and is, bad at self-government; and England is, or used to be, better at that. But was all this really caused by the autocracy? Isn't it far more likely that the autocracy was itself caused by it?

The Tartars certainly made their contribution to the backwardness of Russia, whatever that amounts to. They were not a joke. The immediate physical effects of their irruptions, which were repeated, would alone have put back Russia by many years. They were, when all is said, a barbarian host, however adept in the pastoral arts or tolerant in religion. They were a very real threat to the civilization of the West as a whole. "The Latin world," declares Gibbon, an imaginative historian, "was darkened by this cloud of savage hostility; a Russian fugitive carried the alarm to Sweden; and the remote nations of the Baltic and the Ocean trembled at the approach of the Tartars, whom their fear and ignorance were inclined to separate from the human species. Since the invasion of the Arabs in the eighth century, Europe had never been exposed to a similar calamity; and if the disciples of Mohammed would have oppressed her religion and liberty, it might be apprehended that the shepherds of Scythia would extinguish her cities, her arts, and all the institutions of civilized society." The West escaped this calamity, but Russia did not. Not only were her cities extinguished, as well as her arts and at least some of the institutions of a tender civilization, but she was, as we have seen, totally cut off from all the experimentalism of the West. This alone would have been enough to make Russia backward in the meanings of both Stalin and Conrad. But there were other reasons, deep and latent in the character of the people of the plain, and which worked with the multifold Tartar influences to produce first the Tsardom, then serfdom, then Nicholas I. When we have glanced at some of these we may find our ideas of backwardness enlarged.

The desert, said Renan, is monotheistic. Professor Sarolea, quoting Renan and adapting him, wrote of Russia: "The plain is monarchic and autocratic. In all times and everywhere the plain has invited the invader." Sarolea was illustrating the institution of Tsardom, the central autocratic authority, in terms of holding together a loosely scattered population under pressure from without. The conception is just, and we shall return to it in a moment. But Renan's original notion of the irrelevance of a multiplicity of gods in the immense uniformity of the desert is more literally applicable to the Russian autocracy. Scattered all over the plain are small communities, Russian communities, with, beneath local variations which may sometimes be quite marked, the same thoughts, the same outlook, the same needs. Scattered as they are, they have no internal cohesion. Remote from any sort of common centre, they are in the power of local governors and landowners. Any legislated autonomy for local districts or areas—which might be the size of this country and as far from Moscow as Calabria from London—is bound, because of distance, to cut the common man off wholly from his country's heart. He is prepared to take what comes, good and evil impartially, from the local authorities, but as a citizen of Russia—and he *is* a citizen of Russia—he must feel that somewhere there is a common centre of appeal. There is nothing between him and infinity but the Tsar. "Under God and the Tsar," said the old Russians with a certain pride, "all men are equal." Today they might with even more truth say "Under God and Stalin. . . ." Nor is the contradiction between socialism and an autocracy at all apparent to the Russian mind. "Sometimes I dream," wrote Leontiev in the nineteenth century, "that a Russian Tsar may put himself at the head of the Socialist movement and organize it, as Constantine organized Christianity." That seems to me a remark (and it can be paralleled by the words of many different speakers) of unlimited significance, one of those remarks which, unconsciously, throw a window wide open into the soul of another country. The essence of the character of a nation, as of an individual, is often best isolated by eliminating similarities and looking for disparities, features unique and peculiar to the country in question. The state of mind implicit in Leontiev's innocent declaration is triumphantly Russian and exclusively Russian. It was shared by those who suffered most beneath the Tsardom, the peasant serfs, who attributed their sufferings not to the autocracy but to the jackals of the autocracy who ruled them for their sins, and against whom the only protection was the unutterably remote yet accessible figure, in some ways human and actual, in some ways semi-mystical, of the Tsar.

That is one aspect of the Tsardom. It is a modern aspect. It partly explains why the people clung to the Tsardom, as they did, in their later history, why their revolts, the Stenka Razin revolt, the Pugachev revolt, were never against the Tsardom but always against the nobility. But it does not at all explain how the Tsardom came into being, or why it was upheld by the nobility whom it treated in a disgraceful manner. To begin to understand that we have to qualify Sarolea's observation: The plain is monarchic and autocratic *because it is anarchic.*

I hope I need not stress the fact that we are using the plain as a symbol. It is so used in that paradox. Certainly the autocracy in Russia was called into being (always under the pressure of certain external stresses) because the people of the plain were, and still are to this day, independent to the point of anarchy. They may have received this quality from the pagan gods, or they may have got it from their Slavonic blood: the Poles, it might easily be argued, owe their national disasters to precisely this same quality of independence *à l'outrance,* manifesting itself in an entirely different manner as the result of an entirely different set of natural circumstances. Be that as it may, the Russians certainly have this quality, and if it is not derived from the influence of the plain it is developed and magnified by the nature of the plain, which, with its limitless hinterland, is a constant incitement to secession, brother from brother, clan from clan. There is nothing whatever to stop a perpetual centrifugal drift. At first sight there is everything to gain by it: new air, new life, new land, and all to be got by taking a walk into space. And in face of the perpetual mysteries of space and time and elemental power which, as we have already seen, dwarf the differences between man and man to the point of invisibility, who is better than anybody else? Who is fit to rule whom? Who indeed . . . ?

There is your thesis, as our Marxist friends would say. But now comes the antithesis. Struggling with all his wretched strength against this same elemental power, the individual is helpless. Plainly he must combine with others or die. It is easy to combine in small numbers. You elect a president, an elder, and put the onus of deciding when to plough and when to sow on him. *But* he is one of you and you never let him forget it. He is glad when his term is over. . . . The Russians were doing this kind of thing in the forest of the Dnieper basin before they were called Russians. It is admirable in a small society, and they consisted of a lot of small societies. The Americans are trying to do this sort of thing to this day. But it is not so good in large and complex societies, as the forest-dwellers of the Dnieper began to discover over a thousand years ago. And you have to have bigger units of society, increasingly. You have to band your own community with other communities. But if everybody is as good as everybody else, so every community is as good as every other community; and, in any case, the problems of running it are going to be too involved and complicated for a temporary and reluctant president chosen symbolically as one of you. So you choose one who is not reluctant, who is a different sort of creature from you, and preferably a stranger, saying to him, "Our land is rich; but there is no order in it. Come and rule over us." And then you are free to get on with your life. You are governed by a being *apart*. You accept his rules because everybody else accepts them and you have at least the sense to see that somebody must rule. But the essential thing for the support of your honour is that he is not just a man like you and everybody else, but a being apart and above all laws. That, by the look of it, is the synthesis. It is certainly one way of starting an autocracy.

And I think that, or something very like it, was the Russian way. That is why I said that even if the Ruriki had not come as conquerors they would probably have been invited, as the legend says they were. The early Ruriki were not Tsars. But the process repeats itself on an enlarged scale, with princedoms acting the part of individuals. But princes are not so sensible as peasants. They are prone to fighting among themselves and insisting that each one of them is not only the equal of his neighbours but also better. And it is possible for small and warring principalities to exist side by side in mutual antipathy and destructiveness for far longer than it is possible for small and warring villages. They have richer resources. The synthesis this time can arise only from some overpowering external pressure, the equivalent to a principality of drought and tempest to a small community. For the Russian princes this pressure was the Golden Horde. The Tsardom was their synthesis.

I apologize to Marxists and Hegelians for this irreverence. An invocation of the dialectic in the sphere of poetry was the last thing I had intended when setting out to reflect on what could be no more than a dim and tarnished image of the forces which fashion our human institutions and whose interplay, believe it or not, *is* poetry because it is nothing less than the agonized expression of the thwarted aspirations of the human spirit. The people of the great Eurasian plain aspired to absolute independence of body, mind, and spirit. They got a Tsar, knowing that they had to have a Tsar. And if that is not poetry I do not know what is. Once upon a time, when the Tsardom had temporarily broken down, the Polish nobles who had conquered Moscow invited the boyars to unite with them, to make an end of the Tsardom for ever and to live as free men. The Russians replied: "Your way is freedom for you, but for us it is unfreedom. You do not have freedom but licence. . . . It is easier to suffer injury from the Tsar than from one's brother; for he is our common ruler." And having said that, these Russian boyars, who had recently suffered unforgivable injuries at the hands of an unbridled autocrat, Ivan the Terrible, proceeded to elect a new Tsar, Michael Romanov, giving their lives into his hands with no reservations or safeguards whatsoever. "All," they would seem to have said, "or nothing." And "All—or nothing" might be the slow, implacable systole, diastole, of the faintly heaving plain, which knows nothing of moderation.

It is clear by now, I imagine, that in these chapters I have been concerned neither with writing history nor with trying to make a case for Tsardom or against it. The history has been written by a number of able hands. As for making a case: in this field, as in all others where vital facts are unknown, where even if all the facts were known it would be impossible to assimilate them and re-create their sense, it is possible to prove anything —and then to disprove it. And with no deception. So we are not interested in proofs. The only point I have tried to make, with enough elaboration to bring it alive, is that the Russians are human beings, and that their institutions, above all the Tsarist autocracy, its particular nature and its consequences, are human institutions, not arbitrary accidents, devilish or divine, but the outcome of human and natural forces at work in particular circumstances. The main natural circumstance is the nature of the plain which the Russians inhabit. The main historical circumstance, itself deriving from the plain, was the Mongol conquest. There are plenty of other circumstances. Life is not so simple as all that. But it seems to me that these are more than enough to give life to the dead features of accomplished fact, and to kindle at least the glimmer of an internal vision of those features of Russian life which, regarding them coldly from the outside, so many writers, including the novelist Conrad, saw only as terrible accidents of fate.

We have glanced at the Tsardom from what might be called the high philosophical point of view, and very nice it looks. But when we look at its effect on the characters of both the Tsar and his subjects it is not so inviting. The nobility of modern Russia, for instance, did not owe its existence to ancient foundation and hereditary attributes jealously maintained, but to the favours of an autocrat who could create and who could destroy. And this particular autocrat had collected his strength in the shadow of an Oriental absolutism. The Russian people may not have borrowed from the Tartars, but there can be no doubt at all that their ruler borrowed a good deal. You cannot be a tributary to a tyrant of the most violent habits without drawing certain conclusions about the efficacy of violence. And one has only to compare the first Russian code of laws, the *Russkaya Pravda* of Yaroslav the Wise, a century before the invasion, with the *Sudebnik* of Ivan the Great, the liberator, who finally broke the Tartar yoke, to see what has happened in the interval. The first is an excellent example of an eleventh-century European judicial system. The second smoulders with violence and its corrective is the knout. It has no connection at all with the spirit of thirteenth- or fourteenth-century Europe. Russia has, in enforced isolation, grown away from Europe and in upon herself, and her new autocracy has taken the barbaric taint.

Violence was to be perpetuated in its features for centuries to come. It fitted in all too well in a perverted way with the uncompromising spirit of the plain: "When you do strike— strike hard!" And it came to be accepted by its victims as a fact of nature, so that even after Ivan the Terrible had shattered with panic savagery what remained of national feeling in his boyars, those boyars, or their sons, could still tell the Poles that they did not want their freedom. All this would induce in the nobility a sense of detachment from the real interests of the throne (which are the interests of the country), as distinct from its caprices, and therefore from the people, who are the country. And, in fact, they grew up in a more and more rootless manner, their very real independence of spirit becoming ever more egocentric. Although titles were hereditary, family counted for next to nothing, which is one of the reasons why Russia never developed a "class" society in the Western sense. Each generation saw its own influential nobility, its own high dignitaries, who changed from generation to generation and from reign to reign. These owed the whole of their eminence to the throne and nothing at all to their position in the country: had they, indeed, shown any signs of winning for themselves a position in the country it would have been high treason. They were thus, in so far as they were anything, the temporary agents of the throne, and not at all the champions of the people. In the time of Peter the Great their position was finally clarified and systemized. A table of ranks was drawn up, and it was categorically established that rank was the reward of individual merit, and of nothing else at all. Nothing could be more admirable on paper. But merit very soon had nothing to do with service to the country; it was service to the Tsar, who *was* the country. The Tsar made it quite clear how he wished to be served. All changes came from him. So the Russian great were denied all opportunity of developing initiative. They were place-men.

The moral consequences of a system like this are obvious. Russia totally lacked the tradition of *noblesse oblige,* which was the mainspring of Western civilization for so many generations. In a word, at a time when civilization in the West was being laboriously and painfully shaped by the interplay of character and ambition, leavened by an ever-present sense of responsibility, character in Russia had been extinguished by absolutism; ambition was limited to the task of pleasing the Tsar; a sense of responsibility could not develop for lack of nourishment. Chivalry was unheard of. The astonishing thing is that in these conditions occasional men of moral and intellectual integrity did arise and contrive to stand close to the Tsar without lowering their standards or ending their days in exile. But these were few. And the general impression of the apotheosis of this system, Russia in the reign of Nicholas I, could be summed up by an unsympathetic foreign observer in these words: "From the door of the emperor's ante-chamber, from the high officials of his court down to the sentinel at his gate, every man is an extortioner and a public robber, and all are united in one vast conspiracy to deceive the only man in the empire who cannot be bribed—the possessor of it."

On the other hand, and by the light of nature and the example of liberal Europe, at precisely this time, a new element was creeping into the nobility, into the landowners, into all the people who had put their faith in autocracy. It was as though they were beginning to realize their mistake. There had been revolts in plenty, palace revolutions and peasant uprisings, but never against the autocracy as such. The Decembrist revolt of the most brave and generous-hearted members of the nobility on the accession of Nicholas in 1825 was something different in kind. It was a revolt of principle. It had an idea. And although these men and their families were struck down by the new Tsar with that quiet, contained, pursuing ferocity that was to paralyze the free spirit throughout his reign, the free spirit survived it, and it obtained its sustenance from the West. There were big spiritual changes at work in Russia during the nineteenth and early twentieth centuries. There was a new sense of responsibility. But the autocracy was too firmly established in the hearts of the people, in whose eyes the nobility, through its own fault, had no standing. So that for the last part of its development, paradoxically, the Tsars were protected from enlightenment by the peasants of the plain. These knew nothing of a change of heart in their immediate masters, against whose generations of oppression they had looked for protection from the Tsar. And they continued to look to the Tsar when he alone maintained the harsh rule of the past. They were still looking when everything suddenly crashed. Then the Tsar went, the nobility went, the landowners went, the senior officials went—and only the people were left.

3. THE PEOPLE OF THE PLAIN

IT is time to come down from the Tsars, the princes, and the boyars and think of the ordinary people, the peasants and the working men and women who were left in possession of the plain when those others had been swept away. And the supreme fact to remember about these ordinary people, the Russians of today, is that they are the immediate descendants of primitive agriculturalists who, until the second half of the nineteenth century, were mainly slaves—serfs, they were called. And the supreme fact to remember about serfdom is that the Russian peasant was not a natural slave. The principle of serfdom arose not from any innate servility and submissiveness in the Russian character, but, like the principle of the autocracy, from the Russian's natural independence of spirit, amounting to what is most aptly described as chronic bloody-mindedness. Its ultimate rigour was due to the enervation of the nobility.

In the sixteenth century Ivan the Terrible, the first Tsar of All Russia, was the supreme autocrat of all the land, which cried out for a strong and centralized government as the only possible stay against dissolution. Once more the story belongs to the plain. Here, over immense and vulnerable levels, with the Tartars still in Kazan and on the lower Volga, were scattered the people of Russia. There were few cities; towns were small; compact villages were the exception. Tempted, as we have seen, by the beckoning spaces and interminable river valleys, forced by the poor soil of the forested north to spread themselves out in small communities, there was no cohesion in this population, which yielded to the endemic centrifugal forces of the plain. The Russians were curious. They explored. They were crowded out of the native nest. They explored. They were irked by the exactions of their overlords. They explored.

They hoped for better soil, for better trapping-grounds. They explored. And because the west was barred by the Poles and the Lithuanians and the south by the Crimean Tartars and the Turks, and the north by the ice-bound sea and the Swedes, this exploratory drift was always eastwards and south-westwards, so that soon immense tracts of unknown land were dotted with the settlements of these continental voyagers. Up to a point it was good. But the difficulty of the Tsar was to choose between occupying the widest possible tract of the plain and keeping his people thick enough on the ground to resist the compact spearpoint of sudden invasion. His own main object, further, was to break out in the north-west to the Baltic coastland. Out of this dilemma serfdom grew.

Ivan needed the instant service of his boyars. He had to see that they were well established on estates which were conveniently disposed from the viewpoint of national defence. It was easy to give them the land, but to keep his men on the land and fit for service he had to ensure that there was labour to work the land. Yet in spite of repeated and determined efforts to tie the peasants down, so persistent and unmitigated was their perpetual movement into the unknown, into freedom, or into the domains of the greatest and most prosperous landlords, that, through the years that followed, decree after decree was issued tightening the hold of the landlords on the people of the villages. And finally, in 1594, Boris Godunov formally signed the act of serfdom, which forbade a peasant to leave his master's land on any pretext. All that was not unreasonable. The landowners themselves had been bound to the Tsar's service: they were no longer free to go and fight for the Grand-duke of Lithuania if they felt inclined. And without the binding of the peasants there could be no service to the Tsar. But gradually, as we have seen, the landowners, the nobility, were enervated. Peter the Great turned them into civil servants, with his fifteen official ranks. And when Peter had gone and could no longer bully them, the irresponsibility was complete. The footing of the army was also changed. Serfdom was beginning to lose its historical point. In the reign of Peter III, Catherine the Great's unfortunate and short-lived husband, it lost it entirely. This

Peter signed a decree which released the nobles from all obligations of service to the throne. But the peasants remained tied to the land. Under Catherine and succeeding rulers the laws which forbade their disposal apart from the land to which they were tied imperceptibly relaxed, and soon they came to be regarded as the chattels of the owners of the land—or of the Crown itself.

Whether the Russian serf was better off on the whole than the free English labourer after the enclosures had forced him off the commons and the industrial revolution left him with seven shillings a week to support in a state of freedom a wife and family, it is impossible to say, and in any case it does not affect the principle of serfdom. Nor does the question whether serf-owners were on the whole cruel or on the whole kind or on the whole indifferent. Obviously the Russian serf had a security, if he behaved himself, which the British labourer lacked. There was no workhouse for him. Obviously, too, some landowners were good, others bad, others indifferent, while many were virtually non-existent, leaving the business of running their estates and controlling their serfs to agents, whose main preoccupation was with sending to their masters in St. Petersburg or Moscow the maximum sum compatible with a comfortable rake-off for themselves. Obviously, too, a cruel landowner, isolated in the vast plain, embattled, as it were, in space, and absolute tyrant of his serfs, could indulge in fantasies of cruelty impracticable in a compact society, and under our own system denied to all but such pillars of society as the governors of overseas convict settlements, whither free Englishmen, finding they were not free to eat, were transported for stealing their Sunday dinner. Obviously a benevolent landowner, who was also efficient, could create around him a model community protected from the encroachments of an arbitrary bureaucracy. But all such considerations, being particular and exceptional, and dependent upon personal idiosyncrasy, still do not affect the principle, which boils down to the question of what happens to the characters of men when they enslave and are enslaved. The consequences of slavery which concern us here, because they concern the Russian people to this day, are not cruelty or benevolence, comfort or discomfort, but irresponsibility, lethargy and idleness, fatalistic passivity, and a rooted distrust of government in every form. In other words, we find serfdom, as we found the autocracy, exaggerating the very qualities which brought it into being, and perverting them.

At the time of the Emancipation at the hands of Alexander II, in 1861, there were roughly forty million serfs, three-quarters of the entire Russian population. About half of these forty million were what used to be known as State peasants—*i.e.* serfs of the Crown, as we should say. The other twenty million were owned by individual landowners. Somebody once had over one hundred thousand serfs. The serfs of the Crown were better off than all but the most comfortably placed private serfs. They worked the Crown lands in conjunction with the other peasants of their community, or *Mir,* and although they lacked freedom of movement and were the standing prey of the tax-collector, the police, and every kind of official, they had in part the air of free men, since their submission to authority was confined to their attachment to the land and the payment of dues. The majority of these Crown serfs inhabited the northern regions, where there were few landowners—these, when accorded their grants for services rendered, preferring the South for its climate and its richer soil. So that in the north you found a sturdier peasantry than in the south, and this sturdiness was not altogether accounted for by their more active and variegated life. Part of it came from the fact that they were relatively free in their manner of life within the rigid but ample framework of their bond-slavery to the Crown. They also, paradoxically, lived better on poorer land: there was no master to sell the corn away from the barns and leave them hungry.

The twenty million private serfs belonged body and soul to individual landowners, and it was the existence of these twenty million slaves which corrupted the Russian State so radically that even the removal of the poison by the bungled surgical operation of 1861 did not avail. It was in the blood.

There were two kinds of private serf, the peasant on the land and the house-serf who possessed no land—every kind of personal servant, from scullion to major-domo. Many nineteenth-century Russians seem to have contrived to believe that the serf-owner could not sell his serfs away from the land; but the land-owners knew very well what they could do, and the publication of Gogol's *Dead Souls,* that fantastic study of marginal speculation in terms of human flesh and blood (dead flesh and blood at that), must have suggested new possibilities. It was not always like that, as we have seen. The serf did once go with the land. That was what he was for. But the eighteenth century put an end to that and it was made legal for the owner to do what he liked with his serfs—selling husbands away from their wives, parents from their children, and all the rest of the paraphernalia of unrestricted slavery—including flogging with the knout, conscripting for the army, and deportation to Siberia. But never death. At a time when in England a man could be hung for stealing a sheep the death penalty in Russia was unknown. It was regarded as a savage dream. . . .

Against all this the serf had no right of appeal. And the house-serf was particularly demoralized. His life was far more comfortable, as a rule, than the life of the peasant serf. But the peasant always, in his own eyes, had the land; and the house-serf had nothing. He belonged to no community. He was treated as the chattel he was and advertised in the "for sale" and "wanted" columns of the newspapers. The fact that he was sometimes trained by his owner to become an actor or a musician, or that he sometimes grew into a beloved and trusted companion and steward, is neither here nor there. As a rule he remained one of a teeming crowd of idle and underworked servants—domestic slaves, whose existence in unlimited numbers had precisely the sort of effect on their own characters and the characters of their masters and mistresses that one would expect. The peasant serf was in a stronger position. He had his land; and, indeed, he regarded *all* the land as practically his.

"We are yours, but the land is ours," he would say. He also had his Commune, or Mir, which meant a great deal more to the ordinary peasant than the master himself, who could only get at him through the head of the Mir.

We need not analyse this venerable and fascinating institution. We are touching on these matters, including serfdom itself, not for their own sake, but simply to establish the broad conditions under which the fathers and grandfathers of the present-day Russians lived their lives. You can argue about the Mir for ever. You can use it to prove anything. Remembering what we have seen of the conflict between the individual and the community which is inherent in the plain, it is enough to say now that it was, in effect, a spontaneous banding together of the peasants of one village into a democratic association which ruled all their lives with the utmost rigidity and rigour— a democracy which turned itself into an elective autocracy in the shadow of an absolute autocracy. Or a government beneath the government, and the only one which counted for anything at all.

The Mir, presided over by the village elders, as a rule elected against their will (for it was a responsible position), was also an additional tie to the peasant. For the Mir had its own interest in keeping the individual on the land. Since the Mir, as a community, was held responsible for the collection and delivery of all taxes, and since these taxes were fixed on a *per capita* system based on the last periodical census, regardless of numerical fluctuation in between one census and another, it was in the interests of the Mir as a whole to keep its members. It was similarly with the head of the Mir that the serf-owner negotiated when it came to laying down conditions of service—*e.g.* how much work each serf should be required to perform upon the master's fields.

Thus, as a serf, the peasant was the absolute property of an individual, of his landowner, or of the Tsar. He had no rights, except those which he was able to enforce by custom. While, as a worker in the fields, he was very much the property of his own community, whose laws, to him, were the only laws that meant anything at all and which he had any interest in obeying. His general outlook on life may be summed up like this. To the Mir implicit obedience as a life-and-death matter: the Mir was the living and practical society, which parcelled out to him the land he was to own for himself, dealt with the master on his behalf, arranged the work that should be done in the master's fields, collected his taxes and contributions in kind, sustained him in times of personal misfortune, and, in return, required obedience in all matters regulating the carrying out of his work, and, if he left to work in the towns, a regular contribution from his urban wages, which also kept open for him his place in the Mir should he ever wish to return. The land was his, or, rather, the Mir's. He was the only person who took any interest in the land, who laboured on the land, and who understood the land. The land was there before the master, and it would survive the master; but the peasant, and the Mir of which he was a member, went on for ever. The master was allowed to live on the land, and, on sufferance on the part of the highest powers, and for reasons best known to the highest powers, he was given supreme authority over the people who worked on the land for the period of his tenure. But that was all. He was an outsider. He contributed nothing, but only received. As for the government, with its officials and its police—here was an entanglement of iniquity and corruption which could not exist if only the Tsar had time to get around more and was not misled by false advisers. You defeated the government on every possible occasion, lying to it as best you might, and with the satisfactory feeling of duty well done if you succeeded in a lie. You believed it ever false. Only the Tsar was true. The Tsar was indeed the Little Father, and the golden age would come if only he could dispense with the officials and the landlords. But, of course, that was asking too much. He needed help, poor soul; and how could he know that his helpers were the spawn of Satan? . . . There was the land, the broad Russian land (lately rediscovered by the approved singers of the Revolution); and the land was worked by the children of the land, the peasants of Russia, who owned it and loved it and wrestled with it and hated it and fought for it when called by the Tsar to do so. And there was the Tsar, the supreme fa ther of his people. But between the Tsar who was absolute possessor of all the lands of Russia and the peasants who owned and tilled their tiny strips were the men whom the Tsar must employ as his agents and who shamelessly and mercilessly swindled both him and his people. These were the jackals, upon whose heads all blood lay.

But the faith of the peasants in the Tsar was absolute. When Peter III remitted the obligations of service to his nobility, while leaving unchanged the complementary conditions of serfdom, thereby upsetting the balance of centuries, the peasants, whom, at a stroke of a pen in a weak and pusillanimous hand, this same Peter had degraded to the rank of cattle, were utterly convinced of his own uprightness, were utterly convinced that no Tsar could commit such evil, and that false counsellors had suppressed the second half of the ukase, which would have released them, the peasants, from their corresponding obligations. When the Cossack Pugachev raised up the great peasant rebellion which came nearer to full-scale revolution than any of the innumerable peasant rebellions which for centuries have flared up, now here, now there, in the great plain, and guttered out as quickly, like beacons to presage 1917—when Pugachev came forward and advanced steadily towards Moscow, he owed all his success to the pretence that he was the missing Peter (who in fact had been assassinated as a result of a Court conspiracy—probably at the instigation of Catherine herself), come out of hiding to claim his rightful place and give to the peasants their due. When Alexander proclaimed the Emancipation of the serfs in 1861, but under conditions which made nonsense of it in the eyes of the peasants whom it was supposed to liberate, these again believed that the ukase had been distorted and its sense perverted by the old false counsellors, so that, as given to the world, it in no way represented the real wishes of the Tsar. Finally, in 1917, it was not the peasantry as such who overthrew the Tsar, forced him to abdicate, and later murdered him with all his family. The Tsar, as the Tsar, never stood in danger from the peasants, who would have burned down the houses of all his courtiers and officials in the honest belief that they were liberating their Little Father from the bands of evil men. For the Tsar took the place of God upon earth.

God in heaven was represented by the clergy, who belonged neither to heaven nor to earth, limiting their functions to supporting the temporal power in its government of the masses, and ensuring the spiritual salvation of the masses by insisting on certain ritualistic observances. At no time in the history of the Russian Orthodox Church has it appeared to consider it a part of its duties to act as a moral example and an upholder of ethical standards. On the one side it lacked the Confessional of the Catholic Church, on the other the Evangelical principle of Protestantism. It concerned itself exclusively with fasting and ritual, and the religion it offered, and which the Russians eagerly accepted, was an encouragement to endurance in this world, not to the saving of souls or the perfection of the human spirit on earth. Souls were safe if the ritual and the fasting were observed. As for virtuous behaviour—man is a weak and sinful vessel and no effort he can make to transform himself as a human being can make him less weak and sinful in the eyes of God: he remains a human being. So what can he do? To God he can accord his prayers and fasting, as ordained by the Holy Church. To the Tsar he can pay his taxes. For the rest, as a saved soul and a good subject of the Tsar, he can live as he likes. The remoteness of the Orthodox Church from the living of everyday life by everyday men is symbolized in its very ritual. The Orthodox Mass, far more than the Roman Mass, is a colloquy between the celebrating priest and God, from which, at the height of the Communion, the congregation is excluded by the closing of the altar gates. The priest continues his celebration alone and unseen before the altar, while the choir in the body of the church fills the air with the sombrely impassioned drama of Byzantine polyphony. At these moments the priest is withdrawn utterly from the world of men, which hears nothing of God, but only knows that He is now in the same house with them, separated from them only by the great screen before the altar and the elaborate lamentation of the choir. . . .

Over everything is God, in whose hands our souls repose, and who requires to be acknowledged with certain unambiguous observances. The Tsar is his agent on earth. What man does on earth is neither here nor there provided he obeys the sparse and practical sanctions of God and the Tsar with regard to prayer, fasting, and tax-paying. Nothing else that he can do will improve his position in the eyes of either. So let us get drunk and beat our wives. . . .

By now we should begin to have our own appreciation of the living conditions of these people who lived on the plain. We have registered its climate, which is harsh; its distances, which are immense; its history, which resulted in serfdom; its government, which was by remote-control; its religion, which offered hope of salvation in the most rigid and formal orthodoxy. And we find at one end the Tsar, the supreme arbiter, and at the other end a group of peasants organizing their own communal life beneath an absolute and multiple despotism: the despotism of the elements, of the Tsar, of the Church, and frequently of the individual landowner. By these despotisms the peasant is tied to the land and allowed to get on with his life, within a rigid framework, as best he may, his obligations in the form of taxes and service on the land of his master being such as to exhaust the greater part of his energies, but not quite the whole. On the other hand, for all practical purposes he is left in absolute possession of the land as land to be worked. Nobody interferes.

The land is thus farmed in a peasant manner. We find, as we might expect, a traditional treatment of the land analogous to the three-field system of medieval England, each great field divided into strips, a strip in each field allocated to every peasant. We find the survival of traditional implements, resulting in the shallowest ploughing and consequent vulnerability to drought and famine. We find an irresponsible attitude towards the forests, which are cut down for any reason at all and without the slightest regard to the morrow—with results that have proved disastrous. We find the sort of life arising from this treatment of the land restricted and poor in the extreme, and a peasantry living on the subsistence level and not interested in increasing the yield of each acre, because the surplus will only be taken away from them and sold. We find a very high development of what is known all over the world as the peasant-type: the mixture of liar, sceptic, simpleton, rebel, sycophant, saboteur, grasper, Good Samaritan, passive resister, sanguinary tyrannicide, hard head and soft heart. A mixture which, on examination, sorts itself out into a perfectly simple and explicable duality, the peasant being one thing to the outside world, which, with good reason, he distrusts, despises, and usually detests, and quite another to the members of his own community, whom he trusts and, in adversity, pities in the most practical of ways—a fellow-feeling which, in the case of the Russian peasant, is extended to all unfortunates who have been hard hit by a hard world, whatever their class and condition, a feature recorded time and time again in the diaries of Siberian exiles. And this two-sided human being is unendingly patient. He knows, in his blood, that patience is all. And because of this very patience his outbursts of wrath when they come are violent, unbridled, and appalling. It is not the last prick of the goad that causes him to lash out and burn down his master's house and murder his master's family in hot blood; it is the accumulated poison from all the goading he has endured with dead and absolute patience for so long.

These, then, were the fathers of the men who comprised four-fifths of the people of Russia at the time of the October Revolution, when Lenin, staking everything for their support, told them to take the land for themselves.

For, paradoxically, the free peasants of the twentieth century had less land than the serfs of the nineteenth century. Effectively, that is. Of course they owned more: they were smallholders now. But what they owned in the eyes of the law was now all they had; and as a rule it was not enough. As serfs they had owned nothing in the eyes of the law, but, by virtue of working the land, they had it all. The Emancipation made them free men and gave them a share of their late masters' land (which they had to pay for, after having had it for nothing for so many generations); but that share was frequently insufficient when farmed in the traditional peasant way. And, of course, the house-serfs, now also free men, had nothing but what they stood up in.

These changes in status and condition would in any circumstances have had consequences full of interest; but as it happened the consequences were elaborately complicated by the coincidence of Russia's dawning industrial revolution and also of the introduction of specialized agricultural machinery in the countries of the West. . . . Such, then, were the forces which were moulding the lives of the peasants and the landowners on the one hand, and of the city-dwellers on the other—as we find them mirrored in the works of Chekhov and Turgenev on the one hand and of Gorki and Dostoevski on the other. The broad characters who now dominate the daily life of the great plain are the land-hungry and backward *muzhik* and the new, half-baked farmer-landlord (no longer the owner of serfs who worked his estate for him, fed him, and looked after him in every way from the cradle to the grave, but now an owner of *land,* which he has to work himself with the help of peasant labour), often dreaming of revolutionizing methods of production and often squandering his fortune on machinery which the peasants refuse to work and which in any case is all too often unsuitable for the job it is required to do, often with a dawning conception of his obligations to the peasantry, who are no longer his voiceless children, but are now free men like himself. And in the towns we find the new proletariat of factory workers, uprooted from the soil. And, finally, a growing class of intelligentsia, arising from the development of the towns and the increase in professional occupations, and oscillating between a craving for the sweets of Western culture and an atavistic nostalgia for the breadth and simplicity and incorruptibility of the mighty Russian plain. . . . These characters at the turn of the century were already beginning to change the face of Russia. Even the government of the Tsar was actively engaged in carrying out agrarian reforms (as usual, from above), which showed signs of pushing the agriculture of the plain in much the same general direction as that in which Stalin was later to propel it with such sustained and ferocious vigour.

But there is no need for us to consider all these changes in detail. We are trying to establish the general character of the Russian peasant as it has been shaped by the conditions of his life through the generations, and as it was bound to survive the Emancipation by many decades, and as, in fact, it survived the Revolution and survives among the present younger generation, born on the Collective Farms. We are interested in the Russian peasant because he was, at the time of the Revolution, nearly four-fifths of Russia, so that, one would say, he, above all, was responsible for the Revolution. But what we have so far seen will, I think, have made us wonder how the Russian peasant ever came to make a revolution of the kind that the Russian Revolution has proved itself to be.

We may well wonder. The answer, of course, is that he did not, although he made it possible, and although without him Lenin could never have succeeded. The people who in fact made the Revolution, which in its essential form was very far from a popular and spontaneous reorientation, were the revolutionary intelligentsia, headed by Lenin, and the revolutionary proletariat of the cities. These classes belonged to the other fifth of the population of Tsarist Russia. . . . But the peasants helped. They helped in two ways. First as soldiers, conscripts, who mutinied and made Lenin's seizure of power a possibility. Secondly, as peasants, who, on Lenin's instructions, seized the land for themselves, and, in order to keep it for themselves, fought the White Guards in the civil war that followed. That action gave the Bolsheviks time to consolidate their power and set to work on the real revolution. And the real revolution, which it was left to Stalin to complete, was the industrialization of Russia on socialist lines by the Communist Party, incorporating the revolutionary proletariat. This revolution was not merely executed without the help of the peasants and in spite of the peasants; it was actively and bitterly opposed by the peasants. For it entailed nothing less than the wresting back of the land from the individual peasants and the liquidation of the peasants as a land-owning class, which was what, above all, they had aspired to be, for generations immemorial had aspired to be.

For the real revolution was a deliberate and planned reorientation of the ancient life of a vast and ancient community. It was not a revolt against the throne as such (which, in
any case, had fallen before Lenin's seizure of power). It was a
revolt against a way of living. In the true Russian tradition
it was planned and carried out from above, the directing hand
being no longer the Tsar's but Lenin's, then Stalin's—each of
these men depending absolutely on the support of the Communist Party. It was in fact the dictatorship of the proletariat,
which is not, as many seem to think, an empty term, but a
precise and ruthless fact. For the whole of the Russian Revolution, or reorientation, has been carried out by the city proletariat against the will of the immense majority of peasants,
who, when the Revolution started, formed four-fifths of the
total population of the mighty plain.

The peasant revolt in 1917 was, if you like, a popular revolt,
which occurred within the framework of the great reorientation and which made this possible, although it was entirely
opposed in the general direction of Lenin's revolutionary plan.
Left to itself, and without Lenin, there is nothing to show that
it would have amounted to anything more than a large-scale
variation of the peasant revolts in the familiar tradition of
Razin and Pugachev. It had, that is to say, no direction, no
constructive idea. In due course it would have fizzled out—or,
if the successors to the Tsar (other than Lenin) had proved
incapable of steady government, left the country in a state of
chronic anarchy. Lenin had to take account of this, and he had
to give way a great deal in order to ensure the support of the
peasants both in getting rid of the old system, or anything like
it, for ever, and in clearing the ground for his plan. This he
did with remarkable success. The task of his heirs was, thus,
first to break up the new system which had established itself
among the peasants as a result of Lenin's necessary concessions,
second to impose in its place a system which accorded with
the socialist-industrialist reorientation and was directly opposed to what the peasants wanted, and third to make the
peasants feel that they were active and sympathetic participants
in the destruction of their centuries-old ideals and the imposi-

tion upon them of an alien way of life which they must also be made to feel was better than anything they had ever sighed for in their dreams. This was the task which Germany believed could not succeed. It was complicated further by an entirely new development—the bringing into active participation in the life of Russia of the minor, non-Russian nationalities who, hitherto, had been held in subjection as part of Russia's colonial empire. So that, at the very moment when unity was the most imperative need, the homogeneousness of the Russian people was radically weakened. Russia became the U.S.S.R., and the people of the plain, the descendants of the Eastern Slavs of the Dnieper basin, were henceforth no longer synonymous with "the Russians." New races and new histories had to be absorbed into the concept "Russia," and although the old Russians were still the dominant people, their mental and spiritual horizon began to move decisively towards the East.

Now it is time to shift to Russia as she is today and to see how this fantastic revolution from above, carried out for the benefit of the people and in the teeth of the people, is contriving to work itself out.

III

WHO ARE THESE GREY MASSES?

1. THE LIVING IMAGE

UNLESS he is taken on a conducted tour, the first impressions of the stranger to Russia are likely to be harsh, and especially if he enters the country by the northern sea route and in wartime. Archangel is one of Russia's back doors; and there is a good deal to be said for the back-door approach to anywhere: by the time you get round to the front you know the worst, you know the sort of ideas that have gone into the making of the façade, and you can also judge the amount of effort that has had to be put into the task of keeping up appearances, which is not a thing to be laughed at.

In Archangel there are no appearances. Archangel is a seaport, icebound for half the year, and in peacetime mainly concerned with the export of timber. It is nothing but timber. Far out into the White Sea the water is streaked and dotted with the logs that have floated down from Archangel. The Dvina river itself, when at last you cross the bar, spawns logs and the steamer pushes them aside. The right bank of the winding estuary is composed for mile after mile entirely of timber, timber in unimaginable quantity, in the water, half in the water, out of the water; inert in stacks the size of churches, which look as though they have rotted there for generations, or half alive in the form of wooden wharves and roads and sheds and houses. Immense irregular rafts of timber, a quarter of a mile long, and with little houses built upon them with smoking chimneys, are lugged down the river by Dvina tugs, or self-propelled by some kind of outboard engine. It is impossible to tell where seasoning timber ends and building timber finishes. The people live in the timber, build their houses, their roads, their boats of it, burn it in their engines and in their stoves, and load the surplus into ships. Archangel itself, when you reach it after traversing interminable timber flats, is nothing more than a sudden outcrop of highly organized and sometimes carved and painted timber in the shapes of houses, streets, and public buildings. And then, on the confines of the city, it sinks down again into timber in the mass. And everywhere is utter flatness. There is not a living tree to be seen. The only life comes from the intoxicating quality of the hard northern air with the tang of the distant sea and the distant fir-woods in it, and from the luminous brilliance of the pale-blue sky, which, at sunset and sunrise, produces the majestic effects found only in the desert or at sea.

Against this raw, astringent background the people pullulate in tattered furs.

My own first impressions were as they should be. It was October 1941. Russia had been at war for little more than three months; but already Moscow was directly menaced, and already Archangel, capital of one of the biggest consumer provinces, was being starved. Except as a port for the unloading of war materials from Britain and America, she could play no part in the war effort. So she was treated as a port. Arrangements were made to man the dock facilities at full strength; but nothing else was to matter at all. The government could not afford to send food to people who could do nothing to help with the war. So the people of Archangel got no food.

When I arrived it had been snowing, but the snow had melted into slush, mixing with the accumulation of summer dirt into a thick, porridgy mud which made the steeply raised wooden pavements as slippery as ice and filled vast pot-holes in the streets with greasy water. Urchins rushed up with strident cries, brandishing five, ten, twenty rouble notes which you were supposed to take in exchange for a couple of cigarettes. Over all was a reek of sewage and sickly-sweet *mahorka*, the Russian equivalent of shag, smoked as a rule in a roll of newspaper. I wanted to telephone; but the only call-box in view had been used as a public lavatory; and when I looked in at the public lavatory, belonging to the brand-new and shining river-steamer station, it was easy to understand why. That river station, a resplendent café which was closed (but which reopened later), and a large and imposing new theatre were, apart from the pleasant Admiralty building in the old Moscow style, apparently the only sights in Archangel, through which hunched, grey-faced figures, swathed in black shawls or greasy, ragged sheepskins, plodded their way through the slush with the air of ghouls.

I had come across from Bakharitsa wharf on the other side of the river in the launch of a Russian trade-union official. There had been no time to look at Bakharitsa, and the journey across the water, alive with dozens of remarkably smart-looking launches, and all dominated by the dazzling white paint-work and Italianate lines of the Admiral's streamlined barge, had not prepared me for this; but by the time I had wandered round the town and fought my way back to the public ferry to return I was ready for anything. The ferry, a sizable steam-packet something on the lines of a Mississippi steamer, was packed. But the people who formed the jam, and who ten minutes before had been picking their way through the slush and the pot-holes with the appearance of ghouls, were suddenly amiable and expansive, no longer a scattered, misanthropic mob, but a noisily and gaily chattering crowd—the very mixture one had expected, of ebullient peasant youth, pig-tailed small-town flappers, raw privates in new uniforms, a scattering of amiably condescending Red Army officers, green-capped frontier guards very much off duty, and the age-old patience of peasant old-age. Humanity showed its face. But only to hide it again immediately.

For soon the ferry approached what was meant to be a landing-stage—a heavy platform of waterlogged timber, just awash. At the landward gate leading on to this platform a grey and hideous mob was waiting in silence. In a moment the self-respecting peasants on the ferry were themselves a grey and hideous mob, heeling the ship over in their silent and unanimous surge to the landward railing. I was interested to see how the numerous blue-coated militia, both on the ferry and on the shore, and all with rifles on their backs, would handle these rival mobs. I reckoned without the evident desire of the militia to see how the mobs would handle themselves. For instead of letting the passengers off in a thin stream, and instead of holding

back the waiting crowd until the ferry was cleared, they treated
me to my first Russian inspiration. At a prearranged signal the
gates in the side of the ferry were swung open simultaneously
with the gates on the landing-stage. Five hundred people on the
landing-stage lurched forward towards the ferry, completely
submerging the floating stage. Five hundred people in the ferry
swept down the lowered gangway. A thousand people in two
opposed armies milled about up to their knees in water. Old
women with unimaginable bundles quietly wept. Children
screamed. Soldiers and dockers shoved and cursed. Young
women spat. The battle went on for a long time. The militia
looked on, contributing energetic shouts of *"Davai!"* an extremely Russian form of exhortation which can mean "Come
off it!" or "Get a move on!" impartially. Swept out of the ferry
and on to the landing-stage in the first rush, I managed to edge
out to one side and stood with my ankles in the water, clinging
to a rope which depended from the ferry, until the riot had
sorted itself out. Then, at the height of the mix-up, I was aware
of larger shouts. Two tallish soldiers were focussed in the very
centre of the mob, and they were forcing their way towards
the ferry with the aid of what looked like a battering-ram. But
the battering-ram, now swung up on high, revealed itself as a
stretcher covered with an army blanket from under which two
booted feet protruded. Above all other smells there was suddenly the sickly smell of death. But nobody paused because of
it. On and on the soldiers shoved, pressing back the people who
were trying to get to the land. One at last got a foothold on the
ferry. The stretcher was now raised at a fantastic angle above
the heads of the crowd, who paid no attention, but went on
pushing. Until finally, after a number of false starts, the other
soldier, with the aid of two dockers who caught the stretcher
on their shoulders when it looked as though it would fall and
discharge its burden into the water, managed to climb into the
ferry too, and the corpse was deposited on the ferry's deck.

By the time I touched dry land, twenty-five minutes had
passed. Reflecting on the lessons of these twenty-five minutes,
notably the utter contempt of the ordinary Russian for the

ordinary police, whatever he might feel about the secret variety, and the dramatic and immediate transformation of a pleasant and cheerful boatload of people into a blind and bitter mob, or pack, I ran into a group of soldiers on the main wharf trying to back a horse and cart on the slippery boards. They went about it with that sort of inefficiency which in the warm and sunny South occasionally exasperates but always charms. It does not, however, accord with the savagery of the northern climate, where you have to watch your step. The little horse was slipping about all over the place. With contradictory ejaculations of *"Davai!"* the four soldiers pushed it about and would not give it a chance to find its feet. They were ordinary peasant con-scripts, small, wiry, bullet-headed, and cropped. They were not being cruel. They were being helpful. I watched with my heart in my mouth as the wretched, rough-coated little animal slipped and slithered about on the edge of the wharf. A final, tri-umphant push sent the back wheels of the cart over the edge; the front wheels followed, and then the horse itself, a ten-foot drop into the icy water which was just beginning to freeze. In due course, after various flounderings, assisted by *"Davais"* and futile tugs and a soldier who went down a ladder to try, ineffec-tually, to unharness it, the animal drowned and lay half in, half out of the water with its rough hair streaked and matted and a red discoloration where it had cracked its head. The soldiers were still looking at it when I went away. Next day the cart was gone. It could be used again. But the little horse was still there, and there it remained for many days afterwards until the ice completely covered it. It could not be used again.

By now I was feeling very sick and very angry. So sick and angry that my first sight of a convict gang being led away from the docks did not move me at all and the stupid sentry who stood at the gangway of the ship and whose immediate reaction to the production of my pass was to make an impassive, threaten-ing lunge with his immensely long spike-bayonet, seemed to stand for all the blank and mindless inefficiency of a country which could not afford to be inefficient. I did not know it at the time, but in that one short afternoon I had been granted the most valuable introduction to Russia that could possibly be desired. And that is why I have done my best to share it with the reader, who might well prefer an evening at the ballet.

We shall come to the ballet in due course, but not for some time yet. That belongs to the front of the house, and we are still floundering among the dust-bins at the back. Or the ballet is the flower, which can look after itself and make its own immediate effect, but which cannot tell us how it grows.

You do not see every day a corpse used as a battering-ram even in North Russia, even in wartime; nor do you see a horse being foolishly drowned before your eyes. But you are very much hemmed in by the attitude that finds its ultimate expression in such fantasies, and the demonstration of its logical conclusion helps to fix it in your mind. What it helps to fix is the muddle, the carelessness, of a country in which efficiency has never paid full dividends because people and space have always been "expendable," and the automatic and instantaneous transformation of the kindliest people in the world into utterly self-centred and oblivious beasts when it comes to survival in even its most trivial and impermanent aspects—such as who shall get the last place on the tram. You are very soon aware that physical survival is by no means a *sine qua non* in wartime Soviet Russia, where the devil really does take the hindmost. The Russians are aware of this all the time, and this awareness shows itself in odd ways. Once the point of the moment is carried, once victory is assured, once they have got their foothold on the last step of the tram, or picked up their bread-ration, or corralled their share of timber for the stove, they relax into immediate affability and will go to great lengths to help the next man get his, even to giving up a large part of what they themselves have just won. But it is the winning that seems to be the thing; and since, particularly in wartime Russia and above all in the North, the greater part of life is taken up by precisely the primitive activities I have listed above—the struggle for food, fuel, and transport—the impression of the Russian street crowd is apt to be disconcerting, and it is a long time before you realize that what Maurice Baring and many others have said about the Russians is quite true: namely, that they are the kindest-hearted and most generous people in the world. . . . But they need a base for their generosity. You can't share your last crumb of bread unless you have got it. And getting it has lately been difficult. So we have, repeatedly, these extraordinary transformations from man to beast and back, best expressed, perhaps, in the attitude of a Moscow shopper, who will divide all she has with the neighbour who was unlucky in the scramble but whom, in the course of the scramble, she would cheerfully have slain.

But at first you do not know about this. You see simply the grey-faced, ill-dressed masses, skulking about like lone wolves, then converging in hostile packs, then separating again. They look neither to left nor to right, but straight ahead and slightly downwards, shuffling along in their shapeless felt boots with that peculiarly Russian gait, body bent forward, arms hanging down slightly in front of the body, and, apparently, haunted by the fear of showing interest in anything at all. So that in hard times one of their number may drop exhausted by the roadside and die there in the snow without anybody stopping to help or to enquire.

Another thing you become aware of in the north, and which dominates your ideas, is forced labour in its many different forms. As you sit at breakfast in your hotel you hear the dreadful sound of a woman wailing, half hysterically, in the street outside. And looking out you see thirty or forty women and girls being marched along the frozen street by guards with fixed bayonets, each woman with a small bundle. You do not know where they are going; but you know that they are being marched away against their will, that the call came suddenly and roughly, and that behind them they are leaving homes which are, as it were, still warm, while they trudge through the snow with nothing but their bundles. Most are stony-faced; but one is weeping loudly.

That is the beginning of one kind of forced labour. But you do not know which kind. These stony-faced women may be petty criminals being marched from one prison to another; or they may be minor political offenders, sentenced to hard labour for foolish indiscretions; or they may be women who have evaded conscription, being taken off for enrolment in the women's forces; or they may be housewives turned out of a block of flats, at half an hour's notice, because it is wanted by a government department engaged in fighting the war. You do not know. All you know is that it has, whatever it was, happened roughly and suddenly and without appeal, and that the women are now in the cold, being marched away under guard. And you are harrowed by that wailing, which is like the end of the world.

For forced labour in Soviet Russia, you very soon find, is a term which may mean almost anything, from the sentencing of violent criminals or serious political offenders to a lifetime of brutalization, the effective length of the sentence varying with the endurance or stamina of the individual prisoner, to the drafting of one member of every household in a given street to live for three months in the forest and cut wood against the winter. We shall have more to say about forced labour later on—which may, when you come to think of it, equally include the drafting of a dozen newly graduated doctors to a remote Siberian township where doctors are urgently needed—but the newcomer to Russia only knows what he sees. Entering by the back door and in wartime he almost certainly does not see the worst, but he sees a good deal.

He sees, for instance, toiling in sixty degrees of frost on the construction of a new wartime port—a raw and terrible affair of manhandled timber baulks and splitting ice—a gang of fifty alleged human beings, evidently brutalized beyond description—one gang of fifty among a dozen such gangs, used on this urgent and appalling job with no regard to anything at all but the most rapid completion of the job, as men were used by the builders of the pyramids—he sees this gang being marched back to quarters by a strong guard with fixed bayonets and rifles *at the ready*. Marched is not the word, convoyed, perhaps; they shuffle desperately along the ice-covered wharf, black figures with greasy fur caps hiding half their faces, in the shadow of the rusting walls of merchant vessels iced up for the winter, each with its growing piles of garbage thrown out from the galley on to the winter ice to wait until the spring thaw carries it away. And while the onlooker is speculating on these sub-human figures, speculating on their value as workmen, speculating on how they live when off duty, he observes the furtive glances charged with animal greed which they cast at the heaps of frozen garbage, and he hears the guards shouting to them roughly to keep their eyes to themselves; and then suddenly, unbelievably, one black, stooping figure has detached itself from the horrible procession; like a broken-winged crow it flaps two or three paces out of the line and grabs at a chunk of bread which has rolled away from the nearest garbage-heap; and in that moment, and to the accompaniment of an ear-splitting detonation, vicious in that still and unspeakable waste, the figure pitches forward into the thin snow. . . . The other prisoners shuffle on without a glance at their late companion. The guard who has fired the shot walks up and stirs the black shape with his boot and, satisfied, stumps on after the others, working the bolt of his rifle with a metallic rattle. The indistinct grey twilight deepens into night. But the next day the black shape is still there; and for many days after, embalmed in that frigid air, it lies huddled beneath the dead side of a British steamer, gradually becoming greyer, then whiter, with each fresh fall of fine fragmented snow, until there is nothing but an uneven hummock in the smooth surface of the snow.

Russia is not discreet. She does not seek to hide her middens from herself. From foreigners, perhaps, but not from Russians. They frequently are hidden because everything in that immense plain must be hidden by distance alone. But there is nothing like the careful concealment of German concentration camps. This German concealment was so successful that German citizens could pretend, also successfully, that they did not know of their existence—while in the next breath they will tell you that they dared not actively oppose Hitler, whom they hated, because they were afraid of the concentration camps. . . . There is nothing like that in Russia.

Near one of her larger cities on the way to Asia there was an immense complex of concentration camp and war factory —some square miles of waste land surrounded by barbed wire, packed inside with dwelling-huts and factory buildings, and with modern flats for factory workers just outside the wire. This whole area is dotted with tall watchtowers on stilts, equipped with searchlights and machine-guns. It is impossible from the outside to tell which is concentration camp and which factory, or which bit of barbed wire is put down to keep the prisoners in and which to keep intruders out of the factories. It is a wholly Russian jumble of life in the raw. Children playing on the new greens outside the flats; women shopping with string bags for bread and potatoes in the little shops which go with each block of flats; workmen trudging to and from their work, and convicts under guard building a new road parallel with the old one to the airport—which is placed in the midst of this revealing congeries. The railway runs through it too; and the engine-driver will stop his locomotive half-way across the level-crossing to have a chat with a group of artisans, or a prison-guard, or anyone else in the neighbourhood. There is no concealment. To get to the airport you have to pass right through the heart of this fantastic scene, which is a cross between a Yukon mining township, Lydd ranges at Dungeness, a hasty imitation of Welwyn Garden City, a railway yard, the back areas of the western desert, and a prisoner-of-war cage. The Russians—any Russian using that airport—know all about it. They also know about the mines, the Lena valley, Novaya Zemlya—from which you usually do not come back because you are dead before even a short sentence is concluded. They know all about it. There is no concealment. What, then, do they think —and feel?

We do not know. We know only what we can see. Entering, as we have, by the back door, we have seen what we have seen, and we have drawn our own conclusions, which may have nothing to do with what the Russians feel, but only what we *feel*. And under the weight of these sharp and painful impressions— I have instanced only a handful from a very great number of similar effects—we have quite forgotten all we have read about the socialist experiment, model collective farms, the glorious Red Army, day-nurseries, and the ballet. What we have seen, moreover, is going to influence our general outlook for quite a time to come, inevitably. So that, arrived in Moscow, we shall find ourselves heavily conscious of the Lubianka prison, the horror for which it stands underlined by its gimcrack Victorian office-block façade and its bland position on the great Dzherzhinsky Square in the very centre of the city; we shall see in the downcast faces of the people in the streets that same fear of absolute and arbitrary power and its dreadful expression amid the ice and snow and darkness of the far north that we are beginning to feel ourselves; we shall gaze fascinated at the sprawling, crenellated symbol of that power, the Moscow Kremlin, which houses the men who hold two hundred million fellow-beings in the hollow of their hands, hands so plump and white and soft when spread out on the green baize of the conference table, but hands for so long soaked in the blood of others, first their enemies' and then their friends', that, regarding them, you feel that never again will whiteness stand for anything but falsity and lies. . . . And when you get away from the smell and murmur of the common masses, moving through the frozen city like ghouls, to the hospitality of the Soviet officialdom, glittering enclaves of abundance and luxury, where champagne and enchanting wines from the Crimea, sturgeon, caviar, cold roast chicken and game of every description, decked out with a hundred gastronomical fancies, are served in a shimmer of white linen and crystal chandeliers against a background of dress uniforms and orders—in the midst of grey masses who ask only for bread and for warmth . . . when you get away to this, you feel bitterly that it is nothing but a heartless and cruel mask, a bedizened lie, a projection of unfathomable cynicism to hide the truth—no, not to hide it: it lies all around you—to divert, for five minutes longer, your attention from it. Violence, arbitrary law, sustained privation and undernourishment, blind, trampling stupidity, the uttermost harshness of rule over body and soul impartially, bodily slavery with no compensating freedom for the spirit, forced atrophy of the independent mind without bread and circuses to fill the gap, physical drabness and squalor over all, reflecting perfectly a mood of hopeless apathy. . . .

If that is the impression I have managed to create, we can now set to work. For these are the people, remember, whom, as I proposed earlier, we should love.

I have never read a book about Great Britain by a foreigner who approaches the heart of his subject by way of Dartmoor, Clydeside, and Barrow-in-Furness in a slump. But that is, precisely, our present approach to Soviet Russia. It seems to me probable that the views of a foreigner on the crowds in Piccadilly, to say nothing of the Trooping of the Colours, or life at the Athenaeum or the 400 Club, might be strongly coloured by his impressions of the Depressed Areas and the Black Country if he happened to pass through these first. It is possible, too, that his final picture of this country (if he could bring himself to stay here long enough after such a beginning) might be more just than would have been the case had he gone straight to Claridge's and stayed there: emerging only for shopping excursions in Bond Street, lunch in St. James's, and a week-end in the country. To attain this picture he would require a long time: he would find it very difficult indeed to leap straight from Barrow-in-Furness to Brook Street and take what he found there as a fair sample of the British way of life. Almost everything he saw on the way, his perceptions heightened by the shock of his first experience, would raise a host of awkward questions. But it would be an interesting exercise, and it is an exercise of just that kind upon which we are now engaged.

There is no Barrow-in-Furness in Soviet Russia. But there is Archangel. There is no unemployment; but there is deliberate starvation. There is, indeed, an attempt at Claridge's; but there is no Bond Street. Neither the Kuznetsky Most in Moscow nor the Nevsky Prospect in Leningrad, which gave the nineteenth-century novelists their dash of glitter, could serve that purpose now. And as for St. James's—the Nobleman's Club in Moscow belongs to the Trade Unions and is used for concerts when it is not required by the Procurator-General (Mr. Vishinsky emeritus) as the gilded cockpit of a Purge. So our journey cannot be from Archangel to Bond Street and St. James's. We leap straight from the Bakharitsa station to the interior of the

Moskva Hotel. The Kremlin we cannot penetrate: it has the same air of legend as Mr. Churchill's private cinema. Who, then, inhabits these two extremes, and on what terms? And what do we find in between?

Our first impression is that there is nothing. The grey and faceless citizens of Archangel were free citizens of the U.S.S.R., we recollect, going about their daily business, not the inhabitants of a prison camp. If we have mixed them up in memory with the forced-labour gangs it is because there was so little to distinguish them and because we wrote them off as the population of an outlandish province which was being deliberately starved because it could help so little in winning the war. But now we are in Moscow, and what we see is unchanged. The grey inhabitants of Archangel are now merged indistinguishably with the grey mass of all the Russians, drifting aimlessly, with downcast, expressionless faces and dead incurious eyes, drifting eternally with their curious, tottering gait, through all the cities of the plain—and so obviously doing nothing, going nowhere, that you wonder why they are out in the streets at all. In Moscow the grey mass is broken by the high lights of officers' uniforms, officers of the Army and of the M.V.D.; and sometimes, but not as a rule, a human expression goes with the uniform. But more often than not, all that the uniform does is to accentuate the dead features of its wearer and to emphasize the greyness of the nondescript mob. . . . So that so far what we have seen are the brutalities of convict labour and the brilliance of official high-jinks with the grey and terrifying drift of dead-faced automatons filling the continuum between these two poles.

That, I repeat, is what we have *seen*. It is what every visitor to Russia must have seen from the nineteen-twenties onward until the end of the late war, with one short break in the few years before that war—*must* have seen, if he had used his eyes on what lay before him instead of turning them inwards on what he had read. And what we have seen is nothing less than the physical expression of the anti-Soviet idea that Russia is today nothing more than a police-state run by a gang of gifted thugs for obscure ends known only to themselves. And so? . . . And so, obviously, there is something wrong with what we have seen.

There is no room here for the things we know about. No room for the films of Eisenstein, the music of Shostakovitch, the tales of Mikhail Prishvin; no room for the physics of Kapitza; no room for the lively humanity of Mr. Maisky; no room even for the technical skill of the great factories of the Urals and the Don; no room at all for the spirit that fought a losing war against the most dreaded enemy of all time—and won. For not even a Stalin with the aid of an all-powerful police could force this shapeless grey mass to resist and conquer, as they did, *against* their will—the whole two hundred million of them. . . . Something is obviously very wrong, in spite of the evidence of our eyes. Something is missing from what we see. And the discrepancy between what we see and what we *know* (we need not worry now about what the Kremlin would like us also to believe) is so unbridgeable that we may, by modestly using our eyes, be as hopelessly wide of the mark as those enthusiasts who see nothing but what they have read about in books. At any rate, we have to find out what that something is. But, at the same time, we must not allow ourselves to forget what we *see*, which is the easiest thing in the world when one is hot on the trail of the invisible. For what we see is also evidence. And that is why I think it is a good thing that we have entered Russia by the back door, in wartime, and in the dreary beginnings of winter. We shall not so easily forget the first impressions of our eyes, which otherwise might have been distracted by the glitter of the Bolshoy Theatre or the colour and life of the children in their summer frocks on the green lawns of the Culture Park. No, we must not forget the grey masses. They will pass and repass, drifting aimlessly, before our eyes, and we must keep them in focus even while we contemplate the amazing products of their toil and bitter, bitter sacrifice.

The first thing you notice when you go to a theatre or a concert in Russia is that the people who compose the audience have nothing whatsoever in common with the people in the street outside. They are two completely different sets of people. The theatre audience is alive and individual. You wonder how they got to the theatre, where they come from, and what they do with themselves all day. Surely out of all these hundreds which form the wildly, touchingly, enthusiastic audience, you must, at one moment or another, have brushed past one in the street? But no, you have never seen anything like them before. For there, astoundingly, magically, before your eyes are two thousand eager, vital, highly differentiated individuals—soldiers, artisans, lawyers, doctors, civil servants, working boys and working girls, musicians, students, and all the unmistakable types produced by a complex society—two thousand people who could well be a cheerful cross-section of a great nation in the process of achieving great things. . . . Where, where, do these people live? And who are all those others, the grey-faced masses drifting through the muddy streets outside? . . . Who indeed!

For suddenly you remember that curious glimpse of a dramatic transformation on the Archangel ferry, when, for ten minutes in the middle of the Dvina river, the ghoul-like mob suddenly disintegrated into a cheerful crowd of variegated human beings—and then closed up again to face the other shore. And now, alert and wondering, you see the same thing happening to this theatre audience. The piece is over. The applause has been tremendous. Artists called before the curtain are one with the wildly cheering audience in a delirium of self-giving. But at last the applause must cease and now the magic starts. Between the foyer and the street two thousand individual human beings are silently transformed before your eyes into grey and nondescript particles of the grey and shapeless mass. Even as they stand in the parallel queues to get their fur-coats and goloshes the expression is drained from their faces. As they pass through the glass doors to join in the drift outside, lips tighten, eyes glaze, and the transformation is complete.

But now we have the key. It multiplies itself. It will only be a matter of time before we can follow an individual through a whole series of these fantastic and shocking transformations. Meanwhile our eyes are opened. We know what to look for. The people in the streets are still grey, expressionless, and drab. But they are no longer purposeless. And they are no longer a mass. They are the citizens of the U.S.S.R., a new and mighty nation in the process of fighting the greatest and most ruthless war in history, which came upon them when they were still worn out with the fearful and sustained strain of the greatest and most ruthless social revolution in history. These are the survivors of this revolution, which was really three revolutions, to which each one of them has made an individual contribution, positive or negative. They are also fighting, and slowly winning, this outrageous war—to which each one is making his own individual contribution, positive, as a soldier, an administrator, or a producer—or negative, as a non-participant who starves to feed the active.

They are still drab, and still, where great masses are gathered together, they appear to move with this tentative, aimless drift. But we are now on the trail of people, not grey masses; and as we follow this trail we find that the drabness has three main pressures: one physical, one political, one spiritual. Together they add up to a weight which would crush any Western nation to extinction. Greyness is their armour.

2. THE THREE REVOLUTIONS

WHEN Lenin seized power on November 7th, 1917, he was not the leader of a nation in revolt against the traditional rulers: he was the head of a minority party proscribed by a democratic government that had failed. The traditional rulers had been out of the way since the spring of that year. The Tsardom had fallen in Lenin's absence, and at the hands of an extraordinary combination of artisan strikers, mutinying troops, bourgeois intellectuals, the enlightened nobility, and the magnates of the new capitalism. These were the people who destroyed the ancient fabric. They had no coherent system to put in its place. Lenin had such a system.

Those of my readers who are already over-familiar with the chronology of what is called the Russian Revolution will forgive me for addressing a few pages specifically to those who are not. For once we shall allow ourselves the luxury and indulgence of a few facts, one after another, partly because it seems to me that most Englishmen and Americans have only the haziest notion of the events which made up the Revolution (events which have a very close bearing on the nature of the Russian people, whom we are trying to see in the round, and on the life of contemporary Russia, of which we are trying to get the feel); partly for another reason which will later be manifest.

The year is 1917. The Tsar is Nicholas II, a character of a cultured, obstinate and suicidal imbecility which would have warmed the heart of Damon Runyon. He is still an autocrat, still the Little Father. And although after the bitter but so ineffective revolution of 1905, a revolt against the state of affairs which impelled Joseph Conrad to write his essay called "Autocracy and War" from which we have already quoted freely, he found himself compelled to grant what was called a Constitution, involving the establishment of a Parliament, known as the Duma, it never occurred to him that this institution was anything more than a sort of political bread and circus turn, to be dissolved when it tried to stand in the way of anything he wanted to do. Times, of course, had changed a good deal since the reign of Ivan the Terrible. Moscow was no longer the capital: Peter the Great, in the course of his convulsive effort to turn his country westwards, had built St. Petersburg. The bureaucracy had grown in proportion with the population and free industry. It was now a bureaucracy largely run by Germans, who took a native pleasure in rigidly administering unadministrable laws which it had never occurred to the Russians to take seriously. There had been the beginnings of an industrial revolution, and Moscow was already dotted with the mansions of a new kind of magnate, who needed constitutional government if he was to pursue to the fullest advantage his intricate and international financial and trading manœuvres. There had been the Emancipation, as we have seen. And the new city proletariat, who were called into being by the new factories, lived in barracks and cellars like beasts. The last had lighted a spark in the hearts of the new intelligentsia. Also, the Tsars had had time to develop a sense of responsibility towards the rest of the world, a sense of mission towards humanity as a whole, which made Russia bulk very large among the perplexities of European diplomats. Otherwise things have not changed— things at the top, that is. And the deep quietude of obscurantism which lapped the Winter Palace made it hard, if not impossible, for its occupants to believe that the eternal Russians of the plain might change.

But they could. It is 1917, remember. For two and a half years the Russian masses, the people of the plain, had been fighting an atrocious war against the main weight of the German army, and with no support from the rear. They were badly officered, badly equipped, badly armed, badly fed. There was not enough of anything at all; and what little there was was too often embezzled by the officers of the Q Staff of the Imperial Army, who were the final, phantasmagorial flowering of Tsarist bureaucratic corruption. So that very often the conscripts found themselves floundering in the mud without boots, without food for days on end; and sometimes the second wave of an attack was sent over the top unarmed, with instructions to pick up the rifles of their dead and wounded comrades of the first wave. There was also hunger in the towns, partly the result of inefficient distribution, partly the result of conscripting able-bodied peasants from the fields. Nicholas, under the influence of the Tsaritsa with her German sympathies and her evil advisers, notably the Grand Guignol character Rasputin, the drunken, lecherous, semi-literate holy man from Siberia, had failed utterly in his "mission"; but because he still behaved and felt like an autocrat when he had not a sensible thought in his head, there was no one to stand where he had fallen. The dynasty was tottering to a bleak and whimpering conclusion. For a long time the more intelligent members of the higher nobility on the one hand, and the more ambitious exponents of big business on the other, had had it in mind that Nicholas must be got rid of. Each party wanted a constitutional government; but for different reasons. And now the people were growing very tired and at last impatient. They knew nothing of constitutional governments, but they wanted peace and land and more food. They decided that this unceasing holocaust conducted in the spirit of a comic opera with themselves as the chief victims had to stop. They spoke, therefore. They spoke with the voice of what we have called the revolutionary proletariat.

On the last day of February 25,000 factory workers came out on strike in Petrograd. The strike caught on, and by March 9th there were a quarter of a million Petrograd workers on the streets of the capital, and there was fierce and fatal skirmishing with the police, who, although they had no more notion than the workers themselves that they were assisting in the opening campaign of a national revolution, behaved as though they were conducting a major war, thereby helping to ensure that the revolution would take place. For next day the strike was general throughout Petrograd, and the strikers were busy electing workers' deputies. On March 11th the Tsar dissolved the Duma and prepared to play once more his favourite role of Little Father in a stern and chiding mood. But on March 12th even he must have

begun to feel out of his depth when the strikers were joined
by large numbers of his own bodyguard—the Litolvsky, the
Volynsky, and the Preobrazhensky Guards. . . . On March
14th the workers of Moscow joined with the workers of Petrograd and called a general strike. On March 15th there was nothing for the Tsar to do but sign the instrument of abdication
thrust under his nose by the representatives of the new capitalism, Messrs. Guchkov and Shulgin, who reported that the masses
(who hated the new capitalism a good deal more than they hated
the old nobility) were out of hand. So the Tsar of All Russia
abdicated in favour of his son, Michael Romanov, who was
immediately rejected.

That was the first revolution. On March 15th, 1917, the
Tsarist autocracy came to an end. It was succeeded by a
provisional government pledged to carry on the war. The Prime
Minister of this government was Prince Lvov. Guchkov was
Minister for War. Kerensky, the lawyer, was Minister of Justice.

Lenin, meanwhile, was in Switzerland. His arrival at the
Finland Station in Petrograd, after his journey across German-
occupied Europe in the famous sealed train, took place on
April 16th, a month and a day after the abdication of Nicholas.
He arrived to find an interesting situation, and, from his point
of view, a most promising one. The industrialists and the
Right Wing bourgeoisie in general, who had been only too
pleased to avail themselves of the strong arm of the workers
when it came to forcing the abdication of the Tsar, were now
behaving with consummate foolishness in resisting prema-
turely the movement of the people to whom they owed their
power, and who were far more interested in obtaining peace
and radical economic changes for themselves and their inarticulate comrades than in establishing a constitutional government which would give big business its head. Looking back
from this distance, it seems almost inconceivable that the
Guchkovs and the rest could have imagined for even the wildest moment that they could hold down the lid of this seething
kettle of revolt when even the Tsar had failed. For the Tsar,
as we have seen, stood for something in the eyes of the peasants
and the workers. He stood, amongst other things, for protec-

tion from the predatory Guchkovs. Whereas Prince Lvov, Kerensky, and their friends stood, as far as the peasants were concerned, for Sweet Fanny Adams.

But it is not, alas, within our scope to conduct an enquiry into the mania of the right wing bourgeoisie of wartime Russia. We are in pursuit of Lenin, and the main value of the fact of the Provisional Government to us is that in its constitution, aims, and aspirations, it reflects an almost lunatic unawareness of the real character of the country to which its leaders fondly imagined they belonged.

This delusion was not shared by Lenin. In the first place, he knew that the Provisional Government could not last. In the second place, he knew that although he could seize power—because power, if he waited a little, would fall into his hands with the collapse of that government, or of any other counter-revolutionary government that could manage to push it out by force before it died a natural death—although he knew this, he also knew that he himself would not last unless he could get the support of the peasants, who were not interested in anything at all but peace, and in little plots of land. He knew, in a word, that the peasants, who formed four-fifths of the Russian population, were no more interested in his, Lenin's, ideas of a social revolution than they were in Kerensky's ideas of constitutional government. And to my mind the supreme greatness of Lenin is beautifully illustrated by this cool, unembittered detachment and appraisal of a reality which, if they had had his vision of it, would have plunged his colleagues into the despairing impotence of frustrated idealists. Kerensky, who was not about to devote his life to the elevation of the masses, had to delude himself that he had the masses with him in his attempts to establish a system which was essentially against the people; and when he was at last brought to realize that the people were not with him he cracked. Lenin, who had slaved and suffered all his lifetime for the people, who was about to die for the people (and probably knew it), never for one moment failed in his cold-eyed appreciation of the true facts of the position—namely, that if the people realized the road he was asking them to tread for their own salvation they would turn on him and stone him. This capacity for looking at the facts of life without flinching and without bitterness is a peculiarly Russian quality, as we have already seen, in Lenin raised to the condition of genius. For Lenin was a Russian of the Russians.

"What grounds have we for waiting? I shall be told it can't be done all at once; every idea takes shape in life gradually, in its due time. But who is it says that? Where is the proof that it is right? You will fall back on the natural order of things, the uniformity of phenomena; but is there order in the fact that I, a living, thinking man, stand on the edge of a chasm and wait for it to close of itself, or to fill up with mud, at the very time when perhaps I might leap over it or build a bridge across it?"

Those words were not written by Lenin in exile. They were written by another Russian of the Russians, Anton Chekhov, whom we have chosen to miscall the poet of futility, in his story "Gooseberries."

Lenin did not come alone from Switzerland. He brought with him thirty-two fellow-exiles belonging to the Bolshevik division of the Russian Social Democratic Workers' Party, which was in opposition first to the Menshevik division of that same party, second to the far greater Social Revolutionary Party, which was mainly a peasant affair, third to everything else. The Bolsheviks were a small, compact group of some 80,000 proletarian workers who owed their numerical insignificance and their moral strength to a total rejection of compromise in any shape or form. The Mensheviks, who were compromisers, and who at one time numbered Trotsky in their ranks, who were also (in spite of their name, meaning Minority Men) in the majority of the Social Democrats, had, with the utmost difficulty, been kept at arm's length by Lenin, who knew what he was doing, and whose rigid exclusiveness during the period of his exile had brought him the hostility of many and the reproaches of his closest friends. What he was doing was forging, from outside Russia, a highly tempered instrument which was to cut through the mass of other loosely knit and hopeful political affiliations like a hot knife through butter. For the 80,000 Bolsheviks, and they alone, were the men who carried out the October Revolution and terrified the Western world.

They did not act at once. The Provisional Government, for the time being, was their best weapon. Already early in May the new government was having serious trouble with both the workers and the peasants. The workers paraded the streets with anti-war and anti-capitalist slogans, with the result that Guchkov went from the War Office and Kerensky took his place. The peasants were demanding the land, which the government had no intention of letting them have, and its promises to lay the whole matter of land redistribution before the Constituent Assembly when the time came for it to be convened were met with scepticism and self-help on the part of the peasants. In this they were encouraged by Lenin, who saw that the way to the popularity which must be his if he was to succeed was by promising land for all and peace—and sorting out the mess at a later opportunity. He did so. And meanwhile the Provisional Government's attempt to pursue the war with a new offensive spirit had failed miserably at Tarnopol, and by midsummer the peasants were getting out of hand. In July the Bolsheviks decided to hold street demonstrations, which were put down with shootings and arrests. The party (not yet with a capital letter) was proscribed, and Lenin himself only escaped arrest by slipping away to Finland. But the work of the party went on underground, and its Sixth Congress, held at the end of July, formally adopted the immediate programme of a workers' revolution and the imposition of socialism. Kerensky by that time had become Prime Minister. He had a troubled life. Not only were the peasants and the left wing workers against him (though the Bolsheviks had not yet got control of the workers' Soviets, who were still with him), but he had also to face his own right wing, which was curling round to push him out of his uneasy central position. A plot was laid for Kornilov the Commander-in-Chief, backed by the magnates, to march on Petrograd and install himself as military dictator. Now all the workers fought for Kerensky and Kornilov's own soldiers turned against their general, who was arrested as a traitor. Confusion was complete. The war contin-

ued. And if the old-established government had been unable to
prosecute it properly, the Provisional Government, attacked on
every side, could hardly hope to do as well. The towns were
hungry. The peasants were using their skilful axes on the landowners and burning down their houses. The Bolsheviks, by
publicly backing every show of violence, were becoming known
as the people who knew their own minds and stood for no established interests. By September they had majorities in both the
Petrograd and Moscow Soviets, while Kerensky's own party—
the agrarian Social Revolutionary Party—was split into two
groups, with the left wing trying to steal the thunder of the Bolsheviks. Kerensky was reduced to calling for help from outside,
and the Winter Palace was a scene of anxious consultations, of
hurried comings and goings, on the part of silk-hatted diplomats of the Western powers, whose one preoccupation was to
bolster up the Eastern Front, which meant Kerensky. At the end
of September he made his last despairing throw, by dissolving
the Imperial Council and the Imperial Duma and proclaiming
a republic. But it was too late to save a government which, in all
its dealings during the eight months of its life, never took into
account that fact of its dependence on the people. On October
23rd the Bolsheviks decided that the time had come to give the final push. The programme of an armed rising was approved by
the Central Committee on October 29th. It was carried out on
November 7th.

This was the October revolution. Lenin's revolution. The
Bolshevik party henceforth spelt its name with a capital P. In
Petrograd it was all over in one day. After attempts to storm the
Winter Palace had failed, the order to fire was given to the gunlayers in the Peter and Paul Fortress and to the gunlayers of the
cruiser *Aurora* which steamed slowly up the river with a small
escort of mine-sweepers. They trained their guns. A shell idly
screamed across the November sky of Petrograd, then another,
and another. And to the accompaniment of the compressed
thudding of the heavy guns alternating with the dull crunch of
high explosive bursting free, quick pillars of smoke started up
from the Winter Palace and the dust of falling masonry combined with these to make a thin pall for the would-be constitu-

tion-makers who had reckoned without the people of the plain.

Lenin was in. On that same day, and by the members of his triumphant party, he was elected head of a Council of People's Commissars, and with him Trotsky, as Commissar for War, and Stalin, as Commissar for Nationalities. That was the October Revolution. On the night of November 7th the late members of the Provisional Government sat in confinement in the fortress of Peter and Paul, all except Kerensky, who had got away.

I hope by now the reader has had enough of facts. Before we proceeded with our evocation of the life and people of revolutionary Russia, of the Soviet Union, it was desirable to indicate the sheer, stark confusion which was the inheritance of Lenin, and I have chosen the simplest way to create a sense of confusion, which is to put down a string of facts and dates, one after another. I hope the reader is now feeling confused. If he is, he will feel the shadow of the confusion which all but overwhelmed the Bolsheviks during the first years of their existence as the leaders of Russia, and which, at the same time, made it possible for them to survive. I hope also that he, the reader, has salvaged from confusion the one fact that matters in the least, because it was the one fact that mattered in the least to the Russians: namely, that Lenin was not the leader of a national revolt but a fisher in troubled waters who seized on a national revolt, and aggravated it, to serve his own revolt and to get the people into his power.

Confusion continued, continually augmented, for many years; but during those years the only coherent and consistent note was the voice of Lenin. He won, because he was like the only man in a committee who really knows what he wants. He knew what he wanted and was able for seven years to sustain the shocking burden of talking down the Russians and conducting a death struggle with the rest of the world, because he was a genius of the highest calibre known to mankind.

But we need not detail the confusion. If the reader has got the feel of it, we can now abandon facts and return to our laborious search for truth, for that tiny fraction of truth which

is one man's honest perception of the world around him. We
have seen how the October Revolution was born. It was the
second revolution in eight months. It was over very quickly.
The real revolution, the third revolution, was yet to come, but
already it existed in Lenin's mind. It was to be a long and often
hopeless-seeming struggle. It is impossible to fix the exact
moment of its beginning; but it was under way before Lenin's
death, and it did not finish until, on June 21st, 1941, the Germans invaded Russia. Stalin, no doubt, would not have considered it successfully concluded even then. But on that date it
was all or nothing. And all that Stalin could do was to turn
himself from the leader of a revolutionary party (which the
Communist Party, the heir to the Bolsheviks, still was) into
the leader of a nation at war and behave as though the Revolution was over and hope for the best. It is not impossible that
Stalin did this almost with a sigh of relief, as when the thing one
has worked and striven for is finally taken out of one's hands to
prove itself or perish. There is nothing more to be done. At any
rate, the Revolution proved itself. Just. The proving came in
November 1941, just twenty-four years after the October Revolution, and at the very gates of Moscow.

But before the third revolution, the real revolution, could
begin, Lenin had to establish and consolidate the October Revolution, which most people thought was the whole story. Luck-
ily for him—though at what cost in human lives and suffering!
—the enemy attacked first, and bitterly and persistently, and on
such a broad front, as it were, that Lenin was able to gather
round him and under the banner of the Bolsheviks the great
mass of the Russian people. In civil war, in resistance to foreign
invasion, the people made Lenin strong, so strong that when
the war was over and the invaders had cut their losses and removed themselves, leaving behind them an exhausted and
ravaged land, the people could no longer break away from him.
And, in any case, hundreds of thousands, millions of them, who
had had no use for him before, now looked to him as their
saviour from the men who had come to take their land away
from them. So that, in a high philosophical sense, the Russian
Communists should be grateful to Denikin and Wrangel and

to the governments of the West for uniting the people with the Bolsheviks in defence of the Revolution. But this is too much to expect from men of action, which is what the Bolsheviks very much were and very much still are. And, in any case, like all high philosophy, it would have a flavour of inhumanity and immorality. For you do not, or should not, thank a would-be murderer who advances upon you when you are bound and helpless and whose knife, instead of stabbing you to the heart, slips and cuts your bonds. You rise up and clout him, which is precisely what the Bolsheviks, very understandably, but not very cleverly, and with far too little regard for future moves, are doing to us today.

For we were their would-be murderers. Precisely that. . . . And although we have forgotten this, the Bolsheviks have not. And because, owing to their Marxist blinkers, they have always been wrong about the reason why we tried to throw them down, they still think that we would throw them down tomorrow if we got the chance. The theory upon which this notion is based is the Russian interpretation of Marxist determinism. Marx predicted that the forces of communism would have to fight an international death-struggle with the forces of capitalism, qua capitalism. And when in 1918 the Allies attacked Bolshevik Russia, it never occurred to the Bolsheviks that this attack might be anything but the first round of the capitalistic onslaught upon the revolting proletariat. It never occurred to them, for instance, that it might be inspired by a mixture of motives, generous and mean, idealistic and opportunistic, such as the desire to save the old ruling classes from the cab-ranks of Bucharest, outraged sentimentality at the treatment of the Tsar and his all too innocent family, protection of the financial interests of British stockholders and business men, and, above everything and all else, the imperative necessity of keeping the Eastern front going until the defeat of Germany in the West. And so on. It would not, one would think, call for a very complex and sustained flight of the imagination to realize that these were the emotions of the interveners, and that, with the passage of time, when such emotions had died a natural death, we should forget about them and want to shake hands. But not at all. Although the Russians, in a sense, are the most imaginative people in the world, the Marxist training applied to the Russian temperament precludes the exercise of the free imagination. Marx said that the capitalists would attack for such and such reasons based in the grand dialectic. The capitalists did attack; so Marx must be right. Marx said, further, that the capitalists would continue to attack until they were finally overthrown. The German capitalists did attack and are now finally overthrown. But there are still other capitalists, whose puppets, among others, are the members of the British Trades Union Congress. These have not yet been overthrown. So they will attack. Marx—who knew nothing about the 1914 war, the clumsily brutal murder of the Romanovs, Brest-Litovsk, and the shortness of British memories once their investments are irretrievably written off—who knew all too little, in a word, about life as it is lived by the variegated human animal which makes up the monochrome mob—and *can* change its colour—Marx said so.

May he be proved wrong this time. But the Bolsheviks, the Communists one should now say (but not the Russian people), are so convinced of his rightness and so determined to *prove* him right, that they are now, as we all know, being very troublesome indeed. . . . On the other hand, one of the things Marx did not know about was the Russian temperament, the eternal split in the nature of the people of the plain between the most rigid orthodoxy and an all-accepting anarchy.

This is a digression, and so far we are in the position of Marx, who did not know enough about the Russian temperament. We have to voyage a little farther before we can give ourselves over to direct contemplation of that. And meanwhile we have left the Bolshevik Party deliberating in Petrograd behind a screen of loyal workers, while Germany advances deeply and terrifyingly into the heart of the Ukraine, while Allied diplomats decode frenzied telegrams from their governments telling them that all is lost unless the Russians will go on fighting, while Tsarist officers concoct elaborate plans for holding off the Germans with one hand while beating down the Bolsheviks with the other, and while the condition of the country goes from bad to worse as a result of the internal disorders, industrial and agrarian, which, more than any bloodshed, brought down first an Imperial, then a Republican regime— while Lenin, imperturbable, implacable, and incorruptible, announces that he will get the best peace he can from the Germans, let the imperialistic Western Powers stew in their own juice, and turn Soviets plus Electricity into socialism in Russia.

That was the most important thing he did say. It announced to anyone with ears to hear that what he was interested in was socialism, that he knew he could expect no help from the peasants, and that in order to produce a strong enough class of industrial workers, a proletariat, in short, he proposed to industrialize the country. Marx had said that the dictatorship of the proletariat was the first inevitable stage of the Communist Revolution. But, in Russia, the proletariat was not big enough to dictate, so, before the Revolution could be carried through, the proletariat had to be augmented. The first stage was to provide power to run the factories which would be needed to turn landed peasants into landless factory workers. Hence socialism was Soviets plus Electricity. The factories, besides creating a new working-class, could also be made to increase the amenities of the daily life of the peasants and to produce arms with which to meet the grand capitalistic onslaught when it came. The particular charm of electricity was that it could also produce immediate results in the homes of the peasants, and this it was made to do. The electric lights were called by the grateful peasantry Lenin's Lamps; and thus, with the aid of the force which he designated to dispossess the peasants and turn them into good socialists, he impelled them to acquiesce in their dispossession.

It will have struck the attentive reader that he is being treated to a grossly oversimplified version of the October Revolution. Nothing could be more true. But it seems to me high time that some such simplification was attempted. The sort of drive behind the industrialization of Russia which made it possible for her to fight the army of the most industrialized state in Europe with its own weapons was not obtained by the pious resolution of a host of village peasants, not even by a hundred million of them. And yet precisely the inheritance of Lenin was more than a hundred million peasants, who liked being peasants, and a few million workers, most of whom periodically went home to lend a hand on the farm. That sort of drive cannot be accounted for by any of the popular ideas of the Revolution; and, in fact, the thing most people can never understand is how all these peasants managed spontaneously to achieve all that has, apparently, been done. The answer is, of course, that they did not. With the aid of electricity, Lenin and Stalin between them have managed to reduce the proportion of peasants from four-fifths in 1917 to something over half the population in 1939. Since the total population has been increasing latterly at the rate of some three million a year, there are still nearly as many peasants as there were in 1917, but the industrial population, industrial workers and their families, now amount to some 55,000,000. These are the proletarian dictators upon whom, until the outbreak of the late war, first Lenin, then Stalin, in the last resort depended.

The creation of this proletariat was the industrial revolution which began in Lenin's mind and was pushed to violent lengths by Stalin after Lenin's death. It was not a spontaneous co-agulation of peasants into non-existent industrial areas. And, until the industrial revolution was well under way, the Russian Government could do nothing about the socialization of the peasants themselves. The peasants are now socialized, after a bitterness of resistance and an extremity of suffering quite beyond our Western comprehension. They are socialized, and now, paradoxically, being still born conservatives, but now conservatives of socialism, they will prove to be the main prop of the regime—the regime which created a new proletariat in order to enforce the socialization of the peasants, and which at some time in the not very distant future may well find that pro-letariats are always revolutionary. . . . But this is going too fast.

And if I have overemphasized the arbitrariness of Lenin (though it would be difficult to do so), it is because the point of this arbitrariness seems to me to require making. Lenin's rev-olutions were imposed upon the people from above, like all the great changes in Russian history, which, invariably, have been heralded by the ukase of the autocrat. And the drive has come from above, and still comes from above. In a democratic country the government lags behind the people. In an autocracy the government is ahead of the people. And this was true of the Tsarist autocracy, with the tremendous ukases of Ivan the Terrible, of Peter the Great, of Alexander II, as well as of the Communist autocracy, which is what the Bolshevik autocracy grew into, and which, when it decides in the fastness of the Kremlin that the time has come to abolish the *kulak* and collectivize the peasants, announces its intention by, precisely, a ukase. . . . But in stressing the arbitrariness of Lenin we have to bear very clearly in mind two points. The first is that although the people, the peasantry, the people of the plain, did not want his socialism, they equally did not want any other known or unknown form of government—such as the continued government of the Tsar, the provisional government of Kerensky, the military government of Kornilov, or anything else at all. And when you are faced with a people who do not hold with any kind of government to the point of active resistance, to impose your ideal of a suitable government upon them is very different from imposing your ideal on a people who have a born feeling for the necessity of government and only do not like your particular kind of government. And the second point is that Lenin, although he had this Russian capacity for arbitrariness raised in him to the degree of genius (and this arbitrariness itself, I suppose, comes from the fact that even you do not really *believe* in government, but only perceive the necessity for it), he knew that in the end he would be dependent upon the people, whom he sought to govern against their will, and he was ready to go to extreme lengths in the eyes of his colleagues to conciliate the people and make them accept his rule. He did this so successfully that he won the support of the great majority. And this his successor, whether from temperament, conviction, or a sense of the unbrookable urgency of the hour, or a mixture of all three, failed to do, until he had killed off the more articulate members of the opposition. Whether Lenin would have been as ruthless as Stalin during the years when war with Japan and Germany was seen to be inevitable, we shall never know. Whether Stalin would have been as gentle—or, perhaps, as *tactful,* for Lenin also had a hand of steel—as his master during the first years of the revolution, we shall never know. My guess is that Stalin would have been more ruthless in the early days, and that Lenin would not have needed to be so ruthless, or at any rate to seem so ruthless, as Stalin during the days of the Five-Year Plans. And that is an opinion which seems to have been shared by Lenin himself, who is notoriously said to have written in his will a warning against Stalin's heaviness of hand. But I have never seen this will, and now nobody else will ever have the chance to see it. It is an opinion certainly shared more or less secretly by many Russians in Russia today, particularly by non-Communists of the new intelligentsia and the older peasants and by the relics of the Tsarist dispossessed, who might be forgiven for hating Lenin for dispossessing them, but who, in fact, regard him as the saviour of their country (with their wholly Russian capacity for seeing life whole and seeing it real regardless of its painfulness), while Stalin seems to them very much as he appears to certain intelligent foreigners, such as that great critic Edmund Wilson, as the betrayer of the free and flexible ideals of Lenin. But this is a fallacy. Stalin may be often rough and sometimes clumsy, but, as far as principles go, he has not betrayed his master. And the point I am trying to make is that it is no good sentimentalizing over Lenin and condemning the present regime. They stand or fall together. For nothing could have been less free and flexible than the ideals of Lenin, whose rigidity of mind was absolute, and who went, and would have gone again and again, to any lengths that he dared to bring those ideals to swifter fulfilment. But he had a quicker apprehension of danger than Stalin, or, rather, a quicker apprehension of precisely where the real danger lay, and his character, as distinct from his theorizing, had a freedom and flexibility which enabled him to disguise the real purpose and the waiting horrors of the dreadful journey he had mapped out for his fellow-countrymen, whom he loved. . . . It is in that last word that the final secret of Lenin's greatness lay, and the reason for his acceptance by the people. With all his other qualities, he was consumed with an impassioned hatred for the oppressor and a great and conquering love for humanity as individuals. The people knew this and felt its loss when he was gone.

3. GOVERNMENT, POLICE, AND PEOPLE

A MEASURE of the confusion which the Bolsheviks had to clarify and the internal resistance they had to overcome is provided by three selected facts. The first is that in 1921, four years after the October Revolution and the inauguration of socialism in Russia, Lenin had to take drastic and sustained evading action by announcing the notorious New Economic Policy, the N.E.P., which permitted the establishment of private trading on a limited scale. The second is that although the land was almost immediately declared State property, it was not until 1928, eleven years after the October Revolution, that Stalin was strong enough to force wholesale collectivization upon the peasants; in other words, to take back the land which the Bolsheviks in 1917 had incited the peasants to seize for themselves. The third fact is that the young woman who, in 1921, gave Lenin the bullet wound from which he died in 1924, was not a daughter of the dispossessed classes but a member of the left wing of the Socialist Revolutionary Party, which had split away from Kerensky in the last days of the Provisional Government.

The New Economic Policy was a radical, elaborate, opportunistic, and far-sighted concession to the spirit of private enterprise upon which the Bolsheviks had pronounced anathema. By the outside world it was welcomed with relief as Lenin's own confession of the failure of socialism—which, of course, it was, as far as socialism in Russia in 1921 was concerned. It was to remain in force for seven dreary years, and it was not repealed until four years after Lenin's death, when Stalin simultaneously announced the first Five-Year Plan, which was also the official announcement of the third revolution.

The resistance and confusion which led to the N.E.P. was the outcome of several causes: first, the resistance of the peasants and the old Tsarist officials to socialist ideas; second, the civil war organized by exiled Russian generals and supported by the Western Powers, a war which for three years raged over the plain on a greater scale and with heavier armament and with movements and clashes far more threatening and convulsive than is generally realized outside Russia; third, the actual intervention of the Western Powers in person; fourth, the continuance of the German war and the disastrous peace of Brest-Litovsk, whereby, for a time, Russia had to cede to Germany the agricultural and industrial treasure of the Ukraine; fifth, the various separatist movements after the collapse of Germany in the west, notably the secession of the Ukraine; sixth, the war with Poland, which was a full-dress campaign quite separate from other more general turmoils; and seventh, the great famine of 1921, which was the product of all these causes, plus the age-old climate of the plain.

In 1921 the fighting was over: Lenin and his Bolsheviks had Russia to themselves. But it was a Russia in unspeakable and unimaginable ruin, in which cannibals dwelt on the banks of the lower Volga and starving children roamed the cities and the countryside in organized gangs, stealing and killing to keep themselves alive and overwhelming unwary passers-by like wolf-packs pulling down an exhausted horse and tearing it to pieces as it fell. There were no factories; there were no crops; there were no trains. In the great cities people huddled together in hideous congestion in unheated, unlighted tenements and palaces. In the countryside people swarmed in aimless and exhausted droves in search of food and work, carrying typhus wherever they went. Of all the millions inhabiting the wasted and interminable plain—a prison now, arched by the impassive Russian sky, for the working out of life sentences from which there was no escape; in summer a brazen dust-heap, in winter a frozen desert, in autumn and spring a dreary morass—of all the millions inhabiting this prison, none had a thought for anything at all but keeping alive from one day to the next; and even in that ambition unknown millions failed.

None, that is to say, but Lenin and his Bolsheviks, who had moved from Petrograd to Moscow and now sat in the Kremlin and planned for socialism. For they still believed in the revolution. They still believed in socialism, as a conception greater than life or death, transcending individual man. But though greater than life or death, its realization, paradoxically, depended upon the continuance of life, which, even in Russia, was not infinitely expendable. And Lenin, at any rate, saw clearly enough that the only way to achieve socialism in this ruin was to harness the forces of anti-socialism to his purpose. By announcing the N.E.P. he proceeded to do so, breaking the hearts of some of his most loyal supporters by that act of apparent betrayal. But they could be replaced. For Lenin, by permitting the limited re-establishment of private trading, which was the only kind of trading that could possibly work just then, there being no properly organized State to carry on trading for itself, was enabled to conclude trade agreements with many of his late enemies, the governments of capitalistic countries, with Great Britain, Germany, Austria, Norway, and Poland. At the same time he was able to make use at home of the sort of men he temporarily needed but utterly despised, the Nep-men, as the newly privileged merchant-class was called. Further, as a by-product of this, and doubtless unintentionally, he converted more Russians to socialism than he could have done by more direct methods. For the spectacle of the Nep-men with their wives and mistresses squandering their swollen roubles on gross luxury in the few hotels and restaurants surviving in starved Petrograd and Moscow seems to have bitten extraordinarily deep into the minds of many Russians who were young men and women at the time and had every excuse for hating the Bolsheviks, who had deprived them of their possessions, their homes, their society, and often of their parents and lovers. Many times I have heard the Nep period referred to by Russians who were not at all active sympathizers with the Stalin government in the sort of tone one uses when referring to a period of national shame.

While the Nep-men played a great part in the rebirth of Russian trade and were only thrown out when the country was economically strong enough to do without them, so the peasant proprietors played the dominating part in the recovery of Russian agriculture, and were only dispossessed when the government was strong enough to declare war on them—to declare war, that is to say, on a very large proportion of its people, the people whom, so we are taught at school, it is the function of the government to serve. It depends, of course, on what you mean by "serve." . . . It was then that the term *kulak,* meaning "Clench-fist," originally descriptive of the type of grasping farmer, was determinedly applied to every peasant who preferred working his own personal holding to joining a Collective. *Kulaks,* of course, were only fit for liquidation. But although it was not until 1928 that the government dared call its most individual and most progressive peasants by the same name as the more disreputable elements of the countryside, and although many Nep-men became very prosperous during these years, the process of socialization, initiated by Lenin, was continuing at a great rate all the time. Model collective farms were dotted over the countryside to serve as sign-posts and examples, and the nationalization of industry and trade was steadily forcing private enterprise into an ever-narrowing apron in front of the stage on which the scene-shifters were at work behind the curtain. The scene-shifters were the members of the Communist Party.

The struggle for power among the revolutionary parties did not end with the success of the Bolsheviks' *coup d'état* on November 7th, 1917. The Social Revolutionary Parties, both the right and the left, continued extremely active for some time. When the first elections of the Constituent Assembly had been held in September 1917 under Kerensky, the Bolsheviks had secured only a minority; and when the new Assembly met for the first time in January of the following year and two months after Lenin's *coup d'état,* it showed what it thought of the Bolsheviks by electing as its chairman a Social Revolutionary. Lenin waited no longer. He had had enough of parliamentary government. Already he had quarrelled with his own Council of People's Commissars over the question of combining all left wing parties into a coalition government, as a result of which such familiar revolutionaries as Zinoviev, Kamenev, and Rykov had resigned. Now, the day after its first meeting, he dissolved the Assembly, and, with that act, put an end to parliamentary government in Russia with a decisiveness and despatch which would have been the admiration of the Tsars. The Duma, the first Russian attempt at party government, had been virtually abolished by Nicholas, when he found it would not do his will; the Constituent Assembly, the second attempt, which was to herald the new age, was completely abolished by Lenin, when it would not do his will. Since then there have been no more attempts. For the Supreme Soviet of the U.S.S.R., like every subordinate Soviet throughout that vast realm, is something quite other.

But even then the Social Revolutionaries were active. They blossomed into terrorism, organized revolts in the newly established Cheka, raised demonstrations against the Peace of Brest-Litovsk, assassinated Mirbach, the new German Ambassador, on the one hand, a number of prominent Bolsheviks on the other, and finally, with Dora Kaplan's bullet, put a premature end to the life of Lenin himself.

In due course they were put down, as Social Revolutionaries. But opposition to the Bolsheviks persisted, and it is true enough to say, in the spirit if not in the letter, that the influence of the opposition to Lenin, personified in the Social Revolutionaries, continued after Lenin's death in the opposition of some of Lenin's closest and most trusted supporters to his successor, Stalin. I think particularly of Trotsky, who, while he was far from being a Social Revolutionary, was once a Menshevik, and who believed with passion in the direct method of achieving global communism. And it was not until the great purges of 1937 and 1938 that the heirs to Dora Kaplan, though probably often unconscious of their own ancestry, and thinking that they stood for Lenin as against Stalin, were finally rooted out under pressure of imminent military exigency. By that time there were left in the higher councils of State only a handful of old Bolsheviks in addition to Stalin himself. The rest had either died or been purged away. With them went the last of the opposition.

It is customary to attribute this narrowing down of the

instrument of government to Stalin, the betrayer, as he has been called, of Lenin. But I hope I have said enough about Lenin to make it clear that this is a total, and a dangerous, misapprehension. It was Lenin, as head of the exiled Social Democrats in Switzerland, who forced the issue with the compromisers and divided the party into the Bolshevik and Menshevik groups. It was Lenin who icily, harshly, bitterly, maintained the integrity of the Bolshevik minority, even when it was threatened with effective extinction by the resignations and expulsions of the men who would not go all the way in every matter with their leader. It was Lenin who refused utterly to co-operate with the other parties of the Left in the early days of the Bolshevik rule, when the rulers were so thin on the ground and the opposition nearly the whole of Russia. And Stalin has carried on his tradition, the main difference between the two men being that by his outstanding force of personality and absolute and manifest integrity of purpose Lenin was able to convince more doubters than Stalin, which meant that Stalin had to resort first to intrigue, then force, when persuasion failed.

The foregoing little history is intended to serve two ends. In the first place it is intended to bring home the seriousness of the resistance which the Bolsheviks had to overcome. In the second place it is to show that when he considered it necessary to be unyielding the rigidity of Lenin was absolute and that the cruel eclecticism of his successor is not a Stalin speciality but the inevitable development of Leninism. It is most important for us to realize this today and not to mislead ourselves as to the significance of the Bolshevik revolutions by sentimentalizing about the character and aims of Lenin.

The inauguration of the N.E.P. and the loosening of the rein on the peasants might well give the reader the idea that Lenin was a creature after his own heart, a born master of compromise, who knew when to give way. He knew when to give way, certainly, but the idea that this giving way had any connexion with compromise comes from a complete and dangerous misreading not only of Lenin himself, but also of the Russian character, which Lenin embodied in the highest degree. The very conception of compromise filled him with disgust and nausea. He did not know what it meant. I am not at all sure that even we, the traditional compromisers, nowadays know what it means, so that we confuse, as Lenin confused, humility in face of truth with weakness in face of man, and today those of us who like the word compromise are far too often found using it as a euphemism for any kind of retreat, up to and including moral rout; while those of us who dislike the word have limited it to this unfortunate connotation.

At their best, however, the British compromise because they are insufficiently convinced of the absolute rightness of any single point of view, and this is a mark of a comparatively high state of civilization; at their worst they compromise because they are too timid or idle to press their convictions, and this is a mark of moral and mental inertia. Lenin's capacity to believe utterly in the validity of his own convictions, and the corollary that it was his duty never to betray his convictions, is, at its best, intellectual courage of the highest degree, at its worst sheer bigotry and obscurantism. The difference I am trying to establish is the difference between yielding ground so that you can get it back, with more ground, when you are stronger, at no matter what cost to yourself and to others, and yielding ground for good in order to reach a working agreement with the other fellow, who is also required to yield ground. This is compromise, the other is strategy. Lenin was a born strategist, who had no conception of compromise. In his concessions to private enterprise in business and private ownership of land there was never a suggestion that there might, after all, be something "in" these things, as we should say. The concessions were made because the Bolsheviks were too weak not to make them, and for no other reason at all.

The curious thing is that although it is customary to speak of this sort of fanaticism as intellectual arrogance, it can be argued quite convincingly that it is precisely the reverse, especially within the framework of dialectical materialism, which was the framework for all Lenin's thought. It can, indeed, be shown as humility of the rarest and most self-annihilating order, because it is neither more nor less than a submission of yourself whole-heartedly to the inevitable movement of history and the abdication of your own right to aspire to the wisdom of the gods. I, Lenin, am a Believer. I believe in the historical dialectic of Marx. I believe that all human movements carry within them the germ of their own overthrow. I believe that my function is to lead the overthrow of capitalism. Neither capitalism nor socialism is final. Both are historically necessary and inevitable. I, as the leader of anti-capital, a natural and inevitable movement, must subordinate myself absolutely to this movement and ensure its utmost concentration. Only in this way can my destiny be fulfilled—whereas you, the Social Democrat compromiser, are trying to leap out of the rhythm of history and to arrogate to yourself a power of god-like intervention, judging, as you call it, each case on its merits and inclining now this way, now that way, in a pretence of steering the current upon which you are nothing but a twirling, eddying straw. Vanity and presumption! . . .

It will be observed by now that the last passage might be an exposition of the antithesis between Catholicism and Protestantism. This, though not deliberate, was inevitable. It brings home very sharply the prerequisite for Lenin's uncompromising drive, which, viewed through Protestant eyes, is intellectual arrogance of the most appalling completeness; but viewed through Authoritarian eyes, it is seen as humility raised to the degree of saintliness. Lenin as the servant of a dogma is one sort of creature. Lenin as a free-thinker is quite another. But Lenin was not a free-thinker. He was a convert to a faith. He was a Paul, Paul with the temperament of Ignatius Loyola.

Often enough before this the Communist Party of Russia has been compared to a religious order, but usually in terms of a metaphor or an analogy. There should be no metaphor or analogy about it. It *is* a religious order, with Karl Marx as its head and founder and Lenin as its prophet. And Stalin, whatever his own personal views on life and death, is the orthodox champion of that order in direct succession to Lenin. His opponents are heretics. And the worst heretics of all are not the capitalists, the total unbelievers, but the Social Democrats, who pick and choose in what they believe, applauding Marx for this, defying him in that. The capitalists cannot upset authority. The Social Democrats can.

Communism is to Stalin what Christianity used to be to us. It is no longer the noble flame of a martyred idealism. It is a state of mind. We in this country find it very difficult to understand what the Marxian dialectic means to the Russian Communist leaders, that it is a belief which they take unquestioningly for granted, as something beyond all speculation, as Christians take certain fundamental articles of their faith for granted, so that it colours in some way their every thought and action. Christianity, we argue, or Buddhism, is a faith; Russian Marxism is a philosophy. But this is where we are fatally wrong. Because, in Russia, Marxism is no longer a free philosophy, but a closed faith, or dogma. And its influence permeates even those who are not conscious Marxists, even those who might call themselves anti-Party, just as the influence of the New Testament permeates even those of us who are not active professing Christians. Stalin may or may not believe in the desirability of world revolution; the important thing is that he believes in its inevitability. Until we realize this we shall be hopelessly in the dark.

The tragedy is that up to now the only people who have whole-heartedly resisted communism have been the scum of the earth, rich men seeing their wretched possessions in danger. It would be only too pleasant if it were as simple as that. But communism has little essentially to do with having or not having. For me, the Communists are welcome to all the dividends they can lay their hands on. But the very rich play little part in their philosophy. The Marxist believes that the antithesis of capitalism is the popular revolution leading initially to the dictatorship of the proletariat. He believes that this process is the inevitable and ineluctable riposte to capitalism, which contains the seeds of it. Anything which gets in the way of or complicates this straightforward and clear-cut opposition is irrelevant and pernicious. Social Democracy is especially pernicious because it pretends to the same ends as communism but seeks to compromise. There is no room for compromise in the Marxian religion, which is based on a "natural law" of assertion and counter-assertion, thesis and antithesis. The official Russian thesis was Tsarist capitalistic society. The antithesis (which the Kerenskyites sought to blur) was the October Revolution and the dictatorship of the proletariat. The world thesis is capitalism (represented by America). The antithesis will be the overthrow of capitalism, which can only come as the result of war. This conception is as real and actual to the Russian Communist as the coming of the Messiah to the orthodox Jew or the Resurrection to the Christian. It is a cardinal tenet of faith, and it conditions everything which its believers do and feel. The Russian-Marxist interpretation of history is not a philosophy but a dogma. It should not be necessary to say these things; but when we see pillars of the Christian Church acting as spokesmen for the Russian Communism, it can only mean that such men think of communism as a social system in which there are no millionaires and everybody has enough to eat. It is not. There is no reason in the world why Henry Ford should not have been a Marxist. For the Marxian interpretation of history is not necessarily a monopoly of revolutionaries, who are simply the protagonists of a single dialectical thesis. Henry Ford could have regarded himself as the protagonist of another. He would thereby have found a philosophical, if not a religious, justification for his activities, which he lacked. I make a present of this idea to the weary capitalists of this world. Let them become Marxists and fight for their thesis with all consciousness of their ultimate overthrow but with a new glow of self-righteousness. They are part of a historical process. It is their duty to play their part to the full just as it was Lenin's duty to play his part to the full.

This, I suppose, is a *reductio ad absurdum*. But be that as it may, the only people, as far as I can see, who can never be Marxists are those who do not believe in determinism as presented by Marx. It is still possible to be a determinist of sorts without being a Marxian determinist. All Marxists are determinists, in a word; but not all determinists need be Marxists. For the Marxist, when all is said, has pinned his faith to one single man's view of the ordering of the universe. And since some two hundred million human beings are now directly governed by Marxists, and many more millions are controlled by them, this is a very considerable achievement for a single human prophet, or for Marx and Engels combined—bringing them into the category of Buddha, Jesus Christ, Confucius, and Mohammed. Unless we add Marx-Engels to that list, and realize that they stand for a faith, a faith which is transforming the face of Russia and has the power to transform the face of the world, unless we do this we shall soon find ourselves transformed or liquidated. The great mistake of many pagan societies blotted out by the Christians was that they never found out what it was that was hitting them until it was too late. At the moment most of us in the West have not the faintest idea of what is hitting us. So unless we devote ourselves to the task of understanding this and stop arguing whether it is a good thing for Mr. Rockefeller to have his money taken away from him or not, and to construct a society in which there will be no future Rockefellers, we shall get nowhere. Of course it is a good thing. Who, except Mr. Rockefeller and his friends, could have the least possible doubt on that subject? Where can doubt conceivably exist? What possible justification can there be for allowing one man with an unspeculative lust for money or power to dominate the lives of millions who do not really believe in money or power but only in a peaceful and productive life? Of course it is a good thing to put him under restraint. Of course it is a shocking thing that any human being should have it in his power to force other human beings to do things against their will for the enrichment of their master. Who would argue about that? The only thing to argue about is how to stop that kind of thing without strangling the free development of the individual spirit. Marxism will not help us here. It does not recognize the validity of the human spirit as hitherto understood by us. Meanwhile, we have so weakly allowed ourselves to be bamboozled into *not* thinking about communism as it really is by the wretched men who see in it only a threat to their own skins and possessions, that, reacting naturally and properly against these characters, we find ourselves viewing with sympathy and almost a glow of affection the men who have succeeded in frightening them, forgetting, or ignoring altogether, the fact that these mighty wolf-scarers are motivated by a faith, a creed, a dogma that is incompatible not only with our tolerance of profiteers, but with our tolerance of anything at all.

We seem to have come a long way from the Russian people, the people of the plain. This is not our fault. We have had to contemplate their rulers, who, on the face of it, are such a very long way from them that they have to use a secret police and all the apparatus of tyranny to rule them. There is nothing new in this, as far as Russia is concerned. Also, it takes two to make a tyranny as we understand that term; the oppressor and the oppressed. If the oppressed is not conscious of his oppression there is no tyranny in the accepted sense: instead, there is the order of the hive. But are the Russians bees or are they people?

We have seen them looking grey and undifferentiated and depressed in the murk of wartime winter, and, leaping ahead, we concluded that greyness was their armour. The problem before us is to discover whether this is a purely physical or a mental armour. And what goes on behind it?

One of the first revolutionary actions in 1917 was the abolition of the Tsarist Security Police, the Ochrana. The Security Police was one of those detested institutions which stood for tyranny in the heart of a not yet Prussianized Europe and, within Russia itself, was the symbol of all arbitrariness and evil. The Revolution, as far as great numbers of ordinary Russians were concerned, might almost be characterized as a revolt against the Ochrana. But within a year it was back again, this time called the Cheka. Nobody can reasonably blame Lenin for bringing it back. He had to govern the people, and when he found that police government was the only sort of government they paid any attention to, he had to produce it for them. He would probably have had to do so even if his party had not been fighting for its life in a sea of more or less organized opposition; but the extraordinary character of the times gave him his excuse, without going deeper into the nature of the Russian reaction to authority, and he was able to say, and almost certainly to believe (because even Lenin was not infallible in his appreciations), that when times grew less confused the Cheka would go—or wither away, like the State. The Cheka went in due course, but the Ogpu rose out of its ashes. The Ogpu went in its turn, only to be replaced by the N.K.V.D. which, until a year ago, was the current name for the Ochrana. With the substitution of Ministries for Commissariats it changed its name, but nothing else. It is now the M.V.D. and, as such, it has developed into a mighty and many-headed instrument of State, almost a state within a state. For, if we may now permit ourselves an analogy, Stalin is Philip of Spain, Torquemada is the Public Prosecutor, while the M.V.D. is neither more nor less than the Secular Arm. . . .

There is nothing inherently sinister in those three initials: they stand simply for the Ministry of the Interior, or, in two words, Home Office. But a Home Office run almost exclusively under Regulation 18B of the Emergency Powers Act, with its own armed force to carry out the provisions of that regulation, and its own industries staffed by victims of that regulation who are too valuable to be shot or sent to work in the mines. It is as simple as that, as commonplace, and as paralysing to free initiative of mind and spirit. Or rather, it would be paralysing to free initiative of mind and spirit as conceived by us, who work and think in terms of compromise.

We have seen that Lenin did not know what compromise meant, and we have said that Lenin was a Russian of the Russians, the implication being that the Russians themselves do not know what compromise means. On the other hand we have already spoken, and shall be speaking some more, about the extreme fluidity and openness to suggestions and impressions characteristic of the Russian temperament, which, one would have said, do not go with a single-minded and uncompromising purpose. But it is precisely these two things that do go together. The Russians are indisputably anti-compromisers, and they are equally indisputably "free," in the sense of being all-accept-

ing and, in expansive moments, all-embracing. It is quite easy
to reconcile these apparent opposites, which are seen to be
opposites only if we use the word compromise in its loose connotation, of giving way, instead of in its strict connotation of
dilution. In fact there is no need to reconcile them at all: they
are seen to be inseparable; and, between them, they give rise to
another epithet which we have already employed: anarchic.

Because, to the Russian, the only crime is not to be yourself.
Knowing how far he is from perfection, it never occurs to him
to ask that where he has failed others should succeed. He is all-
accepting because he believes in the fullest sense of the term
and in the very marrow of his bones that it takes all sorts to make
a world. He respects his neighbour's weaknesses and only asks
in exchange that his neighbour should respect his. He also
accepts his neighbour's point of view. Thus it is in Russia that,
inevitably, we find the attempt, carried in Dostoevski to its
logical and most inspired conclusion, to regard all things as
being equally good and to arrive from that at the conception
of the absolute equality of all men: since no living creature is
"superfluous," it follows that the saint is of no more value than
the drunkard, the great discoverer or artist of no more value
than the peasant slave. All is well, provided the drunkard is
a drunkard with conviction and does not, in deference to the
opinions of the saint, try to remain sober on Sundays, and provided the saint is a saint with conviction and does not, in deference to the drunkard, take a glass of vodka on Saturday
night. Such an attitude rules out utterly the characteristic English compromise of, to take an example, the sporting parson, who
in Russian eyes would have proved himself neither sporting nor
a parson—in fact, an *Unmensch*. Such an attitude rules out
utterly the conception of the British policeman who, essentially,
is a link, a human link, between the abstract rigour of the law on
the one hand and human frailty on the other. In Russia you have
the law and you have human frailty, and, on such occasions as
they come into collision, the stronger wins. In order that the law
should win at all it must obviously be very strong indeed. And
all that would be true without politics. But when a country has

to be governed, and when every man regards himself as a law unto himself, and every man is different, it is evident that they have to be submitted to an "overlaw." Left to themselves the Russians would never combine, since combination implies a sinking of differences, a dilution of individuality—compromise, in a word. And this they will not do. But submitted to an over-law they will combine with the utmost readiness, each preserving his own differences as between his fellows and his maker, but, overruled—not diluted—by authority. Such an "overlaw" may be human or elemental.

I have quoted on another occasion, and I quote again, Professor Milyukov's famous remark: "The Russians lack the cement of hypocrisy," because this brings us straight to the heart of our subject. Later, perhaps, we shall talk a little more about the implications of this supremely important truth. For the moment the operative word is "cement." For hypocrisy—taking for the time being that word at its face value—is in fact the cement which holds together in coherent mass the innumerable highly differentiated particles of a nation which, if each retained absolute freedom of action and thought and practised that freedom, could never cohere. We, in this country, are all cement. In every aspect of our daily life one man adapts himself to another, one institution to another, with varying degrees of consciousness, and with the result that no man is what the Americans would call one hundred per cent himself. A Russian would rather die than not be one hundred per cent himself, and so there is none of this perpetual dilution of self when it comes to human and social relationships, sometimes instinctive and involuntary, sometimes deliberate and planned. Yet, if the Russians are to succeed as a people, they must be held together, and if they will not hold themselves together they must be held together by an overriding force. And so, just as the Russians of the earliest days combined together in the Mir in spite of, or because of, their excessive individualism, in order to survive the onslaught of the elements (the overriding force), and just as in later years the Tsars developed serfdom to hold the peasants physically together for purposes of defence and exploitation of the land, so, in the twentieth century, the Bolshevik government has had to return to the device of the Security Police, a perpetual embodiment of 18B, to make them hold together today.

It is not all done by the police. The Russian himself has an instinct which tells him he must combine or perish. And since he cannot combine on his own level he has himself to evoke a superior authority. From this springs his passion for orthodoxy. It does not matter what we say, said Melbourne with the penetrating truth of British detachment at its highest, so long as we all say the same thing. It does not matter what we believe, say the Russians, so long as we all believe in the same thing. Thirty years ago that thing was the Eastern Church. Today it is Marxism. But today's belief in Marxism is much more accurately to be compared with belief in the Eastern Church of two hundred years ago, because, thirty years ago, a large and influential slice of the nation had ceased to believe in the Eastern Church and was thrown back on its own individual resources. I mean the intelligentsia. And if we read the stories and plays of Chekhov we see what happens to Russians when they lack the framework of a common belief or orthodoxy. They go to pieces. Today the intelligentsia finds itself once more incorporated in the new orthodoxy of All Russia, the Marxian religion.

I hope it does not seem too extravagant a jump from the Security Police to religious aspirations. If it does, it means that I have failed in the purpose of this book, which is, precisely, to produce an atmosphere in which such jumps (which are what you have to deal with when you consider the Russian people) do not look like jumps at all. We have already seen how the Russian peasant regarded the source of all oppression, the Tsar, as the Little White Father who could do no wrong. We have already seen how he regarded his religion not as an exhortation to a better life but as an encouragement in adversity. We have already seen how the most active individualists in the world became slaves because of their individualism, and, at the same time, by some instinct, regarded their subservience—to the Tsar, not to the landowners—as a necessary thing. They still have this individualism, and they still have this sense of the necessity for subservience. Their individualism brings them a compensating integrity of spirit, which we lack, and their subservience replaces our political sense.

We have now reached the point from which it is clear that loose talk about hives and ant-heaps, and loose talk about servility, is wholly misleading; further, that to talk of tyranny with the usual connotation of that word in mind is irrelevant. We have reached the point from which, if we cared, we could go forward to prove that the Russians are greater and purer individualists than ourselves, since they never surrender their individuality but only their freedom of action; while we make daily radical compromises involving our individuality in exchange for a limited freedom of action for what is left of it. That, like most arguments, looks very pretty on paper, but it overlooks the empirical fact that it is only by the free exercise of individuality that individuality grows. So that, in fact, although we dilute our individuality, our individuality, through immemorial freedom of action, is strong enough to stand such dilution. Whereas, by restricted freedom of action, the Russian individuality, which he preserves intact, has dwindled. And this, I think, is what has happened in the past, and is happening at a very great rate today.

It is happening at a very great rate today because the demands of the overlaw have been, and still are, too rigorous and too comprehensive and too detailed. This is due to two causes, apart from accidents of personality in Stalin and his colleagues. It is due in the first place to the fact that for the past twenty-four years Russia has existed in a veritable state of emergency, so that 18B has been piled on 18B, and in the second place to popular education. The Ochrana were called upon to hold together an organized and established state inhabited by patriots and loyal subjects of the Tsar. Its subsequent incarnations—the Cheka, Ogpu, N.K.V.D., and M.V.D.—have been called upon first to impose a new organization upon chaos, secondly to create loyalty to new ideas and men, thirdly to prepare for the in-evitable attack from outside. Again, the Tsarist government, aided invaluably and indispensably by the Church, had to pre-scribe a few simple principles of thought for a population that was 90 per cent illiterate and 80 per cent agricultural. The sim- plicity of the compulsory framework left plenty of room for free speculation on the part of the literate intelligentsia. But the Soviet government has had to prescribe a detailed way of thought and life for newly literate millions, a great proportion of these being brought along at a highly artificial rate and capable of as many varieties of error as their own astronomical numbers.

The outcome of this is that the entirely Russian habit of general prescription from above has become today particular prescription from above; and since this prescription goes for all, it absolutely rules out any freedom of action for the new intelligentsia, most of whom, in any case, are so conditioned by the Marxian dialectic that they do not seek such freedom and readily transform themselves into specialized instruments of government policy. As for the masses, being taught to think alike in such detail, they are in fact beginning to become alike. And although if you take a cross-section of, say, the British public, you will find an almost shocking unanimity of thought and feeling, conditioned by the prevailing ideas and con- ventions, these prevailing ideas and conventions are, by and large, the mean of the ideas and conventions of at least very broad classes of society, which have made their own conventions and then been strangled by them, but which, up to now, have revolted in time before strangulation was complete and changed their ideas and conventions. In Russia the ideas and conventions come from above. And the process is making individuals far too much alike.

Let us take an example. Democracy—the burning question. We say, we and the Russians have different conceptions of de- mocracy. That is all right as far as it goes, but it doesn't go any- thing like far enough. The Russian conception is plain and unanimous; within our opposed conception there are infinite variations. But the Russian conception of democracy is not, as we think, a humbug. It means government for the people with the consent of the people. Neither more nor less, and nothing else at all. Our general conception (which, after all, was first upon the scene, so that the onus is on the Russians to find a new word for their variation), means, if it means anything at all, government of the people, for the people, by the people, precisely that, and nothing else. Whether we have achieved this ideal is another matter. We believe in it, most of us, and we say we have it. The Russians say we have not and therefore we cannot believe in it. If, in view of the frequency with which mass deportation is used as an instrument of government, we find it humbug in the Russians to speak even of government of the people for the people, the Russians find it no less humbug in us to speak of government of the people by the people for the people in view of unemployment and depressed areas existing side by side with the mansions of our more prominent financiers, who are known to be, to put it mildly, closer to the ear of the cabinet than the average citizen of the Rhondda valley—and if you succeed in convincing a Russian that we are not, at any rate consciously, humbugging about democracy, he will be appalled by our conception of it. How, he will exclaim, can you conceivably justify the freedom of an individual to oppose a governmental measure devised to benefit the people? . . . And you can go on arguing on that line, or, more accurately, bellowing across that gulf, for ever, because it touches on a national instinct crystallized into a dogma.

We shall return to that dogma in a moment. The point upon which we temporarily dwell is that when discussing these matters, such as conceptions of democracy, with Russians, the answer you receive from one is the answer you receive from *all*, excluding a peripheral fringe of concealed opposition among the heirs to the Tsarist intelligentsia and a proportion of elderly peasants, but not excluding a considerable, but apparently swiftly dwindling, number of Russian patriots who take no stock in the present Kremlin government. *All* Russians. And in their replies there will be no variation at all, no individual slants and sidelights on the over-all flat statement, and no sign of glimmering comprehension of another point of view. *All* Russians. Which means that when you have talked politics with one Russian you have talked politics with the lot. And so perfectly conditioned are they, that even if one or other of them disagrees most violently with this or that policy or measure and, in conversation, ventures to express disagreement (which happens perhaps more often than you would think), it never occurs to him to question the system which forbids him to proselytize his views.

All this, obviously, makes for a certain uniformity as well as the famous unanimity, especially among the very young, whose thoughts about everything under the sun have been conditioned from the cradle. Their uniformity is absolute, and the only variations in it are due to the variations in the party line. This, the line of attack laid down by the Communist Party for the furtherance of communism in Russia, is changed so often in detail, with every change of tactics, that, for the non-Communist, who is not expected to be fully up to date, there is room for a certain latitude of mind while he is catching up on the latest line of thought. But such latitude is superficial. The fundamental tenets are unchanged. And to offer our true conception of democracy to Russian youth is to stimulate the sort of reaction a Mormon might have expected had he chosen to air his views in a Victorian drawing-room—I said our true democracy, and I really think we must insist upon this. For although we are farther than most of us realize from any kind of democracy, the ideal we appear to have in mind is government by the people, which is what the word democracy means. Autocratic government, no matter how beautifully inspired with the ideal of serving the people, is not democracy. The Communists should learn Greek and choose another name for their form of government, or, if they don't believe in Greek, leave Greek words alone.

It should be plain by now that the general idea behind the Russian view of the Soviet government is our old friend the greatest good of the greatest number, and that the Russian inability to compromise is such that the lesser number has to go, while the greater number get more and more alike. There is no room for a free intelligentsia. There is no room for a leaven of minority opinion. And the Russians submit to these limitations not merely with acquiescence but with ardour. "Communism," observes Berdyaev, "has no idea of freedom as to the possibility of choice, but only as to the possibility of giving full play to one's energies when one has chosen which way to turn." The Russians have chosen, and, as we have seen, the Russian character, as moulded by the plain and its history, could not be better suited for the role for which it is now cast. To quote Berdyaev again: "The spirit of the people could very easily pass from one integrated faith to another integrated faith, from one orthodoxy to another orthodoxy, which embraced the whole of life." This it has done. And again: "There always remains, as the supreme thing, the profession of some orthodox faith: this is always the criterion by which membership of the Russian people is judged." And lest we should seem to be unduly wise after the event, let us repeat once more the words of Leontiev: "Sometimes I dream that a Russian Tsar may put himself at the head of the Socialist movement and organize it, as Constantine organized Christianity."

We were talking about the Security Police. It is fairly obvious that if a people is incapable of compromise you will get, between the ruling power and the opposition, a state of war *à l'outrance*. And that, in fact, is what happens in Russia and always has happened. No quarter is given or demanded. The opposition has no more idea of compromise than the established authority, which means that which ever is the weaker goes. Which means that its relics will work underground and employ every conceivable means, good and evil, to overthrow the established power. Which means that the established power must arm itself with a defensive weapon. In Russia this weapon is now called the M.V.D. and it passes from the defensive to the offensive on the least provocation. It is possible that one day there will be no more opposition. The picture I have drawn of the ironing out of Soviet youth into one pattern may suggest that this will be soon. Undoubtedly, should such a state of affairs arise, there would be no more police rule in Russia, and, indeed, such perfection of uniformity and unanimity would signalize, further, the withering away of the State. For if everybody thought the same about everything there would be no need for a state, and this, I take it, is what the Russian thinkers mean by the withering away of the state. Anarchy without tears. It is conceivable that should such a moment arrive the mighty Russian people, identical in their millions in thought and feeling and with none of the striving and the hope that keep the rest of us alive, would have the simultaneous notion of committing suicide. That would be one end to the Russian problem, but I do not consider it the most likely end. There are good and historical human reasons for believing that it will be a long time before uniformity is achieved, even for believing that, before very long, uniformity may be a good deal less marked than it is today, reasons which we shall glance at later. For the moment it is sufficient to state that as long as any kind of opposition to the principle and details of the Kremlin rule exists there will be some form of arbitrary police rule. And this will also remain until the Russians, the Russian people, not merely the Russian government, cease to believe that the means are justified by the end. The Russians do believe this and have always believed it. Ivan Kalita believed it when he sold his soul to the Khan of Tartary; Ivan the Terrible believed it when he rooted out the boyars who complicated his benevolent rule; Peter the Great believed it when he made his inconceivable sacrifices of his own energies and the lives of his subjects for the Westernization of Russia; Nicholas I believed it when he destroyed the Decembrists, the cream of the youthful nobility, with cold and pursuing fury; and so on. And always the Russian people accepted the principle of evil means to benevolent ends, and only kicked when, in detail, or accumulation of detail, the evil was too heavy to be borne. Stalin believes it to this day, and so do the descendants of the people of the plain. Because they believe with the whole of their conviction in the imperative necessity for every man to be himself; and they also have an instinct which tells them that they must cohere and that the only means of cohesion is for a state of war between an autocratic power and the individual, in which the individual will often get hurt.

Now if you really believe that, somehow, the good of the people as a whole is worth more than the sum of the good of the individuals composing it; and if, on the other hand, you do not believe in an absolute and attainable good, but set great emphasis on the separate goods of individuals, you have two opposed conceptions which are absolutely opposed, as in the opposition of Catholic and Protestant. "It seems to me," said a Catholic friend one day, "that all Protestants think far too much of man and far too little of God." And, similarly, a Russian today, and by no means necessarily one of the priestly caste, could observe (if he were capable of an observation of such simple penetrating virtue, which he is not) with no less justice from his inviolable point of view: "It seems to me that you Social Democrats think far too much of men and far too little of Man." Which is unanswerable. We do. The only answer, indeed, is the counter-charge: "It seems to me that you Communists think far too much of Man and far too little of men." Which is also unanswerable. They do.

Impasse.

But how necessary to establish it. Our ancestors were wiser. They were aware of the existence of incompatibles and arranged their lives accordingly, their institutions, their societies, their individual families. Whereas we—we seem to be suffering from a rush of electrons to the brain, a process which is unlikely to be arrested by our latest successful effort in the way of cosmic levelling. We have reduced everything to its common dust and find that we have forgotten what it looked like before it was reduced. You, dear reader, and I are composed of identical electrons, or whatever the latest jargon may be for the ashes and dust of Christian burial; therefore we must be, at bottom, identical. We cannot even credit ourselves with the discovery of this dust. The first man, as he observed between an agony of horror and the wonder of a Cortez the preliminary decomposition of his beloved, the companion of his life, knew all about that dust—we have merely given it a name. We recognize electrons. And we recognize electrons made up into abstract patterns, fundamentals of human behaviour, instincts and complexes. And everybody is composed of the same electrons, or instincts and complexes, therefore everybody is the same. All nations indeed must be the same. We must be, at heart, just like the Russians: they have the same senses, the same fundamental instincts, the same rhythm of life and death shot with all the emotions of the psychologists' spectroscope.

Therefore we will think of them in terms of ourselves, and if that doesn't make sense of what they do, then they must be doing it on purpose. . . . But the first man was wiser. Perhaps because he lived in the fields, he knew that the dust, for a brief span of miraculous years, had made itself into a pattern which was unique and would never in the history of the world occur again.

But we, so intent on our nomenclature, have forgotten the essence of the things we so busily name. And instead of recognizing differences where differences are plain to the eye, we seek to smooth them out and make all things the same: the man in the street and his neighbour; the great man and the small man; the illiterate and the scholar; the Russians and the British. And if in these pages I have been able to establish, not by argument, which can always be demolished, but by suggestion, that the difference between the outlook of the Russian and the outlook of the Englishman is so great as to come into the category of incompatibility, I shall have fulfilled the main hope of this book. Because it is only when you clearly recognize incompatibles that tolerance, understanding, love, begin to detach themselves from infatuation and *Schwärmerei* and grow freely. So long, in a word, as we think that the Russians see life in the same way, fundamentally, as we see it, we shall always be pulling and tugging and nagging and twisting and crying out with the bitterness of exasperation to make them *more* like. But if we recognize clearly that we are unlike, fundamentally and unalterably, and where, then we can relax and begin to think in terms of ways and means. We shall have to decide whether there is room in the world for two such powerful unlikes. And if we decide in the affirmative we can concentrate on developing what we have in common, which is a great deal, and on enjoying the differences—who quarrels with the sun because it is unlike the moon? As I observed, our ancestors were wiser.

We have shown some of the reasons why the Russians show so marked a proclivity for police rule. This seemed necessary for two reasons: in the first place it is an essential item in any exploration of the Russian character; in the second place it is desirable to make it quite clear that the difference between the M.V.D. principle and the Gestapo principle is absolute. The one has come into being by mutual consent between the rulers and the ruled, as a means whereby the multifarious and fearful independence of the ruled may be curbed. The other has come into being as the instrument whereby a race of cynical self-seekers has been dragooned into some kind of public service.

We think too often of the Russian secret police in terms of the atrocious purges of 1936 and 1937. This is a mistake. The secret police is ever present; but as a rule it is not severely felt. The purges were a kind of hysteria which had nothing intrinsically to do with the Russian idea of a secret police. Before the purges Russia was beginning to look up, the people to know happiness and fulfilment. The collectivization of the farms was over and done with, as were the consequent local famines (local, but on a bitter scale) caused by the defensive slaughter of live stock and neglect of crops on the part of the protesting peasants. Although the second Five-Year Plan was still demanding every ounce of disposable energy, life was beginning to grow more colourful. Consumer goods were coming into the shops, and there was a feeling of spring in the air at the end of a long, long winter of privation. Then the obscure Kolylov emptied his revolver into the unprotesting flesh of Kirov, governor of Leningrad, one of Stalin's staunchest supporters and perhaps his closest friend—and for the people of Russia this shot had consequences almost as calamitous for them as the consequences for the world at large of the shot fired by Gavrilo Princeps at his street corner in Sarajevo twenty-two years earlier. For it was the assassination of Kirov, when everything seemed at last set for recovery, when Trotsky had been chased to Mexico and his features expunged from every photograph showing scenes from the life of the early Bolsheviks, when the peasants had at last been brought into line and were rather liking it, those who were left, when the new literacy was beginning to tell, when there was food for everyone and the imaginative labels of Mr. Mikoyan's new canning industries were brightening the grey interiors of the State chain-stores with the allurements of Kamchatka crab and rose-petal jam, when taxis stood in ranks in the new cities, and when Stalin was taking on the aspect of a benevolent patriarch—at precisely this moment all Russia was suddenly turned into a madhouse. Then, by all means, the people were afraid, not the oppositional *fronde,* but the ordinary people of the plain, who had done nothing wrong, contemplated doing nothing wrong, and had never thought of having anything to fear. Then the secret police excelled itself and showed what could be done by such an institution when it was put upon its mettle. And while the outside world devoured the descriptions of the great trials in the hall of columns in the Nobleman's Club, and saw what Mr. Vishinsky was like when there was nobody to oppose him, Russia herself was shadowed with a spectre of fear unprecedented in her history, different not only in degree but in kind. For in the past there had been nothing for the little man to fear who did not step outside the chalk circle (unless, during a brief period, he got himself called a *kulak*). But now nobody was safe. And the names of Yagoda and Yezhov, successive heads of the secret police, cannibals, themselves in the end devoured by the impersonal and gentle Mr. Beria, stood for Terror; so that those, to Russians, unremarkable names took on all the air of sinister and cruel violence which their very appearance has for us, who might, writing a story about evil and absolute tyrants, have invented precisely those combinations of syllables to evoke the horror. Yezhov and Yagoda. Russians today, who regard the name of Beria with detachment, the name of a man with a queer job to do, not the job they would have chosen themselves, but a necessary job, who is doing it reasonably well—Russians who can bear to look at the portrait of the Grand Inquisitor flanking the portraits of Stalin, Kalinin, and the General of the Hour with no more than a suppressed giggle, will turn pale, literally, and tense, if you pronounce the syllables Yezhov or the syllables Yagoda. And, in reaction against those abominations, I have listened to a young Russian of loyal but independent views (for such exist: they come mainly from Leningrad), rhapsodizing about their predecessors, Dzerzhinsky and Menzhinsky—who themselves committed some tough actions—as about founders of the state and upholders of the moral law—say, Jefferson and Lincoln.

It is no part of this book to act as a chronicle for the purges. That has been done too many times already. We need not even speculate about them. Without inside information such speculation is fruitless and one man's guess is as good as another's. There plainly was treason on a big scale, both internal and external, both positive and negative. That is to say, men were plotting for the overthrow of Stalin and the substitution of his late colleagues. While other men, and sometimes the same ones, were plotting the overthrow of Communism by letting in the Germans. Such things need not surprise us. There is no need to believe that Stalin himself assassinated Kirov in order to give himself an excuse to attack where he felt attack was needed. He had no need of that sort of excuse. And, indeed, the killing of Kirov, his friend and putative successor-designate, explains absolutely the way the purges ran. Because now was the only time when Stalin publicly lost his head. He did lose it. In a panic emotional reaction he struck too hard, too bloodily, and altogether too indiscriminately. Messrs. Yezhov and Yagoda were given their heads—only to lose them literally when Stalin suddenly discovered all that they were doing and that soon Mr. Yezhov (Yagoda himself having gone) would be the only Communist left—for it is quite wrong to think of Stalin as unemotional, and his anger and bitterness and fear at the killing of Comrade Kirov must have been terrible in the extreme. He is a Georgian, with a tradition of hot blood. There is nothing detached and impersonal about this pale little man with his impassive exterior, his faintly Mephistophelian eyebrows, his pale, plump hands, his lavender-grey utilities, all veiling the will of a Dancing Dervish, the hot passions of a Caucasian brigand, the lucidity of a Spanish philosopher, and the ruthlessness of a Chinese war-lord. And the beginning of the great purge was almost without a doubt a convulsive act of vengeance, quickly and coldly rationalized into a heaven-sent opportunity to remove everybody, but *everybody*, who might conceivably stand or be about to stand in his way, or in the way of Great Russia. And we need not be surprised by the bitterness, the wildness, the savagery, and the brutal clumsiness of the reaction of the secret police to these plots, and the reckless and wasteful destruction which accompanied this reaction. We have seen enough of Russian history to recognize those symptoms. It was without a doubt a dreadful three years, and it has left traces far more important than the loss of thousands of superior talents. For a time it turned the Russians into a race of informers and internecine denouncers, which by temperament they are not, and it made everybody dreadfully afraid, so that, as never before, each man withdrew into himself and minded his own business. And there is no doubt at all that the downcast look, particularly of the citizens of Moscow, which lies in the immediate shadow of the Kremlin walls, was partly due to the excesses of these purges. And even today people are afraid of things which, almost certainly, they need not fear. Almost certainly; but you can never be sure.

And the point I am trying to make is that this witches' sabbath, although the active and destructive agent was the secret police, and although without a secret police it would not have been possible, is not the stick to measure the M.V.D. with. The great purges were due to an act of revenge, a sudden panic, and a wicked and probably mad chief of police. We do not, or should not, measure the rule of the British in India by Amritsar.

The second point I am trying to make is that it so badly shook people up that they have not yet wholly recovered. It may, for all I know, be to the advantage of the government to have people shaken up; but I do not think so. Men work better, as the Russians did, when they know they will be alive and in the bosom of their families at breakfast-time tomorrow. To live each day as though it were your last is not a satisfactory basis for life, as most Russians and a large number of Western Europeans could now tell us. It is surprising how much the work of today is bound up with plans for the day after tomorrow. And the lack of plans for the day after tomorrow is what is chiefly the matter with Russia, and with authoritarianism as a means of government. You just cannot have plans when authority may ruin them at a blow by ordering you to do this or that quite differently. And without plans you cease to grow. The Russian, as I hope will have emerged from these pages, is able to sublimate his own stunted growth into the growth of the community as a whole. Instead of having his own plans he throws himself into the plans of the community as a whole. And this is much the same as abandoning the notion of personal immortality for a vague idea of continuing, your identity lost, but your life, or whatever it is, going on for ever and for ever in the world spirit, whatever that is, which is so much the richer for this contribution. Some people can derive comfort from such abstractions, others cannot, and insist on their personal immortality. Others, who cannot see any real justification for this, prefer to call it a day when death overtakes them, instead of pretending that they continue as part of a sort of moral Heaviside Layer.

The third point is that it took not the secret police, but the secret police run berserk, to make a marked impression on the buoyancy of the people of the plain.

Let us listen once more to Conrad on "Autocracy and War": ". . . and the coming events of her internal changes, however appalling they may be in their magnitude, will be nothing more impressive than the convulsions of a colossal body. Her soul, kept benumbed by her temporal and spiritual master with the passion of tyranny and superstition, will find itself on awakening possessing no language, a monstrous full-grown child having first to learn the ways of living thought and articulate speech. It is safe to say that tyranny, assuming a thousand protean shapes, will remain clinging to her struggles for a long time before her blind multitudes succeed at last in trampling her out of existence under their millions of bare feet." The last time we quoted those words was before we had got very far with our contemplation of the people of the plain; we had not then looked at them close to. We have still a long way to go before we can feel that we have really seen them, but already, I think, we should be in a better position to decide how far Conrad was right and how far he threw wide of the truth because he wrote out of the experience of an alien, an incompatible, outlook on life.

And nothing could be more important than to decide how far he was wrong, not because Conrad was an authority on Russia, nor even because the words we have quoted contained, when they were written, anything new, but simply because they state with the clarity and economy of a great artist the essence of one way of looking at the Russians, a point of view which, broadly speaking, has been shared for several hundred years by most Western Europeans who have not fallen beneath the spell of the great plain. If it is right, then there is no more to be said. It can be made to cover many of the facts, and it is too much to ask that any generalization should cover all the facts (if it does it ceases to be a generalization and establishes itself as a particular statement). But does it, in the light of what we have thus far seen, cover a majority of the facts, and can those facts be interpreted in other ways? If it does not, and if they can, then it seems to me that we are making progress.

Already I have suggested that Conrad's view of the Tsarist autocracy as an arbitrary cataclysm, having no place in the human chain of cause and effect, like an earthquake, is contradicted by the nature of the plain and the history of the people who have dwelt in it, particularly as it has been affected by Asiatic invasions themselves inherent in the nature of the plain. And now we have to decide whether the grey and nondescript masses, which, to the outward eye, form the city populations of Soviet Russia, ruled with the uttermost rigour by the inscrutable autocrats of the Communist Party in accordance with unalterable doctrine, are in fact blind multitudes, without living thought or articulate speech, and crushed beneath a new tyranny which is the direct heir to the old.

Who are, then, these grey masses? They are neither more nor less than the survivors of one of the most bitter, harsh, and protracted struggles in the history of the world. And now that we know a little more about the instinctive way in which the Russians organize themselves for purposes of government and combination, and have some idea of the intensity and apartness of the idea which rules their governors, we can consider in more detail the particular struggle which ended in the establishment of the third revolution and the conquest of Germany.

4. THE PRICE OF VICTORY

IN less than twenty-five years the people of the plain, the grey masses drifting through the wartime city streets, the bark-shoed peasant women and the old men slaving at the wartime harvest, and the million upon million of drab-uniformed Red Army conscripts, who now swarm over half Europe—in less than twenty-five years these people, driven by a handful of men with an idea, have overthrown a dynasty, changed their religion, learned to read and write and work machinery, carried out an industrial revolution on a gigantic scale, collectivized their immemorial peasant agriculture, and fought and won not only a full-scale civil war in which the enemy was backed and assisted by the great powers, but also several critical minor campaigns against their neighbours, and finally the swiftest and most mechanized major war in the history of the world. And all these things, except the last, were carried out not only by themselves in isolation, but in the teeth of unremitting hostility from the rest of the world, which sought first to prevent their consolidation and then to smash their emergent economy. . . . Those who survived this ordeal are the aimless, grey, and nondescript drifters in the shabby, pot-holed streets. Their greyness is the price of survival.

Remembering the statistical facts of the ruin that was Lenin's inheritance after the Intervention, the civil war, and the great famine; remembering that stability had to be recovered through the medium of officials, managers, scientists, technicians, and educators who in large part had first to be educated themselves; remembering that it was not until 1928 that the Soviet caught up with the production of Tsarist Russia; remembering that once some sort of stability was established there could be no breathing-space because a primitive, agricultural society had to be turned at once into an industrialized state strong enough to support a mechanized army which could stand up to the West; remembering that the third revolution had to be completed in ten years (which was Stalin's accurate estimate of the years of grace allowed him, when he spoke about the urgency of the task in 1931); remembering that in order to build up heavy industry, light industry, with all that stands for in the way of creature comforts and what we call a civilized existence, had to be shelved; remembering, finally, that in order to get machines Russia had to export the food she desperately needed for her own people—remembering all this, we can begin to get some idea of the almost paralysing scarcity not only of things to buy but also of skilled labour. It was not until shortly before the war that consumer goods began to appear in any quantity in the shops, and by the winter of 1941 they were already again a beautiful dream, and a weary people, worn out with a long and bitter struggle against multitudinous adversity, found themselves suddenly back where they had been for so long, and this time with the German army at their throats and sacking the country they had laboured so long to build up. And this shattering disaster occurred at precisely the moment when, for the first time, they were thinking of a little relaxation. . . .

So perhaps the greyness of those masses may be attributed to other things besides the brutality of a Slavonic Gestapo. London itself looked drab, and her citizens haggard, during bad moments of her bombardment from the air. Moscow was also being bombarded from the air, though on a far lesser scale; and her citizens had those twenty-five years behind them. They were also extremely hungry. Greyness is due to malnutrition. Drabness and shabbiness are due to lack of bright clothes. The shambling walk, the expressionless face, are due to the need for reserving your energy. It is less tiring to shamble along with downcast eyes, frequently bumping into your neighbours because your fixed gaze has not seen them, than to stride briskly forward with all your senses alert. It is much less tiring: your movements become automatic and you get along somehow without any noticeable expenditure of effort. It is a technique you learned a long time ago. You probably inherited it from your grandparents who may have shambled thus from village to village in a famine area looking for food; perhaps for hundreds of miles they progressed in that way across the barren plain, using scarcely more energy than you would spend in sleeping. And in any case, grandfather or no grandfather, you yourself have already for many years in your life, during the worst years of revolutionary chaos, had to move with the utmost caution so as not to waste an ounce of precious energy which can only be replaced by food. You had no food. So that now, when war has come again, just at the moment when you had begun to believe that primitive tribulation was at last behind you, the shops having more food than you had ever seen since the early days of 1914, and gay clothes to cheer the sunlight—now, when food is once more short, you fall instinctively into the old energy-saving shamble, which, really the height of disciplined purposefulness, looks from the outside like aimless drifting in limbo. All except the children who, as always, shout and leap about.

Some of these points we have already touched on. Some we have not. We have not, for instance, talked of the task of turning peasants into technicians. We have spoken of the industrial revolution as a stage in the socialization of Russia and the creation of a proletariat; but we have not yet spoken of it as the reply to exterior pressure, which it also very much was. And, so far, we have not spoken of the hostility of the outside world at all. In short, so far we have looked at the three revolutions wholly from the point of view of Lenin, the founder of Russian Socialism. The Western world has appeared only in the role of armed opponents in the initial years. And the rest of the opposition we have indicated has come from within. It was formidable enough. But that alone would not have produced the harsher aspects of life in Russia today. These spring from outside causes.

I am not now suggesting that, inhabiting a friendly world, there would have been no suffering inside Russia. On the contrary. There would have been the civil war—though in less acute form; there would have been the famine of 1921; there would have been the Social Revolutionaries; and there would have been the bitter opposition of the peasants to having their land taken away from them, and all the appalling muddle caused by turning the chief characters of Turgenev's and Chekhov's stories loose in a machine-shop. There would have been the M.V.D.

But all these things would have been felt less acutely, and the whole movement would have been slower. In all probability the third revolution would not even yet have been accomplished, and many, many Russians would be alive today who are now dead. But the Revolution did not take place in a friendly world, and for twenty-five years Russia had to stave off with one hand the pressures from without, while forcing the pressure within to almost intolerable intensity. For ten years with really intolerable intensity. This was the particular mission of Stalin. It was Lenin's task to put Russia on the lines of socialism. It was Stalin's task to achieve socialism and carry through the industrial revolution in a strictly limited time. He knew what was coming.

He knew this because he was a Russian Marxist, and Marx and Lenin had both said that an armed clash between the proletariat and the upholders of capitalism was inevitable. It is important to remember this. Because, whatever the motives of Germany in her attack on Russia, the Russians saw only the final and over-leaping throw of capitalism in its final and degenerate stage, which turned out to be fascism. And because Stalin knew that Germany or Japan, or both, was bound to attack him—Germany, or any of the other great powers of the West, or all together—because Karl Marx had said so, when Germany finally did attack, for whatever reasons of her own, this was a tremendous and unmistakable confirmation of Karl Marx. A confirmation and a vindication. And a dramatic warning that sooner or later the other nations would attack. That means America and Britain, but primarily America, because Britain is supposed to be exhausted. Perhaps she is. But we shall keep these questions until our last chapter of all, because we want to know still more about the present state and condition of the Russians before we consider them in detail. All this is simply to establish the fact that Lenin knew that sooner or later Socialist Russia would be rushed by all or some of the capitalist or imperialist powers. Trotsky also believed this and wished to engineer the overthrow of capitalism in the major powers, partly for the greater glory of Karl Marx, partly to render them innocuous. Stalin also believed this and had the *nous* to realize that any serious attempt to organize revolutions in London, Paris, Washington, and Tokyo would result in the end of his own particular revolution in Moscow itself. In view of that, and knowing that attack would come, the only course open to Stalin was to concentrate hard on building up an armaments industry and a highly trained army to resist attack. This programme was called "Socialism in one country." Out of it arose the first two Five-Year Plans, and linked up with these were the accelerated collectivization of the peasants, the great purges, the wrecking trials, the throwing overboard of foreign technicians, the Ribbentrop-Molotov pact, the strangulation of Finland, the absorption of the Baltic States, and various other strenuous, aggressive, provocative, and conspiratorial activities. As far as the grey masses of Russia were concerned the only thing that arose out of it was Stalin's pronouncement in 1931 that they could not and must not go slow because they had at the most ten years in which to fit themselves up for a struggle with the West. That was because after three years of the first Five-Year Plan people were exhausted and harried beyond endurance and the plan was behind schedule. So they went on under-eating and, for Russians, overworking, in order to turn out guns and tanks with which to save their own country, their revolution, and, incidentally, the Western world.

I think we must realize these things with the utmost clarity. It is too easy to exclaim that we know it already and, having acknowledged our past enmity and our present debt, to go on to the next thing. For the Russians it is still the present thing. It is not enough to know, or to say we know. Before we can leave this question for the next, we have to *feel*. Then we shall see that with all this feverish searching after explanations of the Russian enigma, the answer is all the time under our hand. It is a threefold answer, involving the nature of the Russian people, the dynamic of Russian Marxism, about which we should by now be beginning to have our ideas, and the attitude of the Western world to the three revolutions. We can say, wearily, "All right, we *know*. . . . You've told us! We came to your blasted country when we shouldn't have done and tried to put down your precious government. Forget it. It was a mistake. We all make mistakes. You've made a few in your time. . . . And afterwards we behaved in, to put it mildly, what Charles Shadwell would call an incoherent and inimical manner. Until, that is, the Germans attacked you, which made us realize that you must be all right. . . . Actually, so long as the Germans were attacking you, you were all right. But since they stopped doing this you've been up to your old, unsettling tricks again, which make us wonder if in fact you ever were all right. Even when the Germans were attacking you . . . But for goodness' sake can't you forget the past, let bygones be bygones, and help us to get on with the job of making the world a decent place to live in . . . ?"

But, alas, it is not as easy as that. We are talking in different languages. We know these things: the Russians *feel* them. We must, for a moment, try to feel them too. We have to imagine what we should feel like had the United States of America, outraged by the results of the latest general election, occupied Canada and brought all her energies to bear upon starving the Labour Government out—to make the world safe for democracy, or the American Way of Life. . . . I shall not dilate upon this theme. I merely invite the reader to dwell upon it for a moment and consider his likely feelings as a patriotic Englishman and an inarticulate but convinced believer in the British way of life, which lacks capital letters, but is a way like any other. He would not feel friendly towards America. We are not that far gone. Nor are the Russians—their leaders are statesmen, notoriously not the most trusting members of any society. They are, moreover, Marxists, and believe in the inevitable clash. While as for the people, who are the friendliest people in the world and can forgive with the greatest ease because they know too much about life to take up attitudes in face of it—as for the people, these are the grey and nondescript masses whom we have regarded with well-bred distaste. And their greyness they owe not wholly to the strains and stresses attendant upon the carrying out of a successful revolution, but also very largely to the strains and stresses of carrying out a successful revolution in the teeth of quite highly organized opposition from most of the Western world, including these islands. And the Russian people, weary and grey, although they are the most friendly and forgiving in the world, know this perfectly well. They know that after we had fought them and given it up as a bad job, we continued to vilify, harass, blockade, undermine, and generally make life insupportable for them. And they know that we finished up at Munich with an unsuccessful attempt to turn Hitler away from us and on to them. The Russians, the people of the plain, enjoy colour, luxury, and extravagance as much as anybody in the world, perhaps more than any other people in the world, since they despise comfort, which the West mistakes for luxury, and, living hard, scatter their money in wild fantasies of impermanent splendour; and for a very long time there has been no colour except what they themselves have provided, no luxuries at all, and no relaxation, a deprivation which, for the most gifted time-wasters in the world, has probably been felt as the most bitter of all. This state of affairs they believe they owe to the West. They would forgive the West. They do, astonishingly I think. They would be only too pleased to let bygones be bygones, but their leaders tell them this cannot be done. Because, they say, they are not bygones at all.

The life of the ordinary Russian in the cities, as well as in the countryside, has, for the last twenty-five years, been a drab affair, by our standards an intolerable affair. In wartime its stringency was past belief. And if I keep on harping on wartime it is because life in, say, Moscow in wartime was fairly typical of life in peacetime during the greater part of those twenty-five years. During all those twenty-five years in fact, except for two short interludes. The two short interludes occurred just before the great purges of 1936 and just after, this second interlude being cut short by the war itself with the violent and dramatic suddenness which is a feature of the plain. In June 1941 the shops in the cities were full. There were taxis, ice-creams, plenty to drink, plenty to eat. There was even plenty to wear. By October 1941, with winter just ahead, with the Germans at the city gates, and with scattered but incessant bombing day and night, there was nothing. Nothing at all. There had been no time to build up reserves of consumer goods. Everything, as it came from the new factories, had been put straight into the shop-window, and now the new factories were turning out rations and uniforms and boots for the troops. In no time the shop-windows were empty. And as winter came it was apparent that not only would there be no tinned crab from Kamchatka, no wines from the Crimea and the Caucasus, no caviar from Astrakhan, but there would be no butter and eggs and milk to speak of and, most dreadful of all, not enough bread.

We find it difficult to speak seriously about bread in this country. There is always cake—or something. There really is, in spite of our tedious and celebrated rationing. And whatever people say about the scarcity of food in England, the final, incontrovertible proof that we have enough to live on is that we are all alive. When you begin to think seriously about bread is when you have nothing else. Then it matters very much whether your daily ration is four pounds, or three pounds, or two and a half pounds, or two pounds, or one and a half pounds. It makes all the difference in the world. It makes, precisely, the difference between getting up in the morning and trying to go about your work, or deciding that you will not get up. . . . The Russians call this "lying down." It is an extremely Russian way of saying that you have stayed in bed to die. The gift of the happy despatch is shared by the peasants of all nations. When an old peasant decides that he has done all he need do and is too tired to start it all over again, another sowing, another harvest, he turns his face to the wall and composes himself for the approach of Death, who knows what is expected of him and infallibly appears, if not that day, the next day, or the day after. The Russians, as we have seen, are peasants by blood and tradition, and they too have this gift of the happy despatch, a gift they have jealously preserved even in the heart of great cities. So during that first dreadful winter of the siege of Leningrad, thousands upon thousands of the highly urbanized citizens of the Tsarist, the revolutionary metropolis, lay down and waited for death. I suppose the exact figures are known, but I have never come across them. I have seen 250,000 given as an official figure, but this is certainly too low. From all that has been told me at least half a million Russians lay down and died in that city because they had not sufficient bread. We are being asked to think seriously about bread today. The Russians have had to think seriously about it for a very long time, and what happened in Leningrad, in the winter of 1941, when the city was entirely isolated except for the stupendous ice-road across Lake Ladoga, is what happens when you do not get enough—and when there isn't cake, or anything.

Leningrad was, of course, a special case. It was heroic Leningrad which put up what was perhaps the most wonderful corporate resistance in the history of warfare. For half a million or—if we must stick to published facts, a quarter of a million—a quarter of a million people dead of starvation out of a population of two million is an appreciable percentage. It means one in eight. It makes you wonder, and rightly, about the condition of the other seven in every eight, who managed to get just enough bread. And all the time these people who dragged themselves about managed to keep the Putilov works going to reinforce the Red Army on their sector, which meant just down the road. There were also theatres. And all the time the city was under bombardment from the close-range artillery of the Germans. So that of the people who did not lie down to die, thousands upon thousands dragged themselves to work until they were blown up by a shell, or until they fell down in the street with exhaustion, and the others went on working— or just hanging on. Oh, of course Leningrad was a special case. The government would have fed the people if it could, and it made stupendous and costly efforts to keep the ice-road open. But the other cities were not all that better off. We have seen how in Archangel, which could not help the war, rations were deliberately kept down. Not wantonly, but because they were needed more urgently elsewhere. And in Moscow, with the Germans farther away, life was also very thin. It is not easy for a stranger to gauge the amount of starvation in a Russian city, just because of the fact that people lie down to die at home. Sometimes they go on too long and collapse in the street. But more often they simply do not get up. You are not aware of these. The workers were all right. That is to say, with the aid of canteen meals, they were kept alive and fit for work; but the older people, and the people who could not make a direct contribution to wartime industry, had a terrible time in those first two winters of the war. Most of them got enough bread to keep them going, and, as far as you could discover, most of the ones who died, died because of some illness which demanded more than bread, or because they gave too much of their rations to their children. This was a common failing. You have to imagine a sick mother, dying of undernourishment because she had for too long given too much of her ration to her little boy, in a tiny Moscow room, with no one to help and with her last words making the little boy promise on his soul of honour that he will not stir from the room when she is dead because, if he does so, someone will be sure to come in and squat in that room, the room in Moscow, which is your title to citizenship of that great city, and then, being homeless, he would be forced to go—oh, heaven knew where, but certainly at once out of Moscow— which would mean the end of his special training as an engineer's draughtsman. That kind of thing. . . . For once you found yourself homeless in Moscow during the war, so acute was the housing problem, you were no longer a citizen of that city and were shipped off to wherever more hands were wanted. Having a home consisted in having a room, or a bed in a room shared with others. And so bitter was the struggle for room that if you were a little boy who did not know the ropes and you left your room to go to your mother's funeral—your father being at the front, and therefore, as far as you knew, dead, since letters never came—you faced the very real danger of finding a stranger in that room when you came back, who knew the ropes, and who would swear that he was there by arrangement with your mother. People will do dreadful things in their struggle to arrest the slipping thread of life. And to me the wonder is that the Russians, who have been forced to do such dreadful things for too long, still and always, the moment survival is until the next day assured, show themselves once more unspoilt, impulsive, generous, and invincibly kind.

Life, as I have said, was pretty thin during those first two winters of the war. When there is a complete failure of light and heat in the sort of temperatures which go with the winter of the plain, the whole of life is disrupted. The first thing that happens is that your pipes burst, being immediately frozen. And when, on top of that, your windows have been broken by blast, you are in a very bad way indeed. In this way thousands of apartments in Moscow were made uninhabitable even for the Russians. But I have visited a still-inhabited flat where the floor was covered with ice nearly six inches deep, in which were embedded innumerable chunks and splinters of shattered glass. And on another occasion, trying to find a flat for myself, not only were all the floors in the same state, but, on opening, with the utmost difficulty, the door of the W.C., an extremely modern and up-to-date W.C., one was confronted with a solid block of ice, five feet high and fitting exactly that compact and useful office, in which, gleaming palely, was embedded, like Lot's wife, the whole apparatus, or pan. That was the kind of thing that happened if the heating failed when you happened to be out, or if blast disrupted your pipes. And there was nothing you could do about it until the summer. . . . And all this on next to nothing but black bread, a bite of cheese and frozen potatoes, a bowl of cabbage soup, an occasional cup of straw-coloured tea. For even if you had an intact apartment you still had for weeks on end no electricity and no gas, and for further weeks on end electricity, but not enough to heat by, and nothing but a quarter of an inch glimmer of gas between, say, the hours of 11 P.M. and 5 in the morning. So that if you wanted to heat water for your breakfast tea you had to visit the apartment of a friend living in another district. And the whole of Moscow conversation turned not, as one would expect on food, but on keeping warm. There were, of course, no restaurants where the ordinary Muscovite could go and feed and get warm; and even the one or two restaurants reserved for officials, foreigners, and Army officers on leave, though they would feed you with the utmost luxury, had no heat. You had to keep your fur-coat on to eat, and still were frozen. The theatres had no heating at all. And when the curtain went up a palpable wave of cold air, from somewhere in the region of the North Pole, would advance from the empty spaces of the wings and flies and flood the auditorium with its numbing influence. How the actors and dancers managed to perform I have never understood. But they did.

Of course, if you were a productive worker you got more food. You had at least one hot meal a day at the canteen of your factory or institute, or whatever it was. Not, as a rule, what an English working man would call a hot meal, but a mess of pottage in the form of rich cabbage or beetroot soup, or a sort of buckwheat porridge coloured and flavoured with a thin meat stew. The heavier your work the more you got. But, even then, it was not enough. And I have known a member of the privileged classes, a ballet dancer of great distinction who always had his daily meal, and who was frequently invited to diplomatic parties in addition, to be in such a state of exhaustion from undernourishment that he was too weak to rehearse properly, being forced to keep all his energy for the performance itself.

That chronic weakness, too, turned him, as vital, as colourful, as arbitrary, as Russian a personality as you could desire, the moment he went out of doors, into one more grey particle in that drifting, grey and nondescript mass as to whose identity we have been wondering.

The peasants were better off. The peasants, except in famine, always are. For although the government must have applied, as often before, methods of the utmost severity to collect every grain of wheat or rye or buckwheat for distribution between the army and the city workers, the peasants always had their individual plots, the produce of which they consumed. So that there were always eggs and potatoes in the countryside. And even fowls. You saw them, on railway journeys, being held up for sale over the station railings by the peasant women, to be chaffered over by a thousand half-starved townsmen. You made expeditions, planned, with regard to transport, with the sort of forethought and wangling that must have gone to the first thousand-bomber raid over Cologne, to raid the countryside for half a hundredweight of potatoes, a venture which, success-ful or not, dominated your thoughts and your emotions for two or three months at a time. . . . For the open markets in the towns were empty. There was nothing for the peasants to buy in the shops, so they did not bring their surplus eggs and milk to sell in Moscow at even the fanciest prices, because there was nothing Moscow could give them in exchange for their money. In fact, the only useful currency was vodka and cigarettes. If you had these you had everything—provided you could bring yourself to part with your vodka and cigarettes. This is written about Russia in the days of the late war with Germany, not about Berlin after the defeat of Germany. And by writing it I am trying to kill two birds with one stone. I am trying to show why the people look drab and grey and downcast; and I am hoping to suggest that we are really not the ones to decide what is fair to Germany. Because all the things that horrify us about life in Germany today were being suffered by the Russians in 1941, '42, and '43, when, to put it mildly, the Germans were living well. And they were caused by the Germans.

Up to now we have stressed the background of Russia's suffer-ing, which is compounded, in undeterminable proportions, of Marxist doctrinairism, Russian muddle, carelessness and feck-lessness, Western hostility to the Revolution, and the Russian climate. It seemed desirable to do this because, had it not been for these forces, Russia would have had deeper reserves of fat when the Germans struck, and would not have collapsed so immediately into an extremity of want. For, in fact, Russia had herself recovered from the consequences of all these causes, and, had it not been for Germany, life in Russia during the winters of 1941, '42, and '43 would have been more comfortable for more people than ever in all history. It was not merely a question of suddenly having to sustain an immense army. An immense army had to be sustained with half the grain-lands gone. And half the factories too. In due time, of course, the new Russia east of the Volga, in the Urals, and deep into Siberia on the one hand and deep into Soviet Southeast Asia on the other, came into play. Factories, as we were told, were moved bodily from the Don to the Ural river. Immense areas of rich, uncultivated steppe-land were put under cotton and grain. All these things were undoubtedly done. But not without heart-breaking loss. Anybody who saw the flat cars taking machinery from the Don basin to Siberia, train after train, involving unknown thousands of flat-cars, each with its burden of capstans and lathes, machine-tools, dynamos, and all the rest, all with no protection against the sleet and rain of autumn, all spending days and weeks on the line because of the priority which had to be given to the reserves being hurried from the Far East, the Soviet Far East, for the defence of Moscow and the Volga, and all rusting as they waited, must have wondered what proportion of those machines, with the American and British labels—machines from Detroit, from Youngstown, from Coventry, from Pittsburgh, all collected and rusting in the sleet in the middle of the interminable plain, broken forcibly from their concrete beds, anyone who saw this fantastic sight, must have wondered what proportion of these machines could ever, even in Russia, be used again—and how soon. I have also seen scores and scores of immense and complicated locomotives from the Ukraine railways standing in mile after mile of siding, perhaps ten miles of it, some of them damaged by blast, some of them ruined by near misses, but most of them apparently intact, and all on the way to ruin for lack of a dab of grease on the exposed moving parts. They may still be there for all I know. Or the Russians may have got them to work again. It is impossible to tell. The main point is that the Russians, from the earliest days of the war, were deprived of the grain-lands of the Ukraine, the industries of the Ukraine, the wines and fruits of the Crimea, the cigarettes of Leningrad and Rostov. And although immense quantities of machines and stock were transferred to the East the losses were also immense. That kind of transfer cannot happen just like that with the armoured spearheads of an implacable enemy on your heels and curling round to catch you in front as you run, with the railway junctions being bombed to smithereens, with all your able-bodied men in the Army, with the colossal contradictions between salvaging and destroying which must, which *must*, have taken place, with all your inadequate communications, the few paved roads and the few double railway tracks being required for troops moving at high speed in the opposite direction—and all of this happening just before and during the harvest, so that the fighting retreat against the German tanks was fought out among the endless glory of the corn-fields, and all of it being carried out by the sort of people we saw muddling a simple ferry landing at Bakharitsa wharf, pushing an inoffensive and valuable pony into the water to drown out of sheer helpfulness, the sort of people who laid out, at immense expense in money and labour, the new cotton-fields in Uzbekistan before the irrigation plan was finished, who built the most superb power-station in the world to service a district that would be better served by a station a tenth of the size, by people, too, with defeatism in their hearts. For there *was* defeatism. . . . The glorious Red Army, which was incomparable in all the world, for which the people had starved and sweated and seen their lives broken, some gladly, some reluctantly, some with brooding hostility—this glorious Red Army had completely and utterly failed at the first impact of the armoured West and was moving back at such a rate that the refugees could no longer keep up with it. And all this in face of the shockingly early winter, the one we rejoiced in because it hit the Germans with such vigour. But, as we have seen, winter is no respecter of nationalities, and it dealt some blows to the other side. For instance, after superhuman efforts to convoy countless thousands of cattle from White Russia to the Volga lands, after men had toiled and sweated and fought to get these cattle through, the frosts came and caught them when they were already in safety, and cattle in that condition could no more stand that cold than the foot soldiers of Hitler's armies. They died.

Need we wonder any more about the identity of these grey masses, and the reasons for their greyness? Shouldn't we wonder, rather, how people who can survive such privation and still believe in life are going to fit in with a world which has lost much of its hardness and has got itself detached from any particular purpose—except, apparently, peace. . . . But peace for what?

IV

THE ROAD TO LIFE

1. THE SURVIVORS

faithless and poor
too,

THE Russians want peace too, of course, and they know
what they want it for. They want it to give them a chance
to complete their socialist society and turn it, and the great
land which is its arena, into a country of unparalleled glory,
justice, opportunity, and happiness. It is to be a model to the
world, which, in due course, will emulate it. They think that,
even in their greyness. They have thought it for a long time,
and they have postponed, again and again, the day of glory in
order to be strong enough to fight for it in advance. And now
they have fought for it, and they feel stronger than ever before,
and I think most Russians would agree in feeling that the time
has come for them to have a little of the splendour on account.
Most Russians.

That means most of the survivors, the survivors of the three
revolutions, of the civil war, of the famines, of the collectivization of the farms, of the purges, and finally of this last atrocious
war which has, without a doubt, reduced their number by
at the very least another ten million able-bodied souls. Ten
million is a large number, even out of a hundred and eighty
million. So that when we speak of the Russians today we mean
these survivors, what is left of the people of the plain after a
quarter of a century of convulsive violence unparalleled in the
history of the world, the grey masses, who already, after the
strain of war, are beginning to break up into individual faces.
About the survivor, whether from shipwreck, battle, or concentration camp, there is a special quality of mind and heart
which sets him apart. This quality is shared by the Russians of
today, every single one of whom has looked into the abyss, not
once, but repeatedly. It is an experience which will be with
them always and which will colour all their values. Their one

155

compensation is their impassioned belief in the destiny of Russia and her noble system. It is the sort of belief which many English-men once had about these islands and the Empire. We have lost that belief today. And as a consequence, for the Englishman returning from Russia to this country, although the British people are not grey, although they are more or less alive on all occasions, although they have enough to eat and keep warm with and can therefore devote their minds to other, less primi-tive preoccupations, their life seems brittle and thin, thin, thin —but still not completely threadbare; for we once had a belief, which still colours our attitude to the world, and we may yet find another.

So far we have talked, very generally, about the people of the plain, and the very appearance of the Russians themselves, as we saw them in wartime, is an invitation to speak without much differentiation. But now we must begin to differentiate a little. For it is obvious that not every one of those near two hundred million goes about with a burning, missionary ideal in which a Soviet Kipling poeticizes the findings of a Russian Marx. A great many of them, in any case, are not Russians, but belong to the "Nationalities." And of the Russian peasants in the remote collective farms, the more able-bodied representatives of which our armies have lately encountered in the major cities of central Europe, not very many have thoughts beyond tomorrow's harvest—which is all that they want to be left in peace for. So that when one says the Russian thinks this, the Russian thinks that, we are now, at last, beginning to detach ourselves from the sober, plodding, suffering mass of the people of the plain and focus our dim light upon certain differentiated types. The types, in a word, who make things go. Who are these people, and how can we tell them from the others in their tottering drift through the drab cities of the Union?

First of all, I think, by age. There have been some elderly and middle-aged people who have counted for something in modern Russia. I can think of a few—such as Marshal Stalin, Foreign Minister Molotov, the late President Kalinin; a few decorative generals whose names look good on the Board—Voroshilov, Budyenny—and prevent the army from complaining of inadequate representation in High Places, while keeping the real and more active war-lords in what is considered their proper place; a considerably larger number of artists, scientists, and scholars; and an immense regiment of women of indeterminate age with spectacles and buns and berets, the feminine old faithfuls who occupy minor strategic positions in every institute and organization throughout the Union, and seem, somewhat gloomily, to have escaped the purges which decimated their male counterparts. . . . But even these, the devoted, shrill feminists, the doctors, the scientists, the scholars, the technicians, and the senior bureaucrats, do not count in the way that the very young count. They must have seen too much of life. They must all have secret reservations which render them unfit to build new towns in the desert. For you cannot build new towns in the desert with the sort of speed and prodigality with which Stalin requires them to be built if you have any reservations at all: you can do that only if you believe the new town is to be the salvation of humanity—or an important contribution towards it. And the elderly, even the middle-aged, men and women of Russia have seen enough to know that humanity cannot be saved, not in that absolute sense. Not even by new towns in the desert. You cannot, after all, have experienced all three revolutions and their attendant agonies and still have no secret reservations about the progress of your countrymen, unless you are a knave, or a fool, or a genius—or a Communist. So the number of elderly men who really count for anything at all are all to be found in the inner councils of the Communist Party—a mere handful of them. And what they believe is nobody's business, nor does it in the least matter. They all do their jobs supremely well. They are all, being human, bound to labour and flog themselves in order to keep their jobs. And, in the last resort, the direction they must take is now dictated by the people upon whose support they count, the youth they themselves have created, and which believes certain things which it has imbibed from the cradle from, precisely, these leaders. So that it does not really matter what Mr. Kaganovitch believes. Acting under extreme pressure, the pressure of life or death, Mr. Kaganovitch has revolutionized the Russian railways, has double-tracked the trans-Siberian, laid thousands of miles of new track into this or that bit of the back of beyond, and crammed the marshalling yards with rolling-stock of a size, a solidity, a finish, an impressiveness unsurpassed by anything in America. That is what he is there for. . . . Nor does it in the last resort much matter what Stalin himself believes. I don't say he does not believe all that his friends would like to think he does. He probably does. But what matters is what the young people believe, which is what Stalin says he believes. For nobody, not even Stalin, could turn round and say to those children, Karl Marx is bunk: Socialism is bunk: the Soviets are bunk. Go to it and see who can get rich quickest. He really could not. And so . . . And so, when you contemplate a theatre full of people, the ones who matter are the ones under forty. And the ones who matter most of all are the ones under thirty, who have known nothing at all in their lives but the sort of struggle we outlined in our last chapter. They too merge, in the streets, into the grey and downcast mass, which seems to drain even the freshness of youth of its colour. And they have *nothing* to fear from the M.V.D. But underneath that protective coloration . . .

And I am not in the least talking figuratively. This youth, this Soviet youth, is not one of those Western European abstractions, a half-baked class whom politicians have to flatter in the faint hope that they may trouble to vote in a general election. This youth is running the country. That is why I have said it is important, even in its non-political aspects. It is doing the work. It has all the good jobs. For in Russia today the men whom even we are beginning to know as household names are nearly all young. There is nothing to stop you, given ability and drive, from, at thirty, becoming a field-marshal, an ambassador to a major power, a cabinet minister, the secretary of the Moscow Soviet and a member of the Politburo, the head of a university, of a monstrous industrial trust, the governor of a province the size of the Western Desert, or anything you can think of. And so it will be for some time to come. That is why it is important to know something about the youth of Russia today, and that is why we must say farewell for a time to the conception of the eternal peasant who dwells in the plain. For this youth, which is now beginning to take to itself the commanding position in the country, which, as far as Russia affects the outside world, is beginning to *be* Russia, has different ideas. It has ideas imbibed from Lenin, then from Stalin —who were neither of them eternal peasants. It is the creation of Lenin and Stalin. And it is a lively creation, to say the least.

I don't mean all youth. We can subdivide a little further. We can take away countless thousands of ordinary peasant youth, not very bright, who stay on the farm, who get conscripted into the Army and only live for the day when they can get back to the farm and cash in on their Berlin cameras and watches. These are still very much the immemorial Russian peasant, except that most of them can read or write and very many of them recently have seen something of the world. But although what they mean by the farm is not what their fathers meant by the farm—for the *kolkhoz,* the Collective, is the only background they know, unquestioningly accepted, but of course with infinite grumbling—and although they have some ideas that their fathers did not have, they will never set the Volga on fire. They will age quickly enough, as peasants do, and they will be the conservative element in the country, as peasants will be. With just this difference, that what they will struggle to conserve is the dear old *kolkhoz* and the latter-day trinity: Marx-Lenin-Stalin, Stalin being also the symbol for Holy Russia . . . that, I think, will do to sum up the general religious and patriotic background of modern peasant youth throughout the great plain. The youth that does things, the dynamic youth, originates in the cities, although a great proportion of its numbers still come from a *kolkhoz* background, just as the revolutionary proletariat which Lenin organized for victory was largely recruited from the villages of Tsarist Russia —but urbanized. And this youth, moulded by the old Bolsheviks, now makes the pace and keeps its masters up to the mark.

The reasons for the unlimited power of youth in Soviet Russia are simple enough. In the first place the casualties among the old have been high. In the early days of the Revolution the more intelligent of the then young emigrated in their tens of thousands. Many more were killed in the civil war. Many more died in the famines. What was left were either trained specialists who put up with Lenin and were used by him, or the Bolshevik *élite*. Many of the old specialists, the writers, the artists, the soldiers, the civil servants, the scientists, are still there, having served the new Russia faithfully but with, as we have said, secret reservations. Most of the old Bolsheviks are gone, the victims of innumerable purges within the Party, to say nothing of the great general purges of nearly a decade ago. Most of the old peasants of outstanding ability are also gone, the victims of the liquidation of the *kulaks* and the collectivization of the farms, which they opposed. So that, statistically, the death-rate among the old and middle-aged has been extremely high, which at once gives you a higher proportion of youth to age, a proportion increased still more by the flourishing state of the birth-rate and the extremely early age at which Soviet young women begin to have children, so that the birth-rate is not merely a matter of bigger families, but also of bigger families sooner, which brings the new youth crowding rapidly on the heels of its parental generation. In the second place, of all these young people, almost every one is politically sound and may be trusted with high position. Whereas among the elderly and middle-aged there are deviations. These deviations may be purely negative, or they may be active heresies. Broadly speaking, the great mass of elderly Russians are fairly negative. They may have flamed once with Bolshevik enthusiasm. They may still be good Bolsheviks. But they no longer flame, and they have suffered too much hardship to want to be vigorous any more. Positively, now that Stalin has it all his own way, the deviations are not likely to be spectacular. But it is probably true to say that the surviving old Bolsheviks have seen too much and know too much to be as sharp and sure a tool in the hands of their master as the very young who have seen nothing and know what they do know (which is often a surprisingly great deal) from books. Hence the phenomenon of Mr. Gromyko, who, Stalin thinks, is a better tool than Mr. Litvinov, because he has seen nothing, and can be trusted never to look. But Mr. Gromyko is not characteristic of the kind of youth I have in mind at the moment. He belongs to a very specialized branch. In a word, he is a Communist.

For having divided the young from the old, and the dynamic young from the hobbledehoys, we now come to the most important division of all. On the one hand Party members; on the other hand the others. But this division is not at all what it might seem. It is not, as you would possibly expect, among the Party members that one finds the simple, optimistic pride in Soviet Power (to use a convenient term much favoured in Russia today) which carries the youth of the country to self-immolatory ardours. This is found among the ordinary sons and daughters of the Revolution. The Party members are something other. They provide the initial impetus and they provide the steering. But the engine itself, the drive, is the enthusiasm of countless thousands of non-politically minded young men and women who take their politics for granted, who take Socialism, State Control, and the divinity of Marx and Lenin utterly for granted, as we who are not politically minded take parliamentary government and the constitutional monarchy utterly for granted. What they are working for is a *better* Socialism and a stronger Russia. The Party members are something other. Not for them the simple enthusiasms of the age of innocence. They are the men and women who stand on guard between innocence and all evil, and work and scheme and toil and sacrifice themselves, grimly, to make Russia safe for innocence. Out of the two hundred million Russians there are four or five million Party members, and they form a closed order.

I have said earlier on that there is no question of an analogy between Russian Communism and religion. It is a religion, neither more nor less. The permitted analogy is with the Catholic Church, a Catholic Church which is dominated by the Jesuits. The Communists are the Jesuits—the protectors of innocents, the saviours of souls, the spearhead against heresy, and the upholders of authority. You cannot be all that and still be innocent yourself. In order to defeat the serpent you must have the wisdom of the serpent. And your discipline must be absolute. Entering the Communist Party in Russia is no light matter, al-

though the difficulties set in your way vary from year to year in
accordance with the demands of high policy. Sometimes the
call is for a small, compact, blindly devoted phalanx. Sometimes it is for a mass movement, even at the cost of some dilution. But at all times you surrender your soul and your body
into the keeping of authority, which is the Central Committee.
Before you become a full member of the order there are the
characteristic probations and novitiates. You have to be certain
of your vocation. The Party itself has to be even more certain.
It does not at all follow that because you have belonged as a
child to the Communist Pioneer Organization you will take the
next step and become a *komsomol*—any more than it follows
that if you are educated at a convent you will become a novice.
It does not follow that an enthusiastic *komsomol* will ever be a
full member of the Party, any more than if you become a novice
you will ultimately take the veil. And the atmosphere surround-
ing a young man or woman with faith in the teaching of Marx
or Lenin who is trying to decide whether or not to apply for
membership of the Party is very much like the atmosphere
round a Catholic young man or woman trying to decide
whether to take orders or the veil. Already you are apart among
your friends (all of whom are, of course, fellow-believers). There
is the same solemnity. There are the same malicious imputa-
tions, the same head-shakings, the same hushed envy, the same
defensive reactions among those who do not feel themselves
called. You are doing it because you fancy yourself, because you
think you will get something out of it that the others haven't
got, because you have a hopeless passion for a bishop, because
you are too good for this world, because you are proud, because
you are humble. And you have to satisfy both yourself and your
confessor that you are not doing it for any of these reasons but
because you believe with heart and soul in the doctrine and feel
called irresistibly to give your whole life to its propagation and
its fulfilment. For the protection of the innocent, the salvation
of Russian souls, and the realization on earth of the Marxian
paradise, involving a Strong Russia. If you are accepted you will
be tried. You have been brought up in Leningrad, you love the
society there, you cannot, you feel, live without concerts, good

talk, æsthetic and intellectual stimuli of all kinds. You might have taken—oh, heavens knows what, but any decent job which gave you a chance to work for the fatherland and Socialism and cultivate your own so far undeveloped talents. You will find that you have to do without these things. One day you will get a message telling you to report. And next day you will find yourself in an aeroplane *en route* for some desert land on the far side of Siberia where, with the aid of forced labour, imported experts and the local tribe, in circumstances reminiscent of an Alaskan mining camp, is being raised to the glory of your faith a new cathedral city, designed to turn out fifty million tractors a year in three years' time. And your job is to organize. To organize what? To organize faith which will keep the mob going, which will drive them on to excel themselves when they feel like falling down dead on the job. To fight, to fight, to *fight* the interminable Russian muddles which will see that your city gets twice the amount of cement that it wants but no sand, immense quantities of roofing material but no bricks, half a million pick-axes but no handles, electric lamps by the billion but no electric cable. And in a very short time your innocence will be gone, and you will regard the immense, the devoted labours of your people as a shepherd regards the friskings of his lambs. That will turn you into one kind of Communist. Or, like Mr. Gromyko, you may have a particular kind of brain, when you will be marked out for preferment. And, very soon, having absorbed all that you should know, you will be sent out into the world with the sole job of clearing a space in which the voice of Russia may be heard. You will repeat the words given to you with undeviating loyalty. And if you perceive that these words do not go down very well with the people to whom you are required to address them, you will report this fact to your superior officer, in whom you have absolute confidence, because he has made Russia into one of the three great world powers without troubling whether his words went down very well or not. And if you, as a result of your report, are told to change the sense of what you have said, you will get up and do so, without betraying by a flicker of your eyebrow or an inflexion of your voice that you are conscious of any contradiction.

And if you are told, on the other hand, to pay no attention to
the reaction of others, you will pay no attention. And all this
can be very difficult for a Russian, who likes companionship,
and who is forced to be aloof. His one consolation will be that
of the Christian missionary in the jungle: his unquestioning
sense of superiority over the heathen chieftains. He is right and
they are wrong. And a good envoy of this new young Communist
school would no more dream of insisting that the Kremlin
should change the tone or substance of its message, which he
is called upon to deliver, in deference to the strange mental
habits of his auditors, than the Christian missionary would
question the suitability of the imposition of a sectarian interpretation of the word of Jehovah upon the carefree islanders
of the South Seas, upon the twisted sensuality of darkest Africa,
upon the polite but bitter scepticisms of the Chinese Mandarins,
impartially. It is, when all is said, the word of God. . . .

That is another kind of Communist. There are other kinds
too. The Christian Church has eternally provided a happy-
hunting-ground for the ambitious, the greedy, the lustful, and
the vain. So it is with the Communist Party of Russia. Within
this closed circle you will find all the careerist talent of the
Union. Where else would you expect to find it? For the Communist Party is the seat of all power. But rarely will such men go
on for ever. On the other hand, in this same party you will find
all the saintly elements of the Union, men and women who have
made the final act of abnegation. And the rank-and-file Communist is, by and large, an admirable type. You see him dis-
played, or until quite recently did, in the job of Political Commissar attached to units and formations of the armed forces. The
Army Commissar will always raise a laugh in this country, but
that is only because of a total misconception of his duties, his
character, and his necessity. There are bad commissars, of
course, and there are comic commissars. There are commissars
attached to units of the Red Fleet who have been known to make
the captain put back into harbour when the sea was rough and
they were feeling sick. There are commissars attached to Army
units who have lost battles by contradicting the commanding
officer's orders. And there are commissars of all affiliations who

have used their power to break their enemies. But the ordinary commissar, say the commissar of an infantry brigade, or regiment, occupies a position between a brigade padre and a brigade education officer, and Young Siegfried. He is, that is to say, expected not only to be the source of all instruction and spiritual consolation, but also an example as a warrior. He has to comfort the dying, but only after he has led the way to death. He is the pattern and the stay. And his influence is often very great. If it is not, sooner or later he is removed.

I find myself using the present tense about these commissars, although they were abolished, as such, round about the time of Stalingrad. But it is so difficult to imagine a Russian army or any kind of Soviet establishment without this kind of institution in some shape or form that the present tense is justified. For although the old commissars have now been drawn into the main corpus of the army, those who were good enough being made second in command of the units to which they were attached and finding themselves henceforward in the promotion list (with implications which we shall glance at later), it is perfectly plain to anyone who knows Soviet Russia that in every unit, in every formation, there will be at least one "professional" Communist who will be expected to carry out much the same duties of the old commissar. Nor is this habit of placing "politicals" in the position of watchdogs over the experts by any means an exclusively Soviet one. In principle it goes back to Tsarist Russia, and it has deep roots in the Russian character. It is possible that the reader has already more than a glimmering of the connection between political commissars and the temperament of the people of the great plain.

We have divided the young into the intelligent and politically minded on the one hand, and the unquestioning peasant or day-labourer on the other. The intelligent and politically minded we have divided into the small body of Communists on the one hand and the non-Communists on the other. At the part played by the Communists we have just glanced, and we have seen how they provide the direction and the boost. But the drive and the colour does not come from them. It comes from the young men and women of Russia, all coloured with the Faith, but, most of them, no more dreaming of joining the Party than the ordinary active Christian, in the days when Christians were active, thought of taking orders. They would laugh at the idea, but that doesn't make them any the less Marxist-Leninists. Some are good Marxist-Leninists, some are bad, but all are inescapably imbued with that dogma.

I am sorry if I seem to repeat this point to boredom. But it is a point I have so rarely seen made, so even more rarely taken, and it is so vitally necessary to a proper appreciation of the present-day atmosphere of Soviet Russia, and it *must* be made—and taken. For these are the young people who give Russia its entire atmosphere and colour, once you have penetrated the grey veiling of hard times. These are the young who so much impress the more sympathetic English visitor, say Mr. J. B. Priestley, that when the time comes to say farewell to Russia your predominating sensation is not one of escape from a prison, which, in a sense, Russia is, but of an irrevocable exclusion from all the vitality, generosity, loyalty, and truth which form the expression of the native heart—and a return to a world in which the heart has been degraded into a machine for pumping blood. . . . I don't say that that is a reasoned and balanced summary of the difference between Soviet Russia and Europe. But it is the feeling you have. And it owes by no means everything to Russia. Other sympathetic travellers in Tsarist days have had the same feeling. Today it is magnified, in spite of the grey faces, in spite of the M.V.D., in spite of everything.

I think that by now I may be allowed to use this sort of tone without being accused of *Schwärmerei*. It will not be for long. There will be other hard things to say about some aspects of present-day Russia before we have finished. And what I have said already could be more than enough to exclude me for ever from that country and from what friends I was allowed to make there. Which would be a deprivation. *Could* be, I said, because one can never, with Russia, be sure. And I imagine that what I have said already will have disappointed some who may have thought that what I was providing was an ingenious and subtle denigration of Soviet Russia. So, as usual, when you try to see a thing whole, its shade as well as its light, you may end up by pleasing nobody. On the other hand there may be some who, observing that I am not unconscious of what are commonly regarded as the shades of life in Soviet Russia (and, as I have said, there are more of those to come), will be more ready to credit the high-lights. And one of the high-lights, *the* high-light, is the spirit of Soviet youth, which is irresistible in its colour, its enthusiasm, its generosity, and its warmth. All these qualities, needless to say, are Russian qualities. All are latent in Russian youth. But the Revolution has brought them out and given them a purpose and a means of expression. So that all that we think of when we speak of Russian fervour, Russian love of colour and dance and song, is no longer turned in upon itself and limited in its expression to the wonderful singing and dancing of the people, in which immense and glorious ebullience of spirit is immediately cancelled out by profound lamentation over the fate of man, or in which the most sober thoughts are turned suddenly into a wild, mad whirl of half hysterical defiance, but is *harnessed* to a Five-Year Plan. . . . Which progresses to the music, to the rhythm of the balalaika. Unevenly, that is to say. But it progresses.

And how! . . . For the driving force comes from the young and the very young, who, as I have said, would laugh at the notion of becoming Communists, but who believe that the fulfilment of the plans of the State Planning Department is the way to the salvation of Russia and the world. . . . How can they doubt it? Where there was a wilderness there is now a great city, and they themselves have built it, out of nothing, with their own hands. Beneath the cobbled streets of Moscow run swift electric trains through labyrinthine burrows which they have tunnelled with their own hands, the approaches to which, immense, spacious, underground halls out of Maison Lyons by Sardanapalus, resplendent with every variety of marble, lapis, and strange stones from the Urals, they themselves have helped to construct. In the Asiatic deserts on the way to the borders of India are interminable cotton-fields made to bloom by the great irrigation canals, dug with their own hands. All these things are new, conjured out of nothing, by the will of Stalin in the spirit of Lenin and with the work of the hands of the young men and women of the plain.

"We must work!" cried Irina in *The Three Sisters*. "We must live! Rather any work at all, rather dig ditches, drains, rather sweep crossings, than this life of waking up at nine and drinking tea; starting to get up at eleven and spending the morning dressing—and drinking tea." "To Moscow! To Moscow . . ." she sighs as the curtain comes down on Act Two. "We must work! Work! Work!" echo Masha and Olga and Vershinin. . . . But without conviction. Well, Irina has got to Moscow. The others are dead. But Irina has got to Moscow, and she has found something to work *for*, which was all she wanted, which was all the others wanted. But for the others it came too late. She has worked herself to the bone. She is one of the ubiquitous old faithfuls, with a bun and a beret and a somewhat tight expression. She has worked herself to exhaustion for the new cause, whose chief glory, for her, is that it is a cause. Any cause. And the man who gave her the cause was Lenin, interpreting Karl Marx. For that cause she would suffer all the torments of existence, for anything, anything, is better than the emptiness of the life without purpose and without hope. Her children have never known that life. They were born into the cause, and, with their own hands, and for the greater glory of the Marxist religion, they have hewed and toiled at the foundations of this new state. And they continue to do so.

2. THE ROAD TO LIFE

I SUPPOSE, when all is said, the main task of the imaginative writer, as distinct from the historian or the sociologist, when writing about the people of another country, is, by the presentation of a handful of the innumerable contrasting and often contradictory aspects of the life of that people, to break down the too familiar moulds of oversimplification in the hope that the reader will think again. This, at any rate, is what I have tried to do. We have seen the anarchy and the communalism, the muddle and the efficiency, the silent drift of grey, exhausted faces and the faith in the cause, the coercive harshness of the Security Police and the voluntary ardours of a weary people, the stolid, obstructive, all-enduring passivity of the peasant, and the flame of the Five-Year Plans. And so on. All these aspects and many others we have touched on, and many, many more that we have not touched on at all exist, are facts, facts of the only kind that mean anything at all. And all these contradictions and oppositions are not really contradictions at all, because all are reconciled in the people of the mighty plain, who are human beings, not walking "tendencies." The people themselves are now united in a great society, which includes, as we have said, new elements, with different historical and cultural backgrounds, but which is still dominated by the people of Great Russia.

But now the time has come to look at that society, the Soviet Socialist society, which many have hailed as a new civilization. To have looked at it before would have been a waste of time and also positively misleading. Too many people have tried to examine this society, as an abstraction, an affair of faceless economics, or, scarcely more intelligently, in terms of Western experience and Western standards. With what results . . . For this society has been created by Russians for Russians, and unless we have some idea of what the Russians are, and where they differ from us, any conclusions we draw about that society will throw hopelessly wide of the mark. On the other hand the modern Russian youth is itself partly a product of that new society, so that we cannot hope to know what the young in Russia believe and feel unless we have some conception of the way that society works.

There is nothing particularly recondite about its principles. It is the spirit behind it and the practical applications that are so wholly Russian. It is not enough to quote the whole of the Stalin Constitution, and leave it at that. That is what people do, and then they apply the terms of that celebrated constitution to our own experience. And if they know Russia, and the manner of life in Russia today, they are tempted to regard the whole hocus-pocus as a stupendous and calculated lie; or, if they do not know Russia at all, they envisage the manner of life such a constitution would impose upon us were it applied clause by clause to our own society, with the words of each clause interpreted in our own sense. The result then approaches Utopia. But the Stalin Constitution is neither a thumping lie nor the charter-deeds for Utopia. It is the expression of a Russian way of life based on socialism and moving towards communism.

It seems to me strange that at this time of day it should be necessary to insist that the Soviet Union is a socialist society. The scepticism, rapidly growing, as to this is obviously due to a confusion of Russian Socialism with Russian Communism and an almost total ignorance of the Russian character and its way of looking at life. The whole thing, for our purposes, can be summed up in Article 12 of that famous Constitution, which I shall quote: "Work in the U.S.S.R. is a duty and a matter of honour for every able-bodied citizen, on the principle: 'He who does not work shall not eat.' In the U.S.S.R. the principle of socialism is realized: 'From each according to his ability, to each according to his work.'" That is a very long way from the Communist Utopia. The Russians know that, and never cease to proclaim it. But it is unmistakable socialism. And Article 12

is the Article for which the youth of Russia work and die. It
is also honoured and carried out unambiguously, both in the
spirit and in the letter. One day it will be amended to read:
"From each according to his ability, to each according to his
needs." That will mean that communism has arrived. That
day is not yet, and meanwhile you have socialism, and all the
glitter and panoply and gormandizing of the new privileged
groups have no more effect upon the massive socialist unity of
the Russians inhabiting the plain than the twists and turns
and arabesques of the upper parts have upon the bass figure
of a passacaglia. It might be remarked that the same could be
said about the society of Catherine, the antics of whose glittering Court had no effect on the life of the toiling masses in the
plain that swept away from Petersburg. It certainly might. But
the difference is that the toiling masses today have a socialist
society, and in Catherine's day they did not. This, to the Russians, means a great deal. It means neither more nor less than
that they are working for *themselves.* For just as the peasants
in the days of serfdom felt that they were the real owners of
the land, although their landlord owned them, now every Russian feels that he owns not only the land but everything in it,
and on equal terms with every other Russian. And he does not
in the least mind the bosses, who have to do the hard work of
planning, enjoying certain privileges that he lacks. Of course
he grumbles; but he is not outraged. He will as often as not
take a cynical view of the near-commissar who splashes him
with mud from the shining wheels of his black and shining
limousine; but, by and large, he will recognize the necessity
for his existence. And, in any case, one day his son may ride in
a limousine.

The supreme thing is that everybody has to work, even the
near-commissar in his brand new *Zis.* And you are rewarded
according to the value of your work to the country as a whole.
In return, you are very rigorously required to give according
to your ability. And the greater your ability the more exacting
the demands made upon it. You have indeed to earn your
money, your extra rations, your superior fur-coat, your motor-
car, or whatever it may be. You get nothing for nothing. You

are not allowed to make other people do your work for you while you take the profits. And, if you don't work, you are made to. The celebrated inequalities have increased during the war for two reasons: first, the desperate shortage of consumer-goods, which meant that only a few could have any luxury at all; second, the imperative need for the stimulation at all costs of the utmost possible productiveness. Even then the actual differences have been wantonly exaggerated. If you are in any way important you are rewarded with sufficient creature comforts to keep you in tone for your job; and these comforts come from a pitifully limited pool of luxuries—all home produced. If there were enough to go round, everyone would have them and they would cease to be luxuries; but it will be many a long year before there are enough to go round. On the other hand there would never, never, never be any question of good food being left to rot because not enough people could afford to buy it. Never. The price would come down at once. The Russian people know this, and it means a great deal more to them than the actual existence of luxuries, and even decent comfort. They know there are not enough of these to go round, and it is more important to make life easier for your star aircraft-designer, upon whom the whole industry depends, than for an unskilled peasant labourer in that industry. So the aircraft-designer gets more. Unless he is a professing Communist he will also work better for knowing that he will get more. Not all Russians, as we have seen, are professing Communists. Many of them are very tired men and women who have toiled for years for a tremendous idea which they have only vaguely understood. And they have to be kept up to the mark. It is only the very young who will do everything for nothing; but then they are full of hope and the future has infinite and glorious possibilities.

It is clear enough, then, that the attitude of the Kremlin is based wholly on practical expediency—but *socialist* expediency. Like all systems based on expediency it has its dangers. There is, at the moment, no privileged class; there are only privileged individuals. But since it is plainly impossible to have a society which does not develop a privileged class, we may take it that the sons and daughters and the grandsons and the granddaughters of the present leaders will have, at the very least, a flying start. But even then, they will have to work. And for a long, long time to come there will be such an urgent need for skills of every kind, that the chances of the cleverer among the ordinary people will be as good. And I personally believe that during the next fifty years Soviet Russia will develop a system in which a privileged class, constantly renewed from below, will run a country organized on egalitarian lines. But I do not believe Russia will ever be a democracy in our own sense of that term, which need be no great loss to her citizens. On the other hand there is no insuperable reason against Russia one day attaining freedom of the mind and spirit within a rigid hierarchical framework, once that framework is considered properly bedded down, the sort of freedom Western Europe has known beneath its kings and its priests; but never the freedom of *laissez-faire,* because in Russia that would instantaneously bring about anarchy, which is, sooner or later, the reward of *laissez-faire* in any society, even in a nation of instinctive accommodators like ourselves. As for the state withering away . . .

For the time being, however, the Russians have neither equality nor freedom nor, on the other hand, a firmly bedded hierarchy of privilege and duties. They still move, slowly, blunderingly, tortuously, but with a gathering momentum, towards the state when those will flourish side by side. Inequality does not bother them—inequality of possessions, that is. An ardent young Russian is prouder of his share in the new Metro or one of the new tractor stations than he would be of a private motor-car. Indeed, he is quite naturally and unself-consciously a little contemptuous of private motor-cars—just as in the past he was, though a serf, proud of his share in the land and contemptuous of big establishments. I have sat in the sunlight on a bench in the very charming gardens of Moscow's inner boulevard where it runs down to the site of the megalomaniac Palace of the Soviets, which will never be completed, and the pleasant and imposing Metro station called after that chimera (but the Metro station *is* completed). It was the spring after a hard winter, and all Moscow had its bedding out of doors and was swarming out into the neighbouring countryside to come back laden with green branches. I was sitting with a young Red Army N.C.O., and as we talked, rather sombrely, about the sufferings of the winter that had passed, there swept down past the bordering hedges of the gardens a shining apparition, one of the new and imposing trams which had just appeared, in small numbers, on the streets of Moscow, single-decker affairs with a trailer, but of modern, stream-lined design, spacious inside and steady and silent on the rails, a pathetic but imposing protest against the inadequacy of the city's internal surface transport system (which consists of antique, rattle-trap trams overloaded to the point of break-down), but also a sign of things to come. And at the sight of this apparition my young friend clutched me by the arm, and with eyes alight with pride and a voice husky with emotion, exclaimed: "You see! You see what we can do? And you can still doubt? . . ." And then he breathed the words, like an uncovering and a genuflexion: "Soviet Power . . ." For Soviet Power he lived, for Soviet Power he was ready to die. Soviet Power was the sweeping away of squalor and superstition and the substitution of palaces of light, symbolized by this blessed tram which clattered proudly round the inner Ring of Moscow. And Soviet Power was neither more nor less than the combined and selfless efforts of my young friend himself and all his brothers all over the plain. What did he want with a motor-car? He would have given his boots of an infantryman for the glory of that tram. He had already starved for it for many years. It was his own tram, and soon there would be others. He was now fighting for it and undergoing hardships unsurpassed in history, even in the history of the plain.

That is why all our Western titters about the so-called glories of the Moscow Underground contrasted with the shocking housing conditions of the passengers are so hopelessly wide of the mark. The young men and women of Moscow would rather sleep on park benches and live in the open on a hunk of bread, fetching their water from the public fountains, than see their superb and symbolic Metro denuded of one speck of its shine and glitter to give them more comfort in their private lives.

The young feel this, as I have said, not the old. But it is the young who matter in Russia today. The old will soon be dead.

It is a mistake, too, to think that this enthusiasm is due wholly to perishable illusion, or to ignorance. It goes deeper, much deeper, than that. Of course there are thousands, hundreds of thousands, millions, of Russians who think the Moscow Underground with its escalators is the only Underground in the world and that Tovarisch Kaganovitch, or whoever it was, personally invented the moving-staircase. But even when they know the truth of the matter, it makes no difference. Young Russians who have seen all that Berlin or London could offer still cross themselves with the mystic "Soviet Power. . . ." And their illusions are fewer than one would believe. When my young friend in the boulevard gardens was transfigured by the appearance of his stream-lined tram we were talking of very different things. He had been in the bitter fighting in front of Moscow and Klin which had finally, miraculously, stopped the German drive, and now he had been sent back to take some kind of political course. I think he was being trained as a sort of rank-and-file commissar called a *Politrook*. And he was telling me about the sort of fighting they had had in the first part of that atrocious winter, when certain Russian divisions, including his own, had been reduced to less than half their strength by frost-bite. He was so interested in giving me a picture of those conditions and of the difficulties the new army had had to overcome, that he found himself telling me rather more than he should have done about the troubles with the civilian population who, in the back areas, were, to say the least, unhelpful (consisting at that time almost exclusively of the very old and of children), and, above all, about the corruption and inefficiency of the Q staff, particularly the corruption, which made life almost insupportable for what the Americans call the combat troops, who, on occasions, had found themselves without rations for three weeks at a time because the Q staff had embezzled them. Or, beautifully provided with ammunition for the first objective, a unit would find itself hanging on by its eyebrows and no sign of B echelon, ever. I listened to his story with despondency. It was the story, precisely, that one had heard told so often about Russia in the last war, when

Tsarist corruption, inefficiency, and muddle had sent the un-protesting peasants into the line without food, without arms, sometimes without boots. And when my friend had talked for about an hour I had to ask him whether he still believed in the Soviet regime. I was feeling depressed, for at that time it was of great importance to the rest of the world that the Red Army Q staff should not let the fighting men down. But this young Russian, scrubby in his drab tunic and unpolished belt and hideous fore-and-aft perched on the cropped head of a dreamer, tired and drawn with the dreadful struggle of the winter, stared at me with amazement. "But what on earth," he exclaimed, "what on earth has all that to do with the Soviet regime? All that is *Russia*." He had been telling me his stories, it appeared, simply to indicate the sort of obstacles met with by pioneers when they tried to build a new society.

I agreed that there must be difficulties, but confessed to some surprise that after twenty-five years of his precious new regime there had been a failure to stamp out the very worst scandals of the Tsarist government.

"But of course they're stamped out!" He was bewildered. Of course they were stamped out. Did I imagine for a moment that he would discuss with a sceptic a disgraceful state of affairs which still existed? It was all, emphatically, over and done with. It was already history.

"And all within the year? After twenty-five years?"

But a year in Soviet Russia was a long time! How could I hope to understand? And this particular evil had not been stamped out before because, until it showed itself, nobody knew it existed. They couldn't, heaven help them, do everything at once. Not even in Soviet Russia. And for twenty-five years they had had their hands full, without starting a witch-hunt for hypothetical military embezzlers . . . but now they were stamped out. There would be no more corruption in the Q staffs. Muddle, yes. And plenty of it. But the grafters had been shot.

"All and every one of them?"

"Yes," defiantly, "all and every one of them. You wait and see!"

Well, it certainly seems as though at any rate most of them had been. Certainly after that first winter there was an end to the collapse of front-line units because their Q staff failed. . . . But when it came to muddle—well, I knew a thing or two about that. I knew what my enthusiastic friend did not know—that whole formations of the Red Army were being wiped out for lack of the most elementary security precautions on the part of the Operations staff, and high up, and repeatedly. Whether anyone was shot because of that I don't know. And now my friend, who knew nothing about armies and corps and the sort of blunders that got their headquarters shot up and their divisions encircled, but who did know all about infantry companies and fighting in the bottomless mud of the autumn and the spring and living in holes dug in the snow, was telling me about the same sort of muddles lower down. Quite a fantastic proportion of the Russian casualties, he was telling me, were caused by mines and should never have occurred. You could not, could not get those peasant conscripts to take the most elementary precautions about mines, and so they went up, day in day out, month after month, and with them invaluable equipment, for no reason at all except that they would not learn about mines. It was more than heart-breaking. It sometimes made you despair. . . . And I could sympathize with him, for I had seen the same sort of reckless, feckless, *stupid* waste caused, not by peasant conscripts, but by highly placed officers of the Red Army who would not, would not take the most elementary precautions about certain other things, not mines. . . . It was an uphill task, he said. But it would be done. And now he was back in Moscow learning to be a *Politrook* in order to go back and preach the gospel of efficiency according to St. Marx. . . . I thought of the Red Army soldiers on the quay at Bakharitsa in the far north, muddling their pony over the edge and into the icy river to drown. And at that moment the super-tram went by.

In effect, I was asked to believe in the Soviet regime because beneath its beneficent if rigorous tyranny the people who would not learn about mines, the people who muddled ponies into deep rivers, the people who lost armies because they were too

lazy, or unimaginative, or stupid, or inefficient to take elementary precautions, were able to build super-trams by their
own unaided efforts and for their own use, benefit, and profit.
And I was inclined to think that was a reasonable demand.

The sense of purpose in that land is tremendous and overwhelming. And, as far as the people are concerned, it is a noble
purpose. It is beside the point to sneer at it as a materialistic
purpose. It is not. It is the fulfilment of an altruistic dream
made possible by faith. The objects of its construction are material indeed, and built to serve a material purpose; but the inspiration behind that construction is anything but material. To
prefer the marbled Underground to a room of your own, the
wild material dream of all Muscovites, is the very reverse of
materialism. The Underground certainly gets you about, but
you would rather have a room of your own than a means of getting about a city in which you have no place to rest your head.
The strength of purpose and sacrifice that went into the building of the Moscow Underground had nothing to do with the use
it would be put to. It went to create the symbol and glorification of an idea, and the Moscow Underground is no more a
materialistic construction than the great cathedrals of the
Middle Ages, which were not built as houses of worship *per se,*
or because people wanted cathedrals more than they wanted
cottages, but as the creation of the symbol and glorification of
an idea. It is not materialistic to spend your best years in a
primitive mining-camp, establishing a new metropolis whose
splendours you will never see. It really is not. But this is what
the young of Russia are doing. And when you see them on the
job, as volunteers, or as conscripts, they are indistinguishable
from the forced-labour gangs, whom you also see on the job—
except that they work much harder. Their conditions of living
are the same, the food seems to be the same. I have seen gangs
of young girls working at the toughest construction work in the
far north in the depths of winter. On the job, wrapped like
cocoons in furs and shawls, they were our old friends the grey
and faceless mass. Coming off the job, or in summer when they
could wear summer clothes, they were a bunch of hilarious
high-school girls—and they came off the job to go to a miserable

supper and a suffocating night in the most primitive and over-crowded huts. For months on end. It was *their* job. . . . And these children were not, the majority of them, *komsomolkas*. They were strictly non-political flappers. They belonged to the generation and type of flapper known contemptuously by their immediate seniors, who at one time took no stock in them, as *Fordinkis*, after Henry Ford's mass-produced masterpieces, because, until they were tested, they seemed to have no motive in life but making themselves as like each other as possible, elaborating their hair on stereotyped lines, and painting their nails with the products of Madame Molotov's new and stagger-ingly prosperous cosmetic trust. But when they were tested they too were found to share the new faith of Soviet Power, though they still painted their nails and any other part of them-selves where paint would take; and today in the big cities there are more manicurists and beauty-parlours to the quarter-mile than in any other country in Europe.

Soviet Power is not the same as Russian Power, which is what we encounter in our peregrinating conference rooms. Soviet Power is the power of the new life and the new spirit which is animating the socialist society, of the two hundred million Soviet citizens whose bayonets, when called upon to do so, form the sum of Russian Power, and without which Russian Power does not and cannot exist. That is why the statesmen who deal in Russian Power have to pay a good deal of attention to Soviet Power and could not, even if they wanted to, do any-thing that would contradict that faith, which is expressed very well in the famous Constitution of which the people are very proud.

They hang out flags on Constitution Day; and the first thought of the visitor, heavily conscious of the absolutism of the Kremlin rule, is that either the people are fools, if they really celebrate the Constitution honestly and spontaneously, that Constitution which speaks of the freedom of speech and the freedom of the press and the inviolability of the subject, all of which are made a mockery by the freedom of the M.V.D., or else that the govern-ment are fools, if they force the people to hang out flags, to re-mind the people of the existence of a Constitution of which so much was once expected, but which has been nothing but a mockery since its first inauguration. He is inclined to think that it is the government that are fools, because he has just seen a ballet of extraordinary power and brilliance which is a rendering of the French Revolution and the storming of the Bastille, with Madame Lepeshinskaya first leading a really appallingly impressive march of the whole immense cast, bearing down on the audience in unbroken phalanx, desperately slow, but overwhelming in its rhythmic force—and then crowning it with unexampled virtuosity in a short shirt and a red liberty cap, in a carmagnole of revolutionary triumph. . . . And there he found himself wondering how on earth the government dared put this grey and faceless mob in mind of victorious revolution, in mind of the power of the mob when it comes to barricades. And yet he saw the people cheering this really dreadfully effective symbolization of mob power with something like revolutionary enthusiasm—and never, apparently, thinking for one moment of forming a phalanx then and there and marching with the bitterness and intoxication of despair on the tyrant of the Kremlin. . . . So, by and large, he is confused by the annual celebration of a Constitution that seems a mockery.

But we have seen by now enough of the Russian people to realize where our new visitor has gone wrong. He is looking at Russia, and at the Constitution, through Western eyes, and he is reading the Constitution in terms of Western ideas. For the Constitution is all right, if you are a Russian. If you are a young and ardent Soviet citizen it is doubly all right. And the Constitution, when all is said, is intended for Russians, and, above all, for young and ardent Soviet citizens.

It is all right for a Russian, any Russian, because, as we should by now be feeling in our bones, he is, for the moment, happiest under an autocracy. We have repudiated the Western idea, so magnificently expressed by Conrad, that the Tsardom was a fatal and meaningless accident, a visitation. It arose out of natural circumstances and fulfilled a national need. The original Great Russians of the forests of the north-west, although they had organized enlightened societies of their own, were happy to find their supreme ruler in a Viking prince, to whom all could bow without loss of face among themselves. The fierce autocracy established by Ivan the Great and confirmed with the breaking of the nobility by Ivan the Terrible, may have made the people groan, but it held them together in a way they inwardly realized was necessary.

" 'Can it be possible,' cried our entertainer, 'that there should be any found at present advocates for slavery? . . . Can any, sir, be so abject?'

" 'No, sir,' replied I, 'I am for liberty! that attribute of Gods! Glorious liberty! that theme of modern declamation. I would have all men kings. I would be a king myself. We have all naturally an equal right to the throne: we are all originally equal. This is my opinion, and was once the opinion of a set of honest men who were called Levellers. They tried to erect themselves into a community, where all should be equally free. But, alas! it would never answer: for there were some among them stronger, and some more cunning, than others, and these became masters of the rest. . . . I am then for, and would die for monarchy, sacred monarchy: for if there be anything sacred amongst men, it must be the anointed SOVEREIGN of his people; and every diminution of his power, in war or in peace, is an infringement upon the real liberties of the subject. . . . I have known many of these pretended champions of liberty in my time, yet I do not remember one that was not in his heart and and in his family a tyrant.' "

That was not a Russian boyar to a Polish noble in the Time of Troubles; it was the Vicar of Wakefield at the dinner-table.

There is, of course, as far as the Russians are concerned, rather more to it than that. There is, as we have seen, the centrifugal and anarchic influence of the limitless plain, which, through centuries of Russia's history, beckoned so irresistibly to an independent-minded people to drift ever farther away from any authority at all, *plus* this inborn sense that, if they were to survive as a people in face of the harsh elements and the eager invader, some sort of unifying authority was necessary, that same sense which gave them the communal Mir, which was at once egalitarian and tyrannical. But it had to be an authority in its own right and absolutely apart from themselves, subject to none

of the laws by which they were governed, God-given, if you like
—so that there would never be the shadow of a suggestion that
Authority was simply a jumped-up fellow-creature, which could
not for a moment be tolerated. For under God and the Tsar
all men were equal. And we have seen, indeed, that what
brought about the downfall of the Tsar was not any popular
detestation of Tsardom as an institution, but the host of petty
tyrants who raised themselves after Peter III without responsibility and who could not be controlled by the Autocracy, the
single tyrant, because of immense distances undreamt of by
Parson Primrose.

So the older people, even those who are not particular enthusiasts for the regime, would not expect the words of the
celebrated Constitution to mean what they would mean to us.
I am not sure that even they would be capable of understanding
what they mean to us. Freedom of the press, when not a word
may be published that is not dictated from above; freedom of
assembly, when any spontaneous meeting of protest against the
government would be broken up in five minutes and the demon-
strators deported; secret elections, when there is only one candi-
date; immunity from imprisonment without trial except by
special warrant of the Public Prosecutor, when duplicating
machines and standing orders wait for no special circumstances
—all these things, and many more, make perfectly good sense
to the Russian of the plain, who knows that if he is left to himself with all his fellows he will elect another Tsar (or Commissar,
or what have you) tomorrow, simply to meet the necessity of
creating some kind of order in the chaos of a million claims and
voices, every one of which is as valid as every other. So that what
the Constitution means to him is a guarantee of the *efficiency*
of authority, which will see to it that he is not put upon, as
his fathers were put upon, by jumped-up underlings. Or, at
any rate, not so much. He sees a public and authoritative announcement that the land and everything in it which he has
for centuries believed to be his, in spite of all appearances to
the contrary, is in fact his. And it would never cross his mind
that freedom of the press might conceivably mean freedom to
call for the overthrow of the Authority which is doing the work

of holding him and all his fellows together so that they may live in peace without struggling amongst themselves.

To the very young and ardent it means even more. It means the release and canalization of all those unbounded energies, the impassioned desire to make and build in the wilderness— and for the common good. Authority, the State, the Communist Party, the Great Lord Stalin, is simply the protector of the people, who will jealously guard their privileges and the fruits of their sacrifices from destruction by the evil-minded. The press is free—free to criticize and savage all who do not play their part in the immense and sacrificial task of construction. The people are free to meet—to demonstrate their intoxicating solidarity in the service of their new orthodoxy. The individual will not be arrested without trial—unless he is a renegade and a traitor to the cause, when of course he must be struck down as an enemy of the people, and with no waste of time. As for the single-candidate elections—what does an election mean but the supreme privilege of being allowed, personally and individually, to cast a vote of confidence in your Lord Protector?

And so on.

The opposition, remember, is mostly dead, or lost in the mines of deep Siberia, of Kamchatka, and Novaya Zemlya. These are the survivors.

All this is very nice and simple-minded, but we are not Russian *komsomols* who have just learnt to read and, like the young when they fall in love, are convinced that nobody else has ever felt like this before. We have all manner of complex ideas about the integrity of the human spirit which land us in difficulties undreamt of by our enthusiasts of the mighty plain. We cannot let it go as easily as that.

"The worst crime against humanity of that system [the Tsarist autocracy] . . . is the ruthless destruction of innumerable minds. . . . An attentive survey of Russia's literature, of her Church, of her administration and the cross-currents of her thought, must end in the verdict that the Russia of today has not the right to give her voice on a single question touching the future of humanity, because from the very inception of her being the brutal destruction of dignity, of truth, of rectitude, of all that is faithful in human nature, has been made the imperative condition of her government. To pronounce in the face of such a past the word Evolution, which is precisely the expression of the highest intellectual hope, is a gruesome pleasantry. There can be no evolution out of a grave. Another word of less scientific sound has been very much pronounced of late in connection with Russia's future, a word of more vague import, a word of dread as much as of hope—Revolution."

Well, Russia has had her Revolution, and this is positively the last time we shall draw on the sombre truths of the Polish patriot, Joseph Conrad, brooding on the Russian reverses in the war against Japan—in 1905. The Revolution, we remember, which he, with so many others, then foresaw, was to be, however appalling in its magnitude, "nothing more than the convulsions of a colossal body," because Russia, reborn, would be neither more nor less than a monstrous cretin, and tyranny would succeed tyranny until "her blind multitudes succeed at last in trampling her out of existence under their millions of bare feet."

I speak of Conrad's words as truths because it is nonsense to pretend that what he says is not true from a certain standpoint, the standpoint of a politically alert Western European. We have seen enough in our intermittent survey to bear out the truth of every word he wrote on this subject—given the validity of the standpoint. But we have also seen that from the point of view of the Russians themselves, the mass of the people of the plain, his conclusions were false. We have seen what the Russians think of autocracy and how they fly to embrace it. And what we have seen makes a fair enough reply to the outside view of Russian history from the point of view of the rank-and-file citizen of the U.S.S.R. or subject of the Tsar. And that is something. But we have to go deeper yet. We have to consider this crowning charge of all, the charge of "the worst crime against humanity." We have to consider what sort of provision this Soviet society, this "new civilization," makes for the independent mind and spirit. And if the reply to that question is unfavourable, we have to consider whether or not a nation which stifles intellectual hope has in fact the right to give her voice on questions touching the future of humanity. We begin, in a word, and for the first time, to touch the disturbing problem of Russia in relation to the world. Our world. For what may be good enough for *komsomols* and *komsomolkas* may not be good enough for us. And the regrets for our own lost illusions which we may have experienced in face of the superabundant enthusiasm, the solidarity, the sense of purpose of the Soviet young may possibly be no more worthy of our own trust than the regrets of an adult for the tin soldiers of his innocence, a regret which Stevenson once upon a time derided. Perhaps we have other, more grown-up things to do?

For let us say outright, let us for once make a dogmatic and unqualified assertion: this precious new society, this paradise of *komsomols*, does *not* make provision for the independent mind and spirit—for the mind and the spirit as we understand it, that is. None whatsoever, either by our Western standards or by any other standards, including Russian. It is necessary to say this, because so many people still seem to think there is some doubt upon the subject.

The attentive reader has no doubt observed that this book, though nothing if not personal, contains next to none of those anecdotes about real people which one would expect to find in a personal narrative of this kind. I, at any rate, have been extremely conscious of this deficiency. It is due to two aspects of one cause. In the first place the Soviet government rigorously discourages acquaintance between its citizens and foreigners: there is no law about it, as far as I know, but discouragement by the Kremlin is a harsher and more efficacious deterrent than the written statutes of any other country. In the second place, although because of the curiosity of the Russians it is always possible to make as many friends as you like if you try hard enough and with discretion pushed to the point of fantasy, such friends might find themselves in serious trouble if examples of their innocent conversation found themselves on record in a book by a foreigner. The reason for this is that the citizens of Soviet Russia are, in certain directions, forbidden to think. Though there is, of course, no law about that either.

It is necessary to say this. To think of Russia exclusively in

roseate terms of the new enthusiasms of the young and the faithful, as the land which possesses a purpose of the kind we lack,
is no less wrong-headed than to think of her exclusively in terms
of a middle-aged, resentful, empty-bellied apathy. It is also unfair. It is unfair to the men and women who have suffered intolerably, and died, because they thought thoughts of their own
and were indiscreet enough or brave enough to utter them. It
is unfair to those who are still living, who still think thoughts
of their own and dare not utter them—and would not utter
them even had they a taste for martyrdom: for the martyr without publicity dies the death of the sparrow, which may be recorded in heaven but which is certainly not remarked elsewhere.
. . . At any rate, we should not forget these people, for, when
all is said, they are much more of our kind, of your kind, dear
reader, and mine, than the young and newly lettered enthusiasts
whose solidarity, whose sacrificial generosity, whose sense of
purpose, we, in our irreducible confusion of methods and aims,
are inclined to exalt—because it makes life so simple. Is it, after
all, possible that life is not so simple as all that?

However, as I have said, in fairness to those Russians who,
like ourselves, have failed to attain the sublime simplicity of a
reach-me-down, one-piece credo, a kind of intellectual siren-
suit, admirable for life in the basement, it is necessary to repeat
that "the worst crime against humanity . . . the ruthless destruction of innumerable minds" is practised in Soviet Russia
today with a single-mindedness and an efficiency very much in
excess of that attained by any Tsar who ever lived. The im-
proved technique of elimination which put an end to the corruption of the Red Army Q branch in the first winter of the
war is not confined to the stamping out of erring quartermasters.
The human mind, as we know it and understand and value it,
is also quite stamped out. . . . We seem to hear the echo of a
conversation in the spring sunshine on the charming boulevard gardens of central Moscow.

"The heretics have been shot."

"All and every one of them?"

"Yes," defiantly, "all and every one of them. You wait and
see!"

Well, it certainly seems as though at any rate most of them have been. Certainly since the early thirties there has been little enough come out of Russia to suggest the existence of an original mind inside her.

But, of course, they have not all been shot, or even "sent away." Any more than all the corrupt quartermasters had been shot or sent away. The example of a few was enough to steady the rest. And, scattered over the vast plain today, just as there are aspiring ex-quartermasters hunting for opportunities for the exercise of their talent for graft, so there are thinkers and artists, living perfectly respectable lives, but for ever struggling to introduce into their official epics of stereotyped verbosity disguised glimpses of an inner vision personal to themselves. But the ex-quartermasters have the more hopeful time of it.

The kind of thoughts the citizens of the Soviet Union *are* allowed to think should now be sufficiently clear. Education, of course, has nothing to do with the self-development of individuals. It is a process for turning out good Soviet citizens. . . . But good for what? For building the socialist paradise on earth, of course! But what do you *do* with this paradise when you get it, when you've killed your individual souls in order to get it?—We don't answer frivolous, destructive questions.

But one day, the Russians, being Russians, will ask precisely that question. It is written all over that infinite sky which vaults the infinite plain. And, when they do, things will begin to hum.

Meanwhile they do not, the overwhelming majority; and it is the business of the government to make sure that they do not. It is a fairly easy task just now, because there are so many very exciting things to do, such as learning to drive a tractor, learning to read so that you can decipher the book of instructions that goes with the combine-harvester, building colossal monuments to the glory of your unquestioning faith, in a word, in opening up the country. So that all the government has to do just now is to frighten the scattered independent spirits into keeping quiet and continue, for the rest, with an elementary education based on lies. It is easy enough, and it is done fairly quietly. But that is what Conrad meant when he spoke of the greatest crime against the human spirit . . . "the destruction of innumerable minds."

I don't know what the official defence of this particular outrage is. The Soviet government would not admit it, so there has been no need for it to produce a defence. But there *is* a defence, and it lies deep in the Russian character. The only possible defence is attack. They could say (but I have not heard them say this) that the human mind, as we know it and understand it, is a pernicious cancer of the body politic, which they are in the process of removing in order to substitute an entirely different kind of mind, growing naturally and organically at one with that body. Perhaps that is what the Webbs meant by the term "a new civilization." But I don't think it was. On the other hand, it is nothing like so far-fetched as it sounds. It is the difference between two aims in life, which are opposed and for ever incompatible: on the one hand the striving for the greatest good; on the other hand the striving for the greatest good of the greatest number. Our struggle, for what it has been worth, has, no matter what we may say, been always for the greatest good— and damn the unhappy majority. The struggle of Russia today, foreshadowed in all her history and proclaimed by her great prophets, has been for the greatest good of the greatest number —and damn the glorious minority. And if that is not a radical difference I do not know what is.

Since I am debarred from telling anecdotes about Russians, for the reasons given above, I beg the reader's indulgence for an anecdote about myself. It should be understood that for more than a year I had been steeping myself in the atmosphere of Russia in order to deaden the reflexes of disgust and detestation at the scenes of tyranny and oppression which the Russians did not seem to mind, and which, therefore, were preventing me from even beginning to understand the way the Russians thought and felt, in a word, what they *did* mind. It was the same sort of exercise that a simple-minded citizen of the Soviets might undertake to deaden *his* reflexes of disgust and detestation at the scenes of drilled and highly organized squalor, to which no one pays any attention, in the midst of our own green and pleasant land. One day, after about a year of this discipline, I found in my hands by chance a copy of a book by an English writer perhaps more dear to me than all other English writers; and with it came a sense of stolen delight. For once I would forget Russia and everything belonging to it (Russia which no longer repelled, but now fascinated with an ever-tightening spell) and give myself a rare treat. Opening that precious volume, I should have said that I knew the first paragraphs by heart; but what I found myself reading, and with an eye immediately cold and angry—yes, *angry*, the emotion Mr. Molotov feels when he thinks we are being frivolous, or crooked, or both —what I found was totally strange and so totally trivial and false that I could read no farther than the end of the very first sentence. The shock was extreme, because the sentence which offended, and which I *had* once known by heart, ran as follows:

"Emma Woodhouse, handsome, clever, and rich, with a comfortable home and happy disposition, seemed to unite some of the best blessings of existence; and had lived nearly twenty-one years in the world with very little to distress or vex her. . . ." Just that.

After the first outraged revulsion it became clear that it was time to take stock. It is all very well trying to steep oneself in the atmosphere of Russia, but this was going native with a vengeance. For the first time I was *feeling* with the great Russian prophets, not merely sympathizing, intellectually, with their points of view.

With Kropotkin: "What right had I to these higher joys when all round me was nothing but misery and struggle for a mouldy bit of bread!"

With Dostoevski: "Down with culture . . . the thirst for culture is an aristocratic thirst."

With Belinsky: "I do not want happiness even as a gift, if I do not have peace of mind about each of my blood-brothers, bone of my bone and flesh of my flesh."

With Tolstoy: "A pair of boots is more important than all your Madonnas and all your refined talk about Shakespeare."

All, it will be noticed, Tsarist writers. None of them Communist agitators. All of them Russians. And the irony of that is that each and every one of those writers would have to give their approval to a very great deal of what is happening in Russia today, whereas in Tsarist Russia there was nothing, but nothing at all, they could approve of. And yet each and every one of those writers—for they *were* independent spirits—would, in Russia today, have sooner or later been "sent away," or otherwise liquidated.

We are now at the very hub of the great Russian problem, and each one of us must choose his own "solution," or else leave it admittedly unsolved and draw what comfort he can from the infinite variety of this vale of tears and what pride he can in following his own path while poignantly conscious of the existence of others. For, like the great Russian prophets, we cannot have it both ways. They, in a selfish and disintegrating society, had comparative freedom to express their inner vision and to criticize that society. Today, in a healthy and closely knit society, their successors have no such freedom. And we, we either believe that Miss Austen in her delicate and unemphatic manner has managed and still manages to express the deeper truths about this universe—or else we must find that what she has to say is no longer enough. We, when all is said, belong to the Western world, in company with Mozart and Miss Austen, and their heritage, such as Shakespeare and Bach and Voltaire, and their successors. The Russians do not.

Our world is a world of individual values. The Russians have no individual values—or only one: universal truth, which is a fairly broad affair. For us the universe is something upon which you impose a pattern, a limiting pattern, as all patterns must be. The Russians, believing in the equal validity of everything and everybody under the sun, do not. They reject limitations. And that is why they themselves, today and always, find themselves the appointed piece in a design of monolithic simplicity and procrustean rigidity. Because if you will not make your own pattern, or your own group patterns, if you will not take upon yourself the responsibility or the liberty of selection and rejection—well, if you are to survive as a people, somebody else will have to do it for you, and it will be one pattern for everyone, and what is rejected is rejected for all. For nobody, not even the Russians of the plain with all their breadth and sweep of understanding and acceptance, can exist in a naked universe. And that is why the Russian people, who refuse to make their own selections and rejections, cleave to an exalted authority which will do it for them, and at the same time see in authority a principle of evil. Because, necessary as it is, it is also a confession of their failure to be utterly at one with all the universe and everything contained by it.

All or nothing. . . . Listen to Alexander Herzen in his open letter to the French historian, Michelet:

"Cast into oppressive surroundings, and armed with a clear eye and incorruptible logic, the Russian quickly frees himself from the faith and morals of his fathers. The thinking Russian is the most independent man in the world. What is there to curb him? Respect for the past? But what serves as a starting-point of the modern history of Russia, if not the denial of nationalism and tradition? . . .

"On the other hand, the past of the Western European peoples serves us as a lesson and nothing more; we do not regard ourselves as the executors of their historic testaments.

"We share your doubts, but your faith does not cheer us. We share your hatred, but we do not understand your devotion to what your forefathers have bequeathed you; we are too downtrodden, too unhappy, to be satisfied with half-freedom. You are restrained by scruples, you are held back by second thoughts. We have neither second thoughts nor scruples; all we lack is strength. . . .

"What have we to do with your sacred duties, we younger brothers robbed of our heritage? And can we be honestly contented with your threadbare morality, unchristian and inhuman, existing only in rhetorical exercises and speeches for the prosecution? What respect can be inspired in us by your Roman-barbaric system of law, that hollow clumsy edifice, without light or air, repaired in the Middle Ages, whitewashed by the newly enfranchised petty bourgeois? I admit that the daily brigandage in the Russian law-courts is even worse, but it does not follow from that that you have justice in your laws or your courts.

"The distinction between your laws and our Imperial decrees is confined to the formula with which they begin. Our Imperial decrees begin with the crushing truth: 'The Tsar has been pleased to command'; your laws begin with a revolting falsehood, the ironical abuse of the name of the French people, and the words Liberty, Equality, and Fraternity. The code of Nicholas is drawn up for the benefit of the Autocracy to the detriment of its subjects. The Napoleonic code has absolutely the same character. We are held in too many chains already to fasten fresh ones about us of our own free will. In this respect we stand precisely on a level with our peasants. We submit to brute force. We are slaves because we have no possibility of being free; but we accept nothing from our foes.

"Russia will never be Protestant, Russia will never be *juste-milieu*."

Never, never, never! All or nothing. And if it cannot be all, then let it be nothing!

Or again, in Schedrin's little dialogue between the Russian little boy without trousers and the German little boy *mit*:

"It's the devil that makes you so dense. The devil you've sold your soul to!"

"Then what about you? You've given away your soul for nothing! Is that a good bargain?"

"Better for nothing than for a kopek. What you've given for nothing you can always take back. Sausage!"

So this new society has about it a great deal of the old; or, rather, the people who made it are very like the people who made the old. There is a strong family likeness. This is so precisely what any reasonable person would expect that it would hardly seem worth writing a book to elaborate and underline that very simple truth. On the other hand, too many people still speak as though the Russians of today were an entirely different species from the Russians of yesterday and the day before. What always puzzles me when people make this assumption is what those unfortunate Russians who lived half their lives before and half after the Revolution are supposed to be.

On November 7th, 1917, they woke up as typical characters of old Russia and went to bed revolutionized by the magic of Lenin. It sounds silly to me.

But the first thing that happens when anybody sees just how silly it is and realizes that our old friends the citizens of paradise are really our much older friends, the denizens of the mighty plain—the moment they see this they immediately leap to the conclusion that there has been no change at all. Conrad must have been right. The Kremlin tyranny, which he foresaw, is as absolute, as arbitrary, as soul-annihilating as the Winter Palace tyranny—and a great deal less well-mannered. That is also silly. For by now, I devoutly hope, we can see for ourselves that Conrad was just as right about the shape of things to come, with tyranny piled on tyranny until at last trodden out of existence by the bare feet of the blind and aspiring multitude, as he was right about the Tsarist autocracy. And just as wrong. (And here, once and for all, I apologize to Conrad, one of the great novelists of all time, an aristocrat, a liberal, and a magnificent patriot, for using his tremendous essay "Autocracy and War" as a stalking-horse throughout these pages. I have done this because nowhere else is stated with such force and passion and lucidity an outlook on Russia shared by most Englishmen of his time and by many today, but which seems to me invalid.)

To continue. . . . Once upon a time the Russians submitted to the Tsar because it suited them and because the Tsardom was a reasonable answer to the conditions then obtaining. But it overstayed its mandate, becoming thus perverted. And so you had Nicholas I, and, in due course, the forcible overthrow of that particular autocracy, still long before the great mass of the people had realized that it was the Tsardom that was wrong. Today we find another autocracy, but an autocracy governing quite a different sort of society. This time its subjects are not 80 per cent illiterate peasants but 50 per cent literate peasants and 50 per cent landless manual, clerical, professional, and intellectual workers. The peasants, I have already suggested, will prove to be the conservative element, looking to the autocrat to protect them from the harrying bureaucracy. But the others, whose way of life has broken away from their earthy background, will think increasingly. And, as they mature, they will have the power to modify the autocracy and loosen its tight grip. They have great power. Although there is a strict censorship of current writing there is not much censorship nowadays of the writing of the past. And in the writing of the past there is plenty for the Russians of the present to work upon. It is my own personal belief that the head of the State wishes the Russians to think, those of them who are capable of reading their own classics. Russia is capable of muddles on a transcendental scale; but for a contemporary autocrat to allow his subjects to read what the great Russian spirits had to say about autocracy would be a gaffe of inconceivable proportions—*if he were interested above all in preserving his autocracy*. The peasants on the *kolkhoz* will not read the prophets and the satirists of the nineteenth century, whose ideas might be upsetting in their current state of development. But the people of the towns, and some exceptional peasants, will. And it looks to me as though the head of the State has decided that any Russian with the mental stamina to read such things may be encouraged to think the sort of thoughts they lead to—about, for instance, autocracy. But not all thoughts all at once. Not any wild thought imported, half-baked, from the West. And not any dangerous thought by a jumped-up contemporary writer who may belong to the opposition. For the Russians are all too receptive and plastic, and all too easily thrown off their balance by a new and exciting idea. If they were not, they would never have taken to Lenin.

All this, of course, is highly speculative. But it is speculation based on a fact which I have not yet seen explained in any other way.

There, at any rate, the autocracy is. And it is severe. But it is no longer arbitrary in principle, however much it may be so in detail. It has a purpose. It is a noble purpose, and it is a purpose which all may share: the betterment of the people. It has its seamy side. We have not ignored it. We have seen the sort of things that happen in times of great stringency. But these things are not done for fun. We have seen a whole town go hungry because there was not enough food to go round in a time of crisis, and it was not a very useful town. But nobody goes hungry for the profit of his neighbour. We have not looked very much at the high-lights of the new society. These have been plugged and we know them by heart. But they exist. I have not written at all about crèches and free clinics and workers' rest-homes and parks of culture. These exist, and before the Revolution they did not exist. In principle the Russian knows no fear, provided he works hard and leaves political heresy alone, and no financial worries. His rent is insignificant. His food is cheap (wartime shortages are irrelevant here). His education and his medical attention are free. There is no keeping up appearances. He is left to devote the whole of his energies to getting on with his life and his work and enjoying both with all the zest he can bring to it. And there is in his life a dignity which shines even through the appalling privations of war. It comes from the fact that he does not live at his neighbour's expense. That rule of life, living on your neighbour, upon which the whole of Western society is based, he thinks he is proving to be no rule at all. He always, even in the earliest mists of time, had an inkling that it was not really a rule of life. And to this vague but stubborn conviction he has clung with the utmost resolution through the centuries, with a pig-headed, smouldering passivity. And now he has the chance to prove that he was right all along. And he is doing so.

This, in a word, is what the Revolution has done for Russia. And thinking of the people who have died and suffered intolerably, it should always be remembered that they were the ones who lacked this belief, or who, in one way or another, were suspected of obstructing its fulfilment.

So much for Russian backwardness. . . . You might look at it another way. You might say that through the centuries the Russians did not budge because they cherished this belief in their hearts and, letting the stream of time and all the experimentation of the West pass over their bent heads, clung to it for all they were worth—until somebody said the magic word and they swept into torrential life. From Marx they received a theory. From Lenin a promise. The theory of Marx as dramatized by Lenin was perfectly fitted to set fire to the imaginations of a people whose whole being is a denial of moderation. "All —or nothing." For centuries without end it had been Nothing. Now it was All.

V

THE U. S. S. R. AND THE WORLD

THE U.S.S.R. AND THE WORLD

IT is more than two years since the Germans were beaten. The Russian people are no longer as grey as they have appeared to us in these pages. Towards the end of the war they began to get enough to eat. The shops filled themselves with cheerful goods to buy for hoarded roubles—all manner of unheard of things, rushed back from Hitler's European empire as the Red Army broke ever more deeply into it. Above all, clothes. Clothes of an elegance and a durability that the Russian people had not dreamed of for many years. And, to match the shop-windows, the dull-bleached woodwork of the city housefronts were furbished with new paint, the camouflage stripped from the ancient Kremlin, and the multitudinous domes and cupolas made to glitter with gold leaf. Then came the shocking drought of the summer of 1946, the worst since 1891, which not only put an end to the hopes of unlimited bread, which had been promised by Stalin himself, but also produced a food crisis more serious than anything since the early days of the war, involving almost universal undernourishment and, for uncounted thousands in the afflicted areas, something approaching famine. In spite of this setback, which was all the more cruel because the people were just beginning to relax, and in spite of the fact that tens of thousands of Russians in the western provinces still live in revetted holes in the rubble of their homes and in large dugouts roofed with timber and earth—in spite of all this there is a spirit in Russia today very different from the spirit of black despair during those days of retreat. The people have energy to smile as they go about their daily work. There is a new series of Five-Year Plans to cater to the human needs of human beings, and not merely for the iron furnishings of war, and life is being taken up with a swing and almost with a flourish. But there are not so many Russians as there were five years ago. Nobody appears to know just how many of them died, but the figure may well be fifteen million. That, in numbers, means nearly one in three of the population of Great Britain, or more than one in ten of the population of the United States of America, or a great deal more than the whole population of, say, Canada in the new world or Austria in the old. Fifteen million dead. . . . Even in Russia, the land of immensities, it means that one in every twelve Russians alive in 1941, one in every twelve men, women, and children, has died a violent death, in order that the others might resume their lives with a swing and, if possible, a flourish. And most of these fifteen million were adults.

The survivors will not, of course, forget this. But we seem to have forgotten it. Because now, with this great country shattered, ravaged, and exhausted, with her people strained to breaking-point, and with her adult manhood more than decimated—now, at this moment, there are many loud voices in the West crying out that another war is coming quickly and that this time the aggressor is Russia. And these voices, which cry out of a depth of imbecility, or ignorance, or unimaginativeness which it is truly horrifying to contemplate, are widely believed.

For twenty years the celebrated Russian colossus played no official part in the ordering of Europe and the world. She had not the strength. Then, in the middle nineteen-thirties, she was heard to proclaim, in effect: "Russian power is now reborn. This rebirth has been achieved in spite of the rest of you, indeed, in your very teeth. Our pains were thus immeasurably increased. But we have somehow survived those agonies, and we are now a force to be reckoned with. If you really mean what you say about the peace of the world, about collective security, about the curbing of fascist aggression—if you really mean all this, we should like to let bygones be bygones and help you. We are ready to put this newly born power, achieved by us in your despite, at the disposal of the forces of order. If not . . ." For some time Russia persisted in her offer, in spite of many snubs, until, at Munich, the powers of the West proved finally in her eyes that they were not interested in the peace of the world, but only in their own provisional security, which they showed no particular talent for ensuring. They proved, in addition, that their hatred of Hitlerism was small compared with their hatred of communism, and, in short, that nothing would please them better than to see Germany embroil herself with Russia in a mutually destructive war.

The Russians when, rightly or wrongly, they consider themselves compelled to abandon an ideal, or, indeed, a position of any kind, always do so thoroughly, cleanly, without fuss, without vain repining, without lip-service to a vanished dream, without pretending that their retreat is really an advance, and with a coolness that we, with our shrinking from unpleasant facts, find cold-blooded. It is indeed cold-blooded. They accept their defeat open-eyed and prepare the next position. After Munich they accepted defeat. They had desired, with all the urgency of practical necessity and all the passion of theory, a world of peace through collective security, and the encirclement of the aggressor within a curtain of iron. This desire was brought to nothing by Great Britain, by France, and by America. We in Great Britain wanted security—but not to share with Russia. And so the Russians admitted defeat and applied themselves to strengthening the next position—a very short-term policy, a bad second-best, but the one we had already chosen for ourselves: security for one nation, come what might to the rest. They set about this late in the day; but they had the advantage of a congenital lack of hypocrisy, which enabled them to keep a cool eye on their purpose. We in the West had instinctively perceived that the only way to security for ourselves, once we abandoned collective security, was to turn the German menace eastwards; and this we sought to do, without admitting it even to ourselves (unless Mr. Chamberlain would sometimes mutter his unclear purpose in his sleep). Czechoslovakia was a step in the right direction. But we failed to carry this purpose to an efficient conclusion because we would not admit it, even to ourselves, which made our hand uncertain. The Russians, in reverse, and with their eyes wide open, succeeded where we failed.

By a masterpiece of controlled duplicity, a diplomatic late-cut of unparalleled audacity and coolness, they switched the Germans on to us. The result of this we all know.

Russia can no longer be cold-shouldered. She is there, in the middle of Europe, a big noise at last. A far bigger noise, indeed, than the ordinary Russian imagines. He would be amazed and incredulous if he were told that for the rest of the world he was the biggest noise in existence. Bigger even than President Truman's private bomb. If you could get him to believe it, which is improbable, he would at first be highly gratified. He is so used to being frightened of other people, of those other nations, who so nearly crushed him out of existence through so many weary years, that it would never occur to him that we might now be frightened of him. He would, as I have said, be flattered if he did know and could be persuaded to believe it. And then he would wonder why.

That, as observed, goes for the ordinary Russian. But it is by no means certain that many of the actual rulers of Russia realize quite how frightened we are. They know, of course, that we keep on saying we are frightened. But they themselves are so inescapably conscious of the exhaustion, the vulnerability, and the really desperate need for relaxation, reconstruction, and then relaxation again, on the part of their poor country, that many of them must find it hard to believe that anyone could be so foolish as to be frightened of them. And so they, too, have their perplexities. They wonder why we pretend to be frightened. But it is in their case—except for the very few who can see deeper—a short-lived perplexity; for they have an answer ready to hand. They remember that one way of getting a people into a fighting mood is to magnify a threat to their existence and security. They have used that technique themselves (not that much magnification was needed in this case) to get their own people to fight their way through the first two Five-Year Plans. They are using it again today. They can also remember how for year after year the amazing Adolf Hitler made himself out to be the most frightened man in Europe; and they know he was not frightened at all.

It seems to me that we make—and by "we" I now mean all of us—Russians, Americans, Frenchmen, Englishmen—an absurd and dangerous mistake in attributing to the leaders of foreign governments a clarity of vision, a purposefulness, and a tenacity of design developed to a degree of perfection never found in the human animal. We in this country regard the impassive and magnified photographic stares of Messrs. Stalin, Molotov, Zhdanov, Andreyev, and the rest with a sort of wondering awe which no politician in history has deserved. Their motives wrapped in impenetrable mystery, they plan, they calculate, they conspire. Nothing that they do occurs by accident. None of them suffers from a liver, from toothache, from migraine, from a duodenal ulcer. None of them feels better or worse before lunch or after lunch, with a glass of vodka inside him or without a glass of vodka inside him, on a dry sunny day or on a wet mizzling day. None of them is in any way the victim of his heart when it comes to women, children, or old friendships. They are all—every single member of all the highest Soviet Councils—blood-brothers, without a thought but for the unanimous Plan, without a thought for their own positions, either collectively or in rivalry with one another. And as for the policies of other nations, of, for instance, Great Britain or the United States of America, they have not the least difficulty in the world when it comes to knowing and understanding what the British and Americans are doing and thinking and planning, and why. Everything is allowed for; everything is foreseen.

But why should we make, emotionally, such an extraordinary assumption, when we know it, intellectually, to be untrue? Why should we imagine that any foreign government, including the government of the late Holy Russia, should be any less fallible than we know Messrs. Marshall and Bevin to be? These are the men thrown up by the British and American people to run them. Those others are the men thrown up by the Russian people to run them. There is no reason to believe that politics in Russia, or in any other country, attract a higher type of person than they do in Great Britain or America. It is easy to imagine both Mr. Truman and Mr. Attlee wondering what on earth the

Russians are up to—and, on principle, leaping to predetermined conclusions of the gloomiest kind. We see them doing it. We share their perplexities. We reflect, by our own firesides, in our own pubs, the secret debates round the cabinet table between our own rulers, or representatives, who think Mr. Molotov means black when he says white and those who think he means grey, and those who think that perhaps after all he may mean white. There is no difficulty there. Our governments are foxed by the Russians; we ourselves are foxed by the Russians: obviously, this foxing is part of a deliberate and calculated scheme. . . . But what we have to imagine now is Mr. Truman, or Mr. Attlee, at the head of the Russian State, confronted by the manœuvres of Great Britain and America, two powerful countries led either by iron men above all passions or by foolish puppets manipulated by iron men with their heads and hearts above all passions and their feet in oil (it comes to the same thing). We have to imagine Mr. Truman or Mr. Attlee confronted with this enigmatic spectacle and responsible to the Russian people for getting their guesses right. . . . What perplexities confront them now! And indeed, when the ordinary, intelligent, politically alert Englishman or American himself does not by any means understand what his government is up to —in Greece, in the Ruhr, in Java, in China—how can we expect our Russianized Mr. Truman or Mr. Attlee to know any better? How can they hope to know?

In these pages we have done our utmost to look at Russia steadily, not through Russian eyes, but through the eyes of a stranger to this planet, to whom one set of people, one nation, if you like, is as good as another nation until the contrary is proved. An intelligent stranger, and therefore sympathetic; a stranger, moreover, who knows very well that all nations are ridiculous if only because they cannot at the best contrive to express more than the highest common factor of a group consciousness, which is not very high. . . . What we have seen, I hope, makes sense: it is the image of a living society with its own point of view, which is not the point of view of Great Britain, or France, or the United States of America. If in fact the picture

does make sense, then this book will have fulfilled its main purpose, which has been to provide some sort of a living image of
a distant people whose sudden incursions out of a haze of ob-
scurity into the councils of the West are apt to disconcert us, because we have nothing to which we can relate them. And if this
picture does make sense, it seems to me that already some of the
contemporary actions of Russian statesmen must begin to lose
their air of extreme and arbitrary caprice and to make some sort
of sense themselves. Whether the sense they make is at all re-
assuring is another matter. The thing is, we have been trying to
discover how the Russians think and feel and see. And by now,
as the outcome of accumulated suggestion, we should have some
dim idea of their temperament, of their mental and spiritual
climate, and also of how their general outlook on life and their
particular faith of the moment combine to make a formidable
standpoint from which to view the world. What we have not yet
considered is what, from this viewpoint, they see. We must now,
however sketchily, turn our eyes westwards and try to complete
the picture.

The first thing any Russian statesman sees, looking west, is
an enemy camp. This is the world beyond his own boundaries.
It is a world at present dominated clearly by the United States
of America, and obscurely by Great Britain, which still, in some
unsatisfactory way, is a force to be reckoned with. If we ask him
why he thinks the world is hostile he will be amazed at our
simple-mindedness, or, more probably, he will brush the question contemptuously aside as a misplaced pleasantry. He has
faced, from 1917, from the very day of his grand revolution,
until 1941, the day of the German attack, an openly hostile
world, and he knows what it looks like. He knows well enough
that millions of foolish, well-intentioned citizens of the so-called
democracies, especially in Great Britain, were very far from
hostile during the recent struggle for life; but he also knows
the limitations of these people when it comes to the exercise of
power, and when it comes to replacing the simple virtues of
war with the subtle, elaborate, and exhausting arts of peace.
For twenty-four years, in a word, he fought for the fruits of his
Revolution and the reconstruction of his country, in absolute

isolation and until anyone but a Russian would have been bored
to death by both. When the powers of the West failed to kill it
by force of arms, they set to work quietly to choke it or embarrass
it out of existence by other means. Bolshevism was the named
enemy of the statesmen of every country outside Russia, and
our Russian statesman is a Bolshevik. He saw the crowning
attempt to destroy his system at Munich in 1938, which presented itself to his unsurprised and not very speculative eyes as
nothing less than an attempt to unleash Hitler on to the Ukraine.
With this he gave up trying to co-operate with powers who so
clearly not only had no desire to co-operate, but would have
liked to see him dead. The Molotov-Ribbentrop pact was
Russia's announcement to the world that she proposed henceforward to fight it with its own weapons. It was also Russia's
official recognition of the existence of that curtain of iron which
the powers of the West had rigged up in her face. It was a bad
day for the world when Mr. Chamberlain made his absurd
attempt to arrange the future of Europe without consulting
Russia. Mr. Chamberlain, as far as our Russian statesman
knows, was an Englishman. He stood for England. And today
he finds a million apologists among the British, particularly
among the well-established. It is not, in Russian eyes, the iron
curtain of Marshal Stalin at which we stare so blankly today:
it is the iron curtain of Mr. Chamberlain, one time Prime Minister of Great Britain—but of course it goes back beyond that;
the actual machinery was manufactured and erected by Mr.
Chamberlain's predecessors, with the manifest approval of the
British populace, among others—including the people of
America, who, although not represented at Munich, nevertheless allowed Hitler to march quite a long way and overrun the
greater part of Europe before pulling themselves together. The
Russians, admitting an accomplished act, began to make things
hum on the other side of that curtain. They hummed for several
years.

Then on June 21st, 1941, and under threat of extinction by
German arms, that most doughty anti-Bolshevik of all British
statesmen, the then Prime Minister, announced to an interested
world that the iron curtain no longer existed, and that we were

henceforth allies, friends, and brothers with, precisely, the Bolsheviks. It was a reasonable announcement. It was highly desirable that we should be allies with someone who possessed a fighting army, and there were then no other candidates. Russia herself was in much the same position. But there was nothing in this statesmanlike announcement to suggest to any Russian that it was based on anything but temporary expediency. On the other hand, a great number of Englishmen got it into their heads that it was a confession of faith. What did we think the Russians would do? Dance for joy?

Why should they? What voluntary action of ours had she to thank us for? It was so plainly our only hope to give Russia all the help we could spare to keep her fighting the Germans while we built up our own strength. The fact that this aid was useful to Russia was neither here nor there: emotions of heartfelt gratitude are out of place in amoral situations of this kind. And even if the Russians could have brought themselves to believe in a complete and dramatic change of heart in the British, they could not help observing that after signing the celebrated twenty-year-pact, Great Britain continued to work far more closely with the United States of America, with whom she had no pact, and who made no pretence at all about a change of heart towards the Bolsheviks. Any Russian who assumed, as he would have been entitled to assume, that because of this pact, or treaty, we should range ourselves at the side of the U.S.S.R. in the event of war with, say, the United States, would have been immediately certifiable. And yet, if the pact did not mean this it meant nothing. So, in fact, it meant nothing. And after the war, when the new British Foreign Secretary, well known as an enemy of communism, offered to extend this travesty of an alliance for another thirty years, what did he mean by it? Did he know himself? Certainly he did not mean that we should range ourselves with the U.S.S.R., if necessary against the rest of the world. But if not that—then what?

As for the immediate present—well, there is the Security Council, there is the UN, there is the atomic bomb, there is an anti-Communist Foreign Secretary in Great Britain, and there is, in the United States, a President whose hold on office appears to an outsider to be conditional upon his success in avoiding a single gesture which might annoy any one of an unknown number of groups of voters, all with contradictory views—except about Russia. And even if our Russian statesman did not already assume the hostility of Great Britain and America he would perceive enough of the equivocal in our goings-on to make him very apprehensive indeed. The world as now constituted, with Japan and Germany for the time being out, leaves America, Russia, and Britain as incomparably the most powerful nations on earth, with the rest nowhere. Individually the first two have great power: together we have all power. Why, then, behave as if we had not? Any arrangement based on the assumption that we do not possess this power must, being false, breed falseness. Any attempt to produce a lasting peace without agreement between these three great powers is absurd. To pretend otherwise can be nothing but the outcome of sentimental and frivolous self-delusion, or purposeful double-dealing, or a mixture of both. For even if we truly wished to renounce the advantages of this power, we could not do so; in the last resort our attitude towards other, lesser nations, and, still more, their attitude towards us, is indelibly coloured by the inescapable physical fact that we are stronger. So that even the renunciation of our position would be an act of power, in itself changing the balance of the world. And even the formal and actual abolition of power politics could only be achieved by an act of power on the part of the most strong. We should therefore openly acknowledge the reality of this power, and base our policy upon it.

This is not an easy point of view to oppose, even in theory. In practice it is still more difficult to answer it. For as long as Great Britain and America continue to behave like great powers, while pretending, on a basis of artificial and bogus equality, that we are only two among fifty, every action we perform, separately or together, makes our position more untenable. And not only are we behaving in fact like great powers, while simultaneously declaring that we do not believe in power; we are also, for the time being, as joint disposing agents of the atomic bomb, behaving like the two greatest powers on earth, with the rest nowhere—including, for the moment, Russia.

Such a prospect fills our Russian observer with despondency and gloom. He clings ferociously to what appears to him as the one bit of solid reality in the whole fantastic situation: his precious right of veto. With that veto he can, at an immense cost, which he has weighed, and at an immediate risk, which must cause him frequent nightmares, ensure that the situation is prevented from crystallizing out into an anti-Russian peace which will give the Western powers control over the machinery of that iron curtain erected by the West for its own purposes and now appropriated by Russia for hers. This is not a happy state of affairs; but nobody can end it but ourselves. We desire, we say, a world of peace and plenty. We are not interested in attacking other nations on account of their ideologies, not even Franco's Spain, the heir to Hitler and Mussolini. Certainly not Russia. We want a world without fear of imminent destruction. . . . But all these things, say the Russians, are within our reach. If we are sincere in this desire, it can be realized tomorrow. For if the three supreme powers behave in concert, the most venomous and persistent efforts to disturb the peace elsewhere can be scotched with the greatest of ease. There, Comrades, is your Utopia. It is in our hands. All we need is agreement between us. Can we agree? . . . Not yet! And yet you talk of delegating this immense and beneficent responsibility to a mixed collection of nations and near-nations, some of whom have never had a responsible thought in all their history, most of whom will never agree about anything except under pressure from us—which itself is the exercise of that power from which you profess to shrink. Why? And to give your attitude a still more dubious appearance, if that is possible, you talk of equality with the most backward and corrupt and insignificant nations in the world, while disposing of a weapon which, for the time being, makes you more powerful even than mighty Russia. Why?

To me that seems a sufficiently boding question. To our Russian observer it must blot out the light of the sky.

We could go on like this for a long time. We could, from our uneasy standpoint on the Kremlin wall, reflect, as good Marxists, that although probably neither Mr. Attlee nor President Truman has any desire to attack and conquer Russia, neither of these gentlemen appears to be in full control of his domestic situation, that Mr. Truman presides over a land in which capitalism has got out of hand, and that Mr. Attlee, although no doubt a good Social Democrat with unimpeachable ideals, has been forced to link his country's economy with that of money-mad America. And America is everywhere. For an isolationist nation it is remarkable how she gets about. There is America in China, America in Japan, America in Germany, America in Asia Minor. It is an alarming spectacle. It is the kind of thing that easily becomes an obsession. America is so very close. . . . As for Great Britain—she ought not to count any more, except as an outpost of America. She has fifty million people, mostly urban, whom she cannot possibly feed, and all crammed into an island the size of a pocket-handkerchief. Her people no longer work hard, so that she can't produce enough exports to buy food. Her coal-miners refuse to dig coal, and the government is afraid to make them. She is no longer strong enough to keep her empire, either in face of dissident native populations or in face of the envy of America. And yet . . . And this "and yet . . ." keeps coming between the concentrated gaze of Russia and the looming menace of Wall Street and confusing a perfectly clear-cut issue. For America is predictable (predictable, that is, to Russians: she is running true to Marxian form), while Great Britain is unpredictable. And Leninist-Marxism has no room for the unpredictable. In so many ways Great Britain behaves like a nation in the last stages of capitalism; but in other ways she does not. In fact, her progress is so eccentric that, to account for it satisfactorily, it may be necessary to amend certain clauses of the Leninist-Marxist dogma. Great Britain is undoubtedly undergoing some kind of a social revolution, but a revolution, so far, without violence, without breakdown, without the dictatorship of the proletariat; it is a revolution, to judge by the utterances of the Opposition and certain sections of the British press, most emphatically not desired by the old order. . . . Or is the whole thing a trick, to deceive the wretched proletariat? Because, if there is really a revolution going on in Britain, why doesn't the old order fight for its life? And if there is really a change of heart about the darker aspects of the British Empire, why do the British behave as they do in Malay? And if the present government is really a socialist government and not in the pay of the reactionaries, why do they do their utmost to discourage socialism in Greece? And so on.

We could, as I have said, go on for a long time in this strain. But we can now get down from the Kremlin wall. We have seen enough, I hope, to suggest that suspicion is more than a word. There is no need to enumerate, on our side, the ways in which Russia appears to us to be blocking our honest attempts to push humanity a stage higher on its slow and breath-taking climb from the primeval swamp to the celestial city. They are ever in our minds. By the time these words are printed the examples which are still fresh as I write will be stale and forgotten: there will have been others to take their place. But perhaps our brief and oversimplified essay in looking at the world through Russian eyes has been enough to indicate that by talking about Russian suspicion, and then brushing it to one side as absurd, we confuse the diagnosis with the cure. It is not enough to tell the Russians that their suspicions are unfounded, no matter how loudly we protest, and then expect them to put them away for ever. We first have to find out the root cause of the suspicion; we then have to ask ourselves, seriously, whether, in spite of our good intentions, there may not be some just cause for it; and finally, even if we are assured of our total innocence and are satisfied that there is no just cause, we have to set ourselves to remove the cause, no matter how childish and irrelevant it may appear to us. And if we refuse to do this, we put ourselves precisely on a level with the Russians themselves, who refuse to believe in the fundamental decency of our attitude because so many of its manifestations appear to them unreasonable and absurd.

It will be clear by now that the basic cleavage between Russia and, at any rate, Great Britain, is one of temperament rather than one of principle; and, in the light of the many suggestions which have accumulated themselves during our survey of life as lived in the Soviet Union and in the Russia of the Tsars, it may indeed seem that even where temperament is concerned, the differences between us, striking as they appear, and deep-rooted as they may at first seem, are scarcely more than differences of emphasis. There are other differences, of course. Russia believes in Lenin's interpretation of the Marxist dialectic. We do not. Russia would like to see the whole world achieve communism; we should like to see the whole world governed by a species of parliamentary democracy. Russia is non-Christian, and still too freshly and violently emancipated from the Church to pay the attention which she one day undoubtedly will pay to the greatest teacher in the history of the world. We, on the other hand, are still officially Christian, and thus badly handicapped in our groping but increasingly determined efforts to understand the precepts of this amazing man whom our forefathers turned into an idol. But the main difference, the temperamental difference, as will have been repeatedly apparent in these pages, is the difference between the doctrinaire and the empiricist, the matter-of-fact and the sentimental, the non-compromiser and the compromiser, the whole-hogger and the trimmer: "All—or nothing" versus *"juste milieu."*

The great gift that the Russian brings to the West is the capacity, developed to an extraordinary degree, of seeing things as they are, without blinking. The great gift which we have to offer to the Russians is the quality, sustaining and at the same time mellowing, of hope. Clarity of vision and hope in combination would be the lever of Archimedes: the men of science have already prepared the place to stand upon. But clarity of vision goes too often with an easy defeatism and hope with self-deception. We in this country water our idealism with expediency in our own inimitable manner. Sometimes it seems to be productive; sometimes it does not. The Russians would say it can never be productive. If you cannot be a thorough-paced idealist, they would say, because you find it too dangerous, too wearisome, too costly, then stop pretending to be an idealist and fall back on open expediency. That is the difference between Russian realism, so-called, and British hypocrisy, so-called. Both are romantic attitudes. Half our mystification in face of

Russia is caused by our national habit of considering actions individually, each on its own merits, instead of as part of a larger pattern. The other half is caused by the Russian habit of considering actions collectively, as parts of a whole, and with an awareness of inconsistencies and contradictions which borders on the obsessional. These opposed habits of mind we each apply to our own actions and to the actions of the other. Thus, Russian actions, taken separately, often do not make sense. This is because they are not conceived separately, but as parts of a larger design, which, as a rule, makes very clear sense. Conversely, our own actions, taken together, almost never make sense: they do not form part of a coherent pattern of purpose. But our separate actions usually do make sense—although on the most various levels of human behaviour and consciousness—some on a level of pure expediency, others on a level of high idealism, others on a level in which both expediency and idealism are disconcertingly mixed.

This is plainly a never-failing source of radical misunderstanding. No Englishman would dream of attempting to divine a consistent policy in our attitude towards India, Egypt, Palestine, Germany, the U.S.S.R., the United States, Argentina, Malaya, Greece, Trieste, Persia, the Warsaw Government, Spain, Cyprus, UN, and the atom bomb. He knows very well that there is no such thing as a policy, except the time-honoured (or time-disgraced?) policy of muddling along from hand to mouth and heightening the moral tone of the world by precept, if not by example, where it can conveniently be done without noticeable cost to ourselves. The Russians, however, do not know this—or perhaps, by now, they do? Perhaps they simply pretend not to know? . . . In common with other nations, they are convinced that we must have a policy: life for them is inconceivable without a policy. They do not realize that our policy of having no policy has seemed to us as good and valid as any other. So they look for it elsewhere, and the harder it is to discover the more sinister it seems. In the end they have to admit that it is quite undiscoverable, so they have to invent it. Charity does not enter into this kind of exercise. They very naturally take the lowest common denominator of all our actions and attitudes, which, because these are not inspired by any general purpose except the avoidance of fatigue, is very low indeed. The Russians (and they are not alone in this) take this depth as the moral level of our policy, and armour themselves accordingly. They are fortified in their conclusions, first by past history, secondly by the fact that while the UN is, after all, still a matter of words, Greece, the Ruhr, and the American Loan, Malaya, Persia, and the rest are not. And the Russians have an almost totemistic regard for the deed as distinct from the word, whereas we set an astonishingly high value on words and the mere expression of intentions. Conversely, we make the same mistakes as the Russians, but in reverse. We insist on examining each of their actions separately, without looking for the underlying policy. What *are* they up to in Tripoli? we ask ourselves aggrievedly, never stopping to reflect that they may be up to nothing—in Tripoli.

We have already said that the great gift which Russia brings to the world, intellectual honesty, a remarkable freedom of outlook such as, in the West, characterizes only the artist, has as its reverse a sort of defeatism, which, in those aspects of life we are now discussing, results in a too ready embracing of evil when total good appears to be impracticable. It so rarely seems anything else. . . . We have also said that the indomitable quality of hope, which is the great good our own country offers to the world, has, as its reverse, a proneness to self-deception, leading to hypocrisy. For the time being the Russian has a panacea: his defeatism is transformed into triumphant action, not by hope, but by certain faith. But one day he will suddenly realize the deadly limitations of the Marxist dialectic, with its inescapable implications of puppetry, and then, once more, he will be lost —except that this time, on reflection, he will see that he has indeed achieved marvels in face of the hostile universe, if only with the aid of a delusion. He may then be ready to embrace the despised quality of hope. Thus, gradually, may national characters be amended.

But it is high time our own was amended and hope purged of complacency and hypocrisy. For only then can it, in union with clear-sightedness, become a force to redeem the world.

Our infinite capacity for self-deception may have been well enough in the days when we were the dominant power: we could then afford our moral indulgences. Today we can no longer afford them. When it comes to sheer weight of men the future of the world is in the hands of Russia. Russia will behave badly or she will behave well. There will be no half measures. How she behaves will largely depend on us; and so we can afford no half measures. One would have thought that after comparing the dazzling display of *Realpolitik* which culminated in the Molotov-Ribbentrop affair, with our own dingy essay in the same *genre* which culminated in Munich, we should be chary of ever again entering ourselves for those stakes. And yet, after these long years of bitter retribution, we continue to deceive ourselves with such success that the right hand hardly knows what it is doing, much less what the left is up to. We continue, for instance, to use long and idiotic phrases for short and expressive words, and if we succeed in deceiving ourselves, we certainly deceive nobody else. To take an example of a certain topicality: "The integrity of small nations" is *not* a good synonym for that unhappy monosyllable "oil." It is bad in itself, and its perpetual employment corrupts our judgment and saps our self-knowledge. The fact that the Russians also may employ it is neither here nor there. We force them to employ it. But they never for one moment confuse the two meanings in their heads. But we . . . ? Ask any member of the House of Commons whether, in the last analysis—the *last* analysis, which is the only one that matters, the one on which wars are fought—our interest in Azerbaijan has more to do with an ideal or with oil. . . . I should be surprised if he could tell you: he is so confused by the misuse of words and by trying to run ideals and expediency in harness. On the other hand, any Russian of similar standing could tell you without a moment's hesitation. He would tell you that, in the last analysis, it was oil that counted more—for all of us, Russians, British, and Americans alike. He himself would prefer to stop calling oil the integrity of small nations, admit that Iran has oil, admit that we all want some of it. Because if you admit that sort of thing, as an unfortunate but insuperable fact of life, like the weather, or certain biological peculiarities, there is a chance that you will be able so to arrange affairs that the need can be satisfied without cutting across your moral aims. But if you do not admit the need in so many words, and mix it up inextricably with moral sentiments, in the last result it is the moral aims that go—and for nothing.

Similarly, it neither impresses others nor improves our own state of soul to give away the South Tyrol in one breath and in the next, in connexion with the Julian Marches, to declaim with pompous and false rhetoric that we refuse to bargain with the lives of men and women. . . . Either—or . . . Either we do refuse to bargain with the lives of men and women, in which case we have to discontinue a good many of our present overseas pursuits and dispense with certain accustomed comforts—*or* we admit that we must bargain with the lives of men and women and cease to pretend that we do not. In the one case we assume to ourselves at one blow the moral leadership of the world, to use an unfortunate but popular phrase, a leadership which might well be the death of us as we know ourselves today, but which would not be in vain. In the other, we embrace evil as our good, without the luxury of self-deception and hypocrisy, which weakens the eye and makes the hand unsteady, and thank God for the atom bomb. There is no longer room for half measures. An apparition stalks out of the East, and its cry is "All—or nothing!" We have to make up our minds.

A great many people in both Britain and America like to talk about moral leadership, which they appear to regard as a sort of national compost of good intentions. With this compost they offer to feed the hungry lands, and throw up their hands in outraged indignation because it is not accepted for the first time of asking and on our bare word that it is good. But moral leadership, if it means anything at all, means more than international slumming with a basket of pious hopes. It must mean the deliberate carrying out of ideas which seem to us good for no other reason than their goodness, and regardless of the material consequences to ourselves. In a world of fluctuating values the price of honour remains constant. You cannot be Socrates if you shrink from the taste of hemlock. Or, to bring the matter rather closer home, there are, scattered about the world among a million others, the scarcely settled graves of many young men, who, as individuals, and without dreaming of applying the phrase to themselves, aspired to what is called moral leadership and knew all about the cost.

The highest price is not always demanded. All that is invariably demanded is the willingness to pay it. This willingness will not escape the eye of the most cynical: the true cynic, indeed, the frustrated idealist, the Russian, is the man who, trained to a precise evaluation of the bogus, is the first to discern and acclaim the hard core of the real when it comes before his eyes in the shape of goodness. Unless we are prepared to pay this price, the sooner we stop talking about ideals and attend to our stocks and shares, the better for us and the rest of the world. But I am inclined to think that we should, if we truly understood the issue, be prepared to pay.

The issue is, whether we wish to live as human beings in free association with other human beings or as accidental members of accidental groups of human beings called nations, whose only future is mutual destruction until only one is left. The nation was once a social unit, the sole justification of which was the protection it offered the individual, who, in return for this protection, had certain duties. As the nation grew it acted also as a shield for the development and enrichment of group societies of widely differing attributes. So long as it fulfilled this purpose the sovereign state, or nation, was a reasonable institution: but in no other way could it be justified. Today the sovereign nation has outlived its use: it survives, therefore, as a perversion. For its effect on the individual and on the group is the exact opposite of the effect it is intended to produce. The very existence of a sovereign nation today condemns its unfortunate members to the perpetual fear of violent death: it stultifies all planning for the future, negatives all hope, and, in the end, turns every man the world over into a robot of standardized pattern with standardized preoccupations engaged in a single standardized task—namely, defence. The members of a nation, to keep their souls, their national souls, paradoxically, as well as their individual souls, must cease to belong to nations. Only when they have abdicated their sovereignty, that vain and atrocious burden of futil-

ity, and thus freed themselves from the necessity of spending all
their energies in defending it, can the people of a nation begin to
live as free human beings and devote themselves to the productive and enthralling task of pitting themselves against the universe instead of against each other. But it is not enough to talk
of these things. We have to perform them. And, like all revolutionary actions, the abdication of national sovereignty will have
to start in a unilateral manner. It is not enough to wait until
others also abdicate: we should have to wait for ever—or until
one nation had destroyed the rest.

There is plenty of time, if only we in Britain and America—
and particularly in America—can keep our heads. Russia is in
no hurry. She has all time before her, and she excels at waiting.
She believes, or her leaders believe, that if the Western world
—and particularly America—carries on as it does at present
there will, inevitably, and whether we want it or not, be an
almighty clash between the new communist order and capitalism run riot. This is a fixed idea. But she is in no hurry for that
clash. On the contrary, believing in its inevitability and knowing
her own present weakness, it is in her own interest to put it off
for as long as possible. She would like, above all, to postpone it
until she can achieve her objective with nothing more than a
slight push at the decisive moment—that is to say, when the
enemy is on the verge of revolution within his own camp—as
Lenin waited for his almost bloodless revolution until the Provisional Government was on the verge of breakdown.

We need fear no deliberate aggression from Russia, so long as
we in the West keep ourselves strong and healthy. Being strong
and healthy is not the same as beating our chests and staging
war-dances in front of the "iron curtain." Being strong and
healthy means keeping our own house in order and arranging
the life within it so that all the members of the household are
proud to belong to it and do not look elsewhere for their salvation from oppression. There is no need for heresy-hunts in a
strong and healthy society. And, as I have said, so long as we
can keep strong and healthy, Russia is not to be feared. It is
against the Russian tradition and it is against the Bolshevik
tradition to make a frontal attack on a strong fortress. But once

the fortress is weakened by internal strife, then Russia will show her hand. And, believing in the ultimate incompatibility of the capitalist and communist systems, believing, as I have already said, that some kind of conflict is inevitable, she will do her best to avert a head-on conflict by stirring up internal strife; and at the same time, fearing that the capitalist West—and particularly America—will, in the throes of dissolution, turn to overseas adventures in order to shore up her own tottering domestic structure, she will strain herself to the utmost in the effort to equip herself to fight if she feels herself forced to fight—as she strained herself to the utmost to be ready for the Nazis.

And the moral of this, surely, is that if the West really believes in its way of life, it has one supreme duty: to carry on regardless, refusing to be stampeded by Russian provocation, drawing a line which the Russians must not overstep. This means that the line must be a reasonable line, in which the whole of the people of the West, not merely certain business interests, may believe. It is a line which, had it been drawn two years ago a good deal farther to the east than we can hope to draw it now, might have saved much human suffering and might also have rendered the more equivocal aspects of what is now known as the Truman Doctrine quite unnecessary. . . .

But one thing has to be remembered in drawing this line; and that is that if we expect the peoples of Eastern Europe (and, if it comes to that, of Western Europe and the Far East) to look to the West in preference to the East, we must see that they get the sort of governments they want. We must make it quite clear that the rulers to whom we extend our aid are acting in the interests of the people themselves and not in the interests of our own merchants and financiers. Because, if the line is to hold, everybody behind it must want it to hold. And if the people want socialist governments it is worse than useless for us to sponsor right-wing governments simply because the leaders happen to be friends of ours, with their money in the same stock. In Europe today the staunchest and strongest opponent of Moscow Communism is not the neo-fascist, but the Social Democrat. America seems to find this very hard to believe. . . . It is in a word, not merely at home, not merely in Britain, not merely in America, that society has to be kept strong and healthy, but in all those countries whom we wish to preserve from the spell of Moscow. And the only way to have a strong and healthy society is to make sure that the people and the government are one.

There are two great dangers. Soviet Russia does not desire a conflict; but she fears the inevitability of war, and her diplomacy is inept. The Russians are bad psychologists when it comes to foreign peoples; and this weakness is all the more marked to-day when so few of the leaders of Russia know anything at all about foreign peoples. This means that at any time they may commit some first-class diplomatic blunder which will set the world on fire—unless the rest of the world keeps a very cool head and makes quite clear here and now how far the Russians may go and how far they may not go. Quite clear—and in calm, matter-of-fact tones, without grimaces and without hysteria. The policy of Britain and America since Yalta has been such that even the people of Britain and America, much less the Russians, have now not the least idea of what the Kremlin may be allowed to get away with next. This is dangerous.

The second great danger is the quite fantastic development in America during the past few years of the new dogma of private enterprise and individualism without controls of any kind. America, and until quite lately Britain too, has for long believed in private enterprise and *laissez-faire*. But while Britain shows signs of keeping up with the times, which is really commendable in an elderly nation, America, which one had always thought of enviously as young, resilient, experimental, and beautifully true, has started behaving like a panicky old lady, turning the customs of her early youth into something very much like a religion. This premature senility in what should be a young and virile people, this relapse into the most rigid and hidebound nineteenth-century liberalism, is one of the most interesting features of our age. It is also, as I have said, a stranger. When one speaks of a strong and healthy society one means a developing society, not a dead one. One means a society which is perpetually adjusting itself for the greatest practicable benefit of all its members, not for a ruling caste. Such a society, at certain times and in certain circumstances, may be individualistic, authoritarian, capitalistic or socialistic, conservative or progressive. Unrestricted individualism may be the best thing in the world under certain circumstances. It may be the best thing in the world for America now, at this moment, but it is only a means, not an end. And the frightening thing about the present mood of America, as seen from the outside, is the way in which the American people appear to be exalting uncontrolled individualism into a mystical faith, to which the facts of life have to be fitted, no matter who gets hurt in the process, instead of treating it as one practical expedient among others.

Americans talk today as though unrestricted individualism was the basic principle of all life on this planet, only to be violated at peril—instead of being, as in fact it is, a very recent manifestation of human society with few precedents in history, and those short-lived. I am not attacking unrestricted individualism as a means; only as a dogma. Because if the Americans are going to take a leaf out of the Moscow book and start elevating social expedients into cast-iron dogmas, we are in for a rough passage. It will mean, amongst other things, that America will be running true to Marxian form. If this indeed happens, then the Marxist notion of the ultimate clash will be proved right after all. And if Marx, against all human reason as we understand it, turns out to be as right as all that, then one may expect him to be right in his further particulars, and world revolution will come with blood and fire.

It may be thought that I am being one-sided in urging restraint and coolness and understanding on the peoples of the West. But there is nothing out of order in this. In the first place, I speak the language of the West. In the second place, I know better than to expect any restraint and objectivity from the Russian Marxists, whose possession by a dogma is complete. In the third place, the burden must be ours, because it is we, not the Russians, who believe that we have something worth preserving. It is up to us to take what measures we can to preserve our own values—remembering always that a war of the kind to which we may look forward will write those values off for

ever, no matter who is technically the conqueror, leaving the
way clear for universal totalitarianism as the only possible cure
for universal resultant anarchy.

Russia is a force, potentially the greatest force in the world.
I have tried to give a picture of the Russians, to show, however
dimly, what they are, and how they came to be what they are.
It is the picture of a people of unprecedented strength and fer-
tility, with a great depth of moral purpose, who, at the moment, because of their environment, are playing the old power
game. If they go on playing it they will break up that game
for ever and expose its hollowness—because they are uncompromising, because they are not blinded by self-deception, because they will one day be stronger than any nation in the history of mankind. We are left with the task of discovering how
these people are to fit into the modern world. It is useless to say,
as, with so many tricks of evasion, we often do, that they cannot
fit. If we do not fit ourselves to them, and them to us, then they,
by a single process, will fit us to themselves. They *exist:* a nation
of overwhelming and exuberantly increasing numbers, with
their feet firmly planted in Europe. Russia, in a word, is one
more fact of life, and a decisive one. And it seems to me that the
vitality of our Western culture will receive its great test in the
use it makes of this new fact of life, as real as an earthquake. We
can ignore it: it will overwhelm us. We can seek to destroy it: we
shall destroy ourselves. We can throw ourselves into its arms: it
will absorb us with scarcely a trace. Thus, the only answer, as it
seems to me, is that our whole conception of society, of the way
in which human beings live together, will have to be remodelled
to allow for this new and unprecedented fact.

We have not discussed the great achievements of the Russian
people: these, more or less widely known, form the façade; and
we have been more concerned with getting at the background.
But before we leave Russia it would be as well to enumerate a
brief list of those achievements as they have, up to now, affected
the world—or, rather, the civilization of the West, which, like
the Greeks with their Mediterranean, we habitually regard as
the world.

In our struggle for development and survival as a civilization, the anti-liberal Russian people have contributed with unmeasured blood and suffering to our salvation from the Tartars and the Turks on the one hand, and on the other from Napoleon, Prussia, and Nazi Germany. In other words, but for the Russian people, our civilization, for what it is worth, could not have developed in its present form. On the side of the arts, the Russian people have also contributed largely, and particularly during the last hundred years. They have revitalized our theatre; they have enriched our music; they have revolutionized our conception of the novel, and profoundly influenced, positively or negatively, every Western writer of the last fifty years. In the field of science they have increased our knowledge and command of the material world through their physicists, mathematicians, chemists, biologists, geologists, and archæologists. They have developed and invented new techniques for the conquest of the soil and climate for the purposes of agriculture. In social science they have shown the possibilities of long-term planning for material ends. They have demonstrated the viability of co-operative action on an unlimited scale. In the moral sphere they have filled the world with bold ideas about the social qualities of the human race. They now offer, clumsily, obscurely, and without themselves knowing what they offer, important modifications to our whole attitude towards life and the universe. All this, it seems to me, is an impressive record. It means that for the last hundred years the Russian people have been strongly and radically influencing Western civilization, as it were, in spite of themselves, with by far the greater number of them existing in apparently irredeemable darkness of spirit. In face of the record of this achievement we have to ask what happens when all these millions of sleepers begin at last to awake. We have to ask what happens *now*.